The European Union's Emerging International Identity

Views from the Global Arena

Edited by

Henri de Waele
Jan-Jaap Kuipers

MARTINUS
NIJHOFF
PUBLISHERS

LEIDEN • BOSTON
2013

Library of Congress Cataloging-in-Publication Data

The European Union's emerging international identity : views from the global arena / Edited by Henri de Waele and Jan-Jaap Kuipers.
pages cm. — (Studies in EU External Relations ; 6)
Includes index.
ISBN 978-90-04-23098-9 (hardback : alk. paper) — ISBN 978-90-04-23099-6 (e-book)
1. European Union. 2. International and municipal law—European Union countries. 3. European Union countries—International status. 4. European Union countries—Foreign relations. 5. Treaty-making power—European Union countries. I. Waele, Henri Clemens Ferdinand Jozef Alexander de, 1979- editor. II. Kuipers, Jan-Jaap, 1986– editor.

KJE5057.E87 2013
341.242'2—dc23

2013012994

ISSN 1875-0451
ISBN 978-90-04-23098-9 (hardback)
ISBN 978-90-04-23099-6 (e-book)

This book is printed on acid-free paper.

The European Union's Emerging International Identity

Studies in EU External Relations

Edited by

Marc Maresceau, Ghent University

VOLUME 6

The titles published in this series are listed at brill.com/seur

CONTENTS

ACKNOWLEDGMENTS

Various persons have contributed to the successful publication of this volume. In particular, we would like to express our gratitude to Lisa Hanson and Alexandra Mitton at Brill/Martinus Nijhoff Publishers for their most excellent guidance during the preparatory stages. In addition, we are grateful to the peer reviewers of the Studies in EU External Relations series, whose invaluable comments and suggestions have greatly benefited the overall quality of the manuscript. Moreover, we would like to thank Fiorina Argante and Marion Grevinga at Radboud University Nijmegen for their untiring practical support. Above all however, we are indebted to Tristan Naber for his assiduous editorial assistance.

All chapters were finalized on 1 February 2013, and reflect the law as it stood on that date. Only to a limited extent could subsequent developments be incorporated.

HdW/JJK
Nijmegen/Amsterdam

CONTRIBUTORS

Geert De Baere is Assistant Professor of EU Law and International Law at the Faculty of Law of the University of Leuven, and Senior Member at the Leuven Centre for Global Governance Studies. He studied law at the University of Antwerp and at King's College, Cambridge. In 2005, he was a Visiting Research Fellow at Columbia Law School in New York. From 2007 to 2009, he worked as a *référendaire* in the chambers of Advocate General Eleanor Sharpston at the Court of Justice of the European Union. His publications include *Constitutional Principles of EU External Relations* (OUP, 2008) and *Federalism in the European Union* (edited with Elke Cloots and Stefan Sottiaux, Hart Publishing, 2012).

Henri de Waele is Associate Professor of European Law at the Radboud University Nijmegen, and currently also serves as Guest Professor of European Institutional Law at the University of Antwerp. He studied Dutch, International and European Law in Nijmegen and Leuven, obtained his Ph.D. from Radboud University Nijmegen, and was awarded the Diploma in European Union Law at the European University Institute in Florence (2009). He has authored two monographs, various book chapters, co-edited two other volumes, and published articles and case notes in inter alia the *Common Market Law Review, European Constitutional Law Review, European Public Law* and *Legal Issues of Economic Integration.*

Rudi Delarue is Director of the ILO Office for the EU and the Benelux countries (since June 2008). Prior to taking up this post, he was a principal administrator at the European Commission since 1999, where he held posts relating to international affairs and to EU social dialogue. Between 1987 and 1999, he was Senior Advisor at the Belgian Christian trade union confederation (ACV/CSC) dealing with regional, national, EU and international labor issues and collective bargaining at Belgian and EU level. Mr. Delarue obtained his law degree from the University of Leuven in 1986, and subsequently pursued European studies at the College of Europe in Bruges. He has published on Belgian, EU and international labor issues.

Jan-Jaap Kuipers is an Associate at De Brauw Blackstone Westbroek in Amsterdam. Previously, he worked as Assistant Professor of European

Law at Radboud University Nijmegen. He studied EU Law at the University of Maastricht, and obtained his Ph.D. at the European University Institute in Florence with the dissertation *The European Union and Private International Law* (Martinus Nijhoff Publishers, 2012). He has published widely on EU and private international law issues, inter alia in the *Revue Internationale de Droit Comparé, European Law Journal, Common Market Law Review* and the *Rabels Zeitschrift für ausländisches und internationales Privatrecht.*

Joris Larik is a Researcher and Ph.D. Candidate at the European University Institute in Florence. His dissertation is on foreign policy objectives in European constitutional law. He obtained a B.A. from the University of Dresden, an LL.M. from the University of Leiden, as well as an M.A. from the College of Europe in Bruges. He received the Manfred Wörner Award for the best essay on a NATO-related topic in 2007/2008. In the spring term of 2012, he was a Visiting Research Scholar at the University of Michigan Law School.

Esa Paasivirta is a Member of the Legal Service of the European Commission in Brussels, and an Adjunct Professor in the Faculty of Law at the University of Helsinki. He graduated in law from the University of Turku and the University of Helsinki, and obtained his Ph.D. in international law from the University of Cambridge. At the European Commission since 1997, he has worked mainly in the area of external relations, including in 2004–2008 as First Counselor and Legal Advisor in the Commission Delegation to the United Nations in New York. Before, he worked as the Legal Advisor of the Energy Charter Secretariat (Brussels), at the Finnish Ministry for Foreign Affairs (Helsinki), and the International Trade Centre UNCTAD/WTO (Geneva). He has published extensively in the areas of international law and EU law.

Tamara Perišin, Ph.D., M.Jur. (*Oxon*) is Professor at the Department for European Public Law, University of Zagreb. She teaches the Jean Monnet Modules 'EU and WTO in a Comparative Perspective' and 'EU Internal Market Law'. She has studied or conducted research at the University of Oxford, the T.M.C. Asser Institute, Georgetown University, University of Michigan, Central European University, the European Court of Justice, and the Max Planck Institute for Comparative Public Law and International Law. She is the author of *Free Movement of Goods and Limits of*

Regulatory Autonomy in the EU and the WTO (Asser Press, 2008), and has published numerous articles.

Laura Puccio holds a B.Sc. in International Economics and Management from Bocconi University in Milan, an M.A. in International Affairs from the Institut d'Etudes Politiques in Paris (Sciences Po), and an LL.M. in Comparative, International and European Law from the European University Institute in Florence. She is currently a Ph.D. Candidate in Law at the European University Institute. She has been Visiting Scholar at Columbia Law School in New York and a Visiting Researcher at the Department of Economics of the Université Libre de Bruxelles. Her work focuses mainly on trade law (WTO and EU trade law and policy) as well as international and European monetary law.

Thomas Streinz is a Research Associate at Noerr LLP in Munich and a Ph.D. Candidate at the Ludwig-Maximilians University in Munich. He studied Law and Economics at the University of Bayreuth, International Trade Law at Bond University in Australia, European and International Public Law at the Ludwig-Maximilians-University of Munich and Competition Law and Policy at the London School of Economics. During his legal practice training (Referendariat), he spent five months working in the institutional team of the European Commission's Legal Service.

Tamara Takács is a Senior Researcher at EU Law at the T.M.C. Asser Institute and Academic Programme Coordinator of the Centre for the Law of EU External Relations (CLEER). She completed her Ph.D. at the School of Law of Utrecht University and the T.M.C. Asser Institute in The Hague in 2009. She was Lecturer (2008–2009) and subsequently Assistant Professor at the School of Law of Utrecht University (2009–2011), and taught European Union Law as Adjunct Associate Professor at American University Washington College of Law in the Spring semester of 2011.

Joren Verschaeve is a Ph.D. Fellow at the Centre for EU Studies of Ghent University. He holds a Master's degree in EU Studies from Ghent University (2011). His research focuses mainly on the European Union's role in the Development Assistance Committee (DAC) of the Organization for Economic Co-operation and Development (OECD), but also extends to the EU development cooperation and multilateral aid architecture.

ABBREVIATIONS

AB	Appellate Body
ACP	African, Caribbean and Pacific countries
AFSJ	Area of Freedom, Security and Justice
AG	Advocate General
AI	Amnesty International
APEC	Asia-Pacific Economic Cooperation
ASEAN	Association of South East Asian Nations
ASEM	Asia–Europe Meeting
ASIL	American Society of International Law
AU	African Union
BRICS	Brazil, Russia, India, China, South Africa
BSP	Biosafety Protocol
C	Communications series of the Official Journal of the European Union
CARICOM	Caribbean Community
CCICA	Chicago Convention on International Civil Aviation
CCP	Common Commercial Policy
CDDH	Comité Directeur Droits de l'Homme
CEACR	Committee of Experts on the Application of Conventions and Recommendations
CEB	Chief Executive Board
CEE	Central and Eastern European
CETS	Council of Europe Treaty Series
CFI	Court of First Instance of the European Union
CFSP	Common Foreign and Security Policy
CHG	Civilian Headline Goal
CITES	Convention on International Trade in Endangered Species of Wild Fauna and Flora
CoE	Council of Europe
CoM	Committee of Ministers
COREPER	Committee of Permanent Representatives
CSDP	Common Security and Defence Policy
CSR	corporate social responsibility
CT	Constitutional Treaty
DAC	Development Assistance Committee

DAG	Development Assistance Group
DER	draft explanatory report
DEVCO	Development Cooperation
DG	Director General / Directorate General
DLI	draft legal instrument
Doc.	document
DSB	Dispute Settlement Body
DSU	Dispute Settlement Understanding
EAEC	European Atomic Energy Community
EBA	European Banking Authority
EBRD	European Bank for Reconstruction and Development
EC	European Community
ECB	European Central Bank
ECHR	European Convention on Human Rights and Fundamental Freedoms
ECJ	European Court of Justice
ECOFIN	Economic and Financial Affairs
ECOSOC	Economic and Social Council
ECSC	European Coal and Steel Community
ECtHR	European Court of Human Rights
EDC	European Defence Community
EDF	European Development Fund
EDRC	Economic Development Review Committee
EEA	European Economic Area
EEAS	European External Action Service
EEC	European Economic Community
EESC	European Economic and Social Committee
EFTA	European Free Trade Association
EIDHR	European Initiative for Democracy and Human Rights
EIOPA	European Insurance and Occupational Pensions Authority
ENP	European Neighbourhood Policy
EoL	exchange of letters
EP	European Parliament
EPC	European Political Cooperation
ESCB	European System of Central Banks
ESDI	European Security and Defence Identity
ESDP	European Security and Defence Policy
ESIL	European Society of International Law
ESMA	European Securities Market Authority

ESS	European Security Strategy
ETS	European Treaty Series
EU	European Union
EURIMF	EU representatives to the IMF
FAC	Foreign Affairs Council
FAO	Food and Agriculture Organisation
FTA	free trade agreement
GATS	General Agreement on Trade in Services
GATT	General Agreement on Tariffs and Trade
GB	Governing Body
GC	General Court of the European Union
GSP	Generalised System of Preferences
HDI	Human Development Index
HR	High Representative of the EU for Foreign Affairs and Security Policy
HRC UN	Human Rights Committee
IACHR	Inter-American Court of Human Rights
IAEA	International Atomic Energy Agency
ICAO	International Civil Aviation Organisation
ICC	International Criminal Court
ICCPR	International Covenant on Civil and Political Rights
ICISS	International Commission on Intervention and State Sovereignty
ICJ	International Court of Justice
ICTR	International Criminal Tribunal for Rwanda
ICTY	International Criminal Tribunal for the Former Yugoslavia
IDI	Institut de Droit International
IFI	international financial institution
ILA	International Law Association
ILC	International Labour Conference
ILO	International Labour Organization
IMEC	industrialised market economies
IMF	International Monetary Fund
IMFC	Interim Monetary and Financial Committee
IMO	International Maritime Organization
IO	international organisation
ISAF	International Security Assistance Force
JHA	Justice and Home Affairs
KFOR	Kosovo Force

L	Legislation series of the Official Journal of the European Union
MDGs	Millenium Development Goals
MFN	Most Favoured Nation
MLC	Maritime Labour Convention
MoU	memorandum of understanding
MPI	Multidimensional Poverty Index
NAT	North Atlantic Treaty
NATO	North Atlantic Treaty Organization
NCB	national central bank
NGO	non-governmental organisation
NSC	NATO Strategic Concept
OAS	Organization of American States
OECD	Organisation for Economic Co-operation and Development
OIC	Organization of the Islamic Conference
OJ	Official Journal of the European Union
OMC	Open Method of Coordination
OSCE	Organisation for Security and Co-operation in Europe
PACE	Parliamentary Assembly of the Council of Europe
par.	paragraph(s)
PCA	Partnership and Co-operation Agreement
PCD	Policy Coherence for Development
PCIJ	Permanent Court of International Justice
PfP	Partnership for Peace
PIL	private international law
PJCC	Police and Judicial Cooperation in Criminal Matters
PSC	Political and Security Committee
R(E)IO	regional (economic) integration organization
RTB	regional trading block
QMV	qualified majority voting
Res.	resolution
RtoP	Responsibility to Protect
SDR	Special Drawing Right
SEA	Single European Act
SG	Secretary General
SPS	Agreement on the Application of Sanitary and Phytosanitary Measures
TBT	Agreement on Technical Barriers to Trade
TEC	Treaty establishing the European Community
TEU	Treaty on European Union
TFEU	Treaty on the Functioning of the European Union

TFG	Transitional Federal Government
TPC	Trade Policy Committee
TRIPs	Agreement on Trade Related Aspects of Intellectual Property Rights
UfM	Union for the Mediterranean
UN	United Nations
UNCLOS	United Nations Convention on the Law of the Sea
UNCTAD	United Nations Conference on Trade and Development
UNDP	United Nations Development Programme
UNEP	United Nations Environment Programme
UNESCO	United Nations Educational, Scientific and Cultural Organisation
UNFCC	United Nations Framework Convention on Climate Change
UNGA	United Nations General Assembly
UNHCR	United Nations High Commissioner for Refugees
UNMIK	United Nations Mission in Kosovo
UNSC	United Nations Security Council
UNSG	United Nations Secretary General
UNTLOS	United Nations Tribunal for the Law of the Sea
VCLT	Vienna Convention on the Law of Treaties
WEOG	Western European and Others Group
WEU	Western European Union
WHO	World Health Organization
WTO	World Trade Organization

CHAPTER ONE

THE EMERGING INTERNATIONAL IDENTITY OF THE EUROPEAN UNION – SOME PRELIMINARY OBSERVATIONS

Henri de Waele and Jan-Jaap Kuipers

1. Introduction: The Rise of a Capricious Global Player

In countless respects, the European Union constitutes a most remarkable legal experiment. For one thing, it is the product of an unprecedented process of integration between formerly sovereign nation-states. Over time, the construct evolved into a hybrid of supranational and international forms of governance which transcends classic Westphalian norms.[1] On the global scene, as an original composite structure, it cannot unreservedly be assimilated to federated actors. Apart from the enduring external presence of the EU Member States, until recently, the convoluted set-up was exacerbated by the unhelpful duality of a Community functioning alongside (or sometimes instead of) the Union.[2] Consequently, problems of demarcation have beset both the legal and the diplomatic field, and to an extent, such difficulties still persist today.

Internally, as has been richly documented elsewhere, the first regulatory steps focused on economic objectives.[3] A phase of gradual broadening and intensification ensued which, facilitated by the European Court of Justice's 'implied powers doctrine', has had a bearing far beyond the relations between the Member States.[4] As envisaged by the Court, this conscious commitment to common internal and external policies was

1 Ian Manners, 'Normative Power Europe: A Contradiction in Terms?', (2002) 40 *Journal of Common Market Studies*, p. 240. European Council President Herman Van Rompuy has recently typified the EU as "maybe the most sophisticated club of states that ever existed" ('The European Union in a Changing World', Speech by President of the European Council Herman van Rompuy at the India International Centre, 10 February 2012, EUCO 25/12).

2 See e.g. Koen Lenaerts and Eddy De Smijter, 'The European Union as an Actor under International Law', (1999–2000) 16 *Yearbook of European Law*, pp. 126–136.

3 See e.g. Mauro Cappelletti, Monica Seccombe and J.H.H. Weiler (eds.), *Integration through Law*, Berlin: Walter de Gruyter 1985.

4 As known, the kick-start was provided in Case 22/70, *Commission* v *Council* (ERTA), [1971] ECR 263.

bound to translate into a more refined profile vis-à-vis the outside world, and indeed at present, the Union's system of internal measures can no longer be separated from its international relations counterpart.[5]

For several years though, the shaping of a genuinely autonomous role of the EU in the global arena has been hampered by a significant amount of ambiguity surrounding its international legal personality.[6] On the one hand, the presence of a European Community – which did possess that quality – offered a convenient substratum for Union action. On the other hand, this made it seem unwise or unnecessary to bestow a similar status upon the latter. Evidently, such confusing asymmetry did little to raise Europe's profile in international legal traffic.[7] The situation was partly remedied in 1999, by according the EU treaty-making competence under the Common Foreign and Security Policy, and wholly resolved in 2009, following the dissolution of the EC and its integral replacement by the EU.[8] Both these renovations have brought some much-needed clarity, paving the way for the rise of a uniform global identity.

At this particular juncture, one might wonder whether the label 'international organization' may still be applied to the product of the remarkable integration experiment. Some have argued that it may be properly understood in federal terms, others regard the franchise as a highly advanced, but not intrinsically unique species.[9] While the academic debate is bound to rage on, the ECJ, as known, has trumpeted the view

---

[5] Panos Koutrakos, 'Legal Basis and Delimitation of Competence', in: Marise Cremona and Bruno De Witte (eds.), *EU Foreign Relations Law – Constitutional Foundations*, Oxford: Hart (2008), p. 171; Marise Cremona, 'External Relations and External Competence of the European Union: The Emergence of an Integrated Policy', in: Paul Craig and Gráinne de Búrca (eds.), *The Evolution of EU Law*, Oxford: Oxford University Press 2011, p. 217.

[6] See e.g. Ramses Wessel, 'Revisiting the International Legal Status of the EU', (2000) 5 *European Foreign Affairs Review*, p. 507; Marise Cremona, 'The Union as a Global Actor: Roles, Modes and Identity', (2004) 41 *Common Market Law Review*, p. 553.

[7] Compare for instance the common, but misguided expectation among observers in the early 1990s that the move from the single EC structure to the three-pillar EU structure at Maastricht signaled a fundamental shift from civilian to military power: see Manners, *supra* n. 1, p. 237.

[8] Pursuant to the entry into force of the Treaty of Amsterdam and the Treaty of Lisbon, respectively. The provision (*ex* Article 24 TEU) that accorded CFSP treaty-making competence was not unequivocal, as it did not make clear whether such agreements were to be concluded by the Council acting on behalf of the Member States, or by the Council on behalf of the EU as such. The latter supposition gradually became dominant, giving rise to the idea of the Union possessing 'presumptive international legal personality'. See further Wessel, *supra* n. 6.

[9] The two opposing lines are magisterially defended in respectively Robert Schütze, *From Dual to Cooperative Federalism: The Changing Structure of European Law*, Oxford: Oxford University Press 2009, and Bruno De Witte, 'The European Union as an International Legal

of a new, innovative, and largely self-contained legal order.[10] To be sure, this position has reinforced the actorness of the erstwhile Community and current-day Union, further buttressing claims to participation in international organizations alongside the Member States. At the same time, unfortunately, the great zeal with which the Court has sought to prevent the European legal order from being 'contaminated' by norms and principles considered alien and possibly deleterious, has also negatively impacted the latter's stature. For starters, in the eyes of outsiders, this tenacious shielding conveys the unfavorable impression that the local norms are regarded as superior. The stance is moreover problematic in light of the general theorem that domestic law cannot be invoked as a justification for not respecting international commitments.[11] Conversely, in some cases, it offers the Member States unacceptable leeway for operating outside the constraints of bilateral and multilateral agreements, by working through semi-permeable supranational institutions.[12]

The refurbished Article 21 TEU stipulates that in its external action, the Union endeavors to advance, inter alia, democracy, the rule of law and human rights. Its ultimate success on the world stage however is not solely determined by its institutional set-up, the internal allocation of competences, or the judicial agenda. Autonomy too may be self-proclaimed, but requires a conscious acceptance by, and an active collaboration with,

---

Experiment', in: J.H.H. Weiler and Gráinne de Búrca (eds.), *The Worlds of European Constitutionalism*, Cambridge: Cambridge University Press 2012, pp. 19–56.

[10] ECJ, Case 26/62, *NV Algemene Transport- en Expeditie Onderneming van Gend & Loos* v *Nederlandse administratie der belastingen*, [1963] ECR 3; Opinion 1/91, *Draft agreement relating to the creation of the European Economic Area*, [1991] ECR I-6079; Opinion 1/00, *Proposed agreement on the establishment of a European Common Aviation Area*, [2002] ECR I-3493; Joined Cases C-402/05 P and C-415/05 P, *Yassin Abdullah Kadi and Al Barakaat International Foundation* v *Council and Commission*, [2008] ECR I-6351; Case C-308/06, *The Queen, on the application of International Association of Independent Tanker Owners (Intertanko) and Others* v *Secretary of State for Transport*, [2008] ECR I-4057; Case C-366/10, *Air Transport Association of America and Others* v *Secretary of State for Energy and Climate Change*, Judgment of 21 December 2011, n.y.r.

[11] Jan Klabbers, 'The European Union in the Global Constitutional Mosaic', in: Neil Walker, Jo Shaw and Stephen Tierney (eds.), *Europe's Constitutional Mosaic*, Oxford: Hart Publishing 2011, pp. 298–299. For illustrations, see id., *Treaty Conflict and the European Union*, Cambridge: Cambridge University Press 2008; Eileen Denza, 'Placing the European Union in International Context – Legitimacy of the Court's Case Law', in: Maurice Adams, Henri de Waele, Johan Meeusen and Gert Straetmans (eds.), *Judging Europe's Judges – The Legitimacy of the Case Law of the European Court of Justice*, Oxford: Hart Publishing (forthcoming, 2013).

[12] As implicitly recognized in the *Air Transport Association of America* judgment (*supra*, n. 10): see Brian Havel and John Mulligan, 'Flying Too High? Extraterritoriality and the EU Emissions Trading Scheme', <http://eutopialaw.com/2012/02/02/958>.

other dominant global players. The pithy question posed in the 1970s, commonly attributed to Henry Kissinger, "Who do I call if I want to call Europe?", strikingly reflects that indeed, it are not just the EU Member States themselves that need to be persuaded to acknowledge and support the Union's role on the global scene.[13] Illustrative of this fact are the strenuous efforts of the E(E)C to 'upgrade' its status in multilateral forums, which repeatedly encountered resistance from countries that had little understanding of its constitutional dynamics, and were keen to preserve a more traditional international relations landscape.[14] At least from a law in the books vantage point, the entry into force of the Lisbon Treaty ought to mark a decisive change, which should eventually allow us to formulate an answer to Kissinger's question.[15] Much continues to depend nonetheless on how the Union is actually being perceived, whether other global players have grown accustomed to it in its various incarnations, and whether its refurbished architecture will prove able to dispel, or at least mitigate the earlier reluctance. It is to these questions, which are gaining in topicality, yet have been receiving still too little scholarly attention so far, that this volume is dedicated.

2. EU External Relations – A Nebulous Legal Patchwork

Undeniably, there is a byzantine quality to Union's external relations framework. While the bewildering complexity may be downplayed by labeling it as a 'layered' or 'multi-level constitution', this does little to attenuate the grave contrast with unitary states, 'pure' federations and international organizations.[16] The Union's internal modus of decision-making and its representation to the outside world are, alas, essentially different things.[17]

---

[13] Cf. Christian Tomuschat, 'Calling Europe by Phone', (2010) 47 *Common Market Law Review*, p. 3.

[14] Frank Hoffmeister, 'Outsider or Frontrunner? Recent Developments under International and European Law on the Status of the European Union in International Organizations and Treaty Bodies', (2007) 44 *Common Market Law Review*, p. 43. In this respect, also note e.g. the protracted refusal of the Soviet Union to recognize the legal personality of the EC.

[15] Tomuschat, *supra* n. 13. See also Peter Van Elsuwege, 'EU External Action after the Collapse of the Pillar Structure: In search of a New Balance between Delimitation and Consistency' (2010) 47 *Common Market Law Review*, p. 987.

[16] Cf. J.H.H. Weiler, 'The External Relations of Non-Unitary Actors: Mixity and the Federal Principle', in: id., *The Constitution of Europe*, Cambridge: Cambridge University Press 1999, p. 168.

[17] As emphatically noted in the contribution by De Baere and Paasivirta to this volume, with regard to EU-UN relations (Chapter 2).

For starters, the relevant Union competences are fragmented and scattered all over the Treaties.[18] Although at first glance, the Common Foreign and Security Policy may appear to be an all-encompassing cadre, spanning the whole gamut of EU external competences, upon closer inspection, it turns out to have a limited reach. Alongside the powers tucked away in the TFEU, it occupies a separate position and carries a paramountly residual character.[19]

Next, when peering inside a little bit longer, one is easily confounded by the multitude of organs, bodies and offices whose roles and powers are unhelpfully underdefined. Exemplary is the fuzzy order of play between the High Representative, the President of the Commission, and the President of the European Council.[20] In the absence of proper guidance in the TEU or TFEU, pragmatic behaviour from the incumbents is the only rule to avoid tensions or turf wars.[21] Working groups, committees and agencies are also rich in supply. The latest installment is the European External Action Service, which might promote cohesion, but simultaneously excites frictions, by necessarily curtailing national diplomatic autonomy.

The crucial component parts are the twenty-seven countries that buttress the overarching structure. Yet, largely due to the concept of shared powers, they find themselves not integrally enveloped by EU policies, retaining instead a potentially clamorous presence on the global plane.[22] After all, the kernel of the national legal orders lies in foundational norms with an independent claim to legitimacy, beyond the remit of the Treaties.[23] The upshot is a nearly unfathomable patchwork, consisting of closely interwoven, though poorly delineated components.

---

[18] Knud Erik Jørgensen and Ramses Wessel, 'The Position of the European Union in (other) International Organizations: Confronting Legal and Political Approaches', in: Panos Koutrakos (ed.), *EU Foreign Policy – Legal and Political Perspectives*, Cheltenham: Edward Elgar 2011, p. 266.

[19] Piet Eeckhout, *EU External Relations Law*, Oxford: Oxford University Press 2011, p. 170; Henri de Waele, *Layered Global Player – Legal Dynamics of EU External Relations*, Berlin-Heidelberg: Springer 2011, p. 23.

[20] See Art. 15(6), Art. 17(1) and Art. 27(2) TEU. On the role of Union delegations, see also Art. 221(2) TFEU.

[21] Cf. Mauro Gatti and Pietro Manzini, 'External Representation of the European Union in the Conclusion of International Agreements', (2012) 49 *Common Market Law Review*, p. 1703.

[22] As outlined in the contribution by Puccio to this volume (Chapter 9), as regards the EU's representation at the IMF, matters are compounded further by the division between Euro and non-Euro area countries, and the participation of national central banks.

[23] Christina Eckes, 'Protecting Supremacy from External Influences: A Precondition for a European Constitutional Order?', (2012) 18 *European Law Journal*, p. 233.

Whereas the European Court of Justice has ordained already several decades ago that there must a principal display of unity in international representation, this has not been realized overnight, with much still being left desired today. Both in the process of negotiation, conclusion, and in the fulfillment of the obligations undertaken under a mixed agreement, the ECJ specifically obliged the Union and the Member States to work in close association.[24] Within multilateral forums as well, they are to pursue positions that mutually reinforce one another.[25] In the latest case law it has gone even further, to the minds of some requesting a virtually unlimited form of obedience.[26] With the entry into force of the Lisbon Treaty, the duty of sincere cooperation has become of explicit general application, now covering both the Member States and the Union institutions.[27] Additionally, various provisions stress the overriding requirement of consistency in EU external action. Of course, both the duty of sincere cooperation and the principle of consistency are of critical importance for attaining the objectives spelled out in Article 21 TEU. In reality though, the stability of the entire construction rests on the willingness of the national and supranational institutions concerned to give priority to the *effet utile* of EU law.[28] In line with the Court's precepts, and codes of conduct drafted by the Commission, the Union and the Member States quite adequately coordinate their actions in practice. At the same time, this has not prevented departures by the latter from earlier agreed positions, or deliberate attempts in multilateral forums to reduce the voting power of the EU itself.[29] Thus, the desired structural unity may well prove illusory without deeper integration, in the absence of stronger enforcement tools than the

---

[24] ECJ, Opinion 1/78, *Draft International Agreement on Natural Rubber*, [1979] ECR 2871, par. 34. See also e.g. Case C-459/03, *Commission* v *Ireland* (Mox Plant), [2006] ECR I-4635, par. 175.

[25] ECJ, Opinion 2/91, *Participation of the Community in ILO Convention No. 170 on Chemicals at Work*, [1993] ECR I-1061, par. 36–38.

[26] ECJ, Case C-45/07, *Commission* v *Greece* (IMO), [2009] ECR I-701; ECJ, Case C-246/07, *Commission* v *Sweden* (PFOS), [2010] ECR I-3317; see Andrés Delgado Casteleiro and Joris Larik, 'The Duty to Remain Silent: Limitless Loyalty in EU External Relations?', (2011) 36 *European Law Review*, pp. 524–541.

[27] For earlier reflections, see Christophe Hillion, 'Mixity and Coherence in EU External Relations: The Significance of the Duty of Cooperation', *CLEER Working Papers* 2009/2; Marise Cremona, 'Defending the Community Interest: The Duties of Cooperation and Compliance', in: Marise Cremona and Bruno De Witte (eds.) *EU Foreign Relations Law – Constitutional Fundamentals*, Oxford: Hart Publishing 2008, pp. 125–169.

[28] Eckes, *supra* n. 23, p. 231.

[29] For illustrations, see Hoffmeister, *supra* n. 14, p. 66.

instigation of infringement procedures *ex post facto*.[30] It would seem that a true global powerhouse does not follow automatically from twenty-plus countries pooling their sovereignty, in order to reach common decisions in the foreign policy field.[31]

3. On, Off or In-Between Seats – The Union's Dealings with International Organizations

Notwithstanding its complex and inimitable anatomy, the EU maintains differing relations with numerous international organizations, general as well as specialized.[32] Thereby, its most intensive participation takes the form of either full membership or observer status.[33] As a rule of thumb, full membership is mainly found in areas where the Union possesses extensive competences.[34] That holds true, for example, for the World Trade Organization, while the EU is a mere observer in the International Labor Organization.[35] Its position has however shifted over time, often in sync with alterations to the EU Treaties resulting in an expanse of its powers. Conversely, while only a small number of international organizations allow other such organizations to become full members, their constitutions are not cast in stone either.[36]

Nonetheless, whenever the Union as such is refused admittance, some sizeable discomfort arises, especially when it holds exclusive external competences in the domain concerned.[37] In situations like these, the EU purports to stay in the picture by using the Member States as a conduit,

---

30 Art. 258–260 TFEU.

31 Reflection Group on the Future of the EU, 'Project Europe 2030 – Challenges and Opportunities', May 2010, p. 36.

32 Article 211 TEU, which stipulates that "[w]ithin their respective spheres of competence, the Union and the Member States shall cooperate with third countries and with the competent international organisations", deals out a mandate for this practice.

33 While the exact modalities can vary, observer status normally entails a right to speak and not to vote, nor to propose candidates at elections for governing bodies.

34 Jørgensen and Wessel, *supra* n. 18, p. 268; cf. Hoffmeister, *supra* n. 14, p. 54.

35 The ECJ confirmed that the Union's predecessor was capable of joining, or even founding, such organizations in Opinion 1/76, *Draft Agreement on the establishment of a European laying-up fund for inland waterway vessels*, [1977] ECR 741, par. 5, and in Joined Cases C-3, 4 & 6/76, *Cornelis Kramer and Others*, [1976] ECR 1279, par. 17–18.

36 As demonstrated e.g. by the willingness of the FAO to amend its statute in 1991, so as to allow for membership of regional economic integration organizations.

37 As is e.g. the case with regard to the ILO. The tension is highlighted further in the contribution of Delarue to this volume (Chapter 6).

expecting them to behave as 'trustees of the common interest'.[38] This even holds when not all Member States take part in the organization concerned.[39] As their legal status is not wholly clear, agreements concluded by these 'trustees of the common interest' may then turn out to be a recurrent spot of bother. However, when the relevant issues resides within the purview of EU competence, there is good reason to consider those binding upon the Union.[40]

Consonant with the reluctance flagged above, even when the Union possesses the necessary competence to accede, the Member States are frequently unenthusiastic about it actually doing so. Hereby, they appear adamant not to dilute their own influence in the organizations concerned.[41] Where the Union moreover holds exclusive powers in the relevant domain, and the Member States persist in dealing with the issues themselves, their posture could be qualified as an egregious violation of the duty of cooperation. A nefarious corollary is that the organization itself and the other contracting states may gain the erroneous impression that the subject-matter lies (chiefly) within the scope of national competences.[42] Now that the EU, with the entry into force of the Lisbon Treaty, has gained in stature, power and coherence, one would expect such cases of overt obstruction to diminish. Equally, an increasing number of organizations that hitherto denied access, might contemplate the idea anew, either as a once-only favor, or as part of a wider strategy of 'opening up'.

In the post-Lisbon era, the Treaties contain multiple provisions that spell out how, when legally permitted to do so, the Union should conduct itself in international forums. They often render the High Representative responsible for expressing the EU's positions, and aligning the views of the Member States.[43] The diplomatic missions and delegations are similarly bound to cooperating, and to contribute to the formulation

---

[38] Marise Cremona, 'Member States as Trustees of the Union Interest: Participating in International Agreements on behalf of the European Union', in: Anthony Arnull, Catherine Barnard, Michael Dougan and Eleanor Spaventa (eds.), *A Constitutional Order of States: Essays in European Law in Honour of Alan Dashwood*, Oxford: Hart Publishing 2011, p. 435; cf. ECJ, Opinion 2/91, *supra* n. 25, par. 5.

[39] See Art. 34 TEU.

[40] Inge Govaere, Jeroen Capiau, An Vermeersch, 'In-Between Seats: The Participation of the European Union in International Organizations', (2004) 9 *European Foreign Affairs Review*, p. 176.

[41] Ibid., p. 171.

[42] Ibid., p. 173.

[43] Art. 27 and Art. 34 TEU.

and implementation of common approaches.[44] When adhered to in good faith, these instructions go some way in alleviating the problem of an EU that occasionally still finds itself stuck 'in-between seats'. Perhaps the most notable progress so far was made at the UN, with the adoption of Resolution 65/276 by the General Assembly.[45] Bouncing back from a failure at the first attempt in 2010, the Union was finally accorded an enhanced observer status in the UNGA, inter alia awarding it speaking rights, the right to circulate documents and to present proposals or amendments. It is not clear however whether, and if so in what way, this arrangement also applies to specialised UN agencies.[46] The implementation of the Lisbon Treaty has also been hampered by an absence of political guidance with regard to EU representation at other multilateral organizations, and the slightly overdue creation of the EEAS. Nevertheless, with regard to the Union's dealings with international organizations, even when not every asymmetry is likely to be overcome, a page does look certain to be turned.

4. External Impact and External Perception – The View from the Global Arena

There is certainly no dearth of literature on what, competence-wise, the EU can do in relation to the Member States, how it can do this, and has done it.[47] By the same token, sundry scholars have attested already that the latest renovations are poised to reinvigorate the conduct and scope of the Union's external relations.[48] Comparatively less attention has however gone out to the question of its external impact, and to (possible changes in) how it is being perceived by its international partners. To be sure, in the past decades, it has stepped up its efforts with means, money and manpower to make a tangible difference across the planet. As known, the EU is at present the largest dispenser of official development assistance, has sent out thousands of aid workers, soldiers, policemen and judges

---

44 Art. 32 and Art 35 TEU.

45 Resolution A/RES/65/276, 10 May 2011.

46 UN Document A/65/856, 'Participation of the European Union in the Work of the United Nations – Note by the Secretary-General', does propose to extend its working sphere to subsidiary organs of the UNGA.

47 Jørgensen and Wessel, *supra* n. 18, p. 273.

48 Paul James Cardwell, 'EU External Relations Law and Policy in the Post-Lisbon Era', in: id., *EU External Relations Law and Policy in the Post-Lisbon Era*, Berlin-Heidelberg: Springer 2011, p. 5.

in missions around the world, engaged in peacekeeping on the Balkans and in the African Great Lakes region, training police in Kosovo, Iraq and Afghanistan, combating piracy off the coast of Somalia. It regards itself as constructive in world trade negotiations, ambitious in climate talks, and forthcoming in the reform of the international financial institutions, recognizing the seismic shifts in global economic power.[49] All the same, many political scientists regard it above all as a standard-setter, and have qualified Europe's attainment as more normative than empirical.[50] This does not mean to say that the Union's civilian or (fledgling) military powers are unimportant, but that views on its concrete achievements need to be augmented: for, the most important factor shaping its international role is arguably not so much what it does or says, but what it ideologically stands for.[51] As noted, according to the restyled Treaty provisions, EU external action is nowadays expressly predicated on the advancement of democracy, the rule of law and human rights. From a macro-perspective, its strong commitment to fundamental rights represents no less than a crucial characteristic, rendering the Union normatively distinct from other polities.[52]

As yet, this dimension has not been sufficiently appreciated. Whereas they do habitually focus on issues of representation and kept an open eye for the Lisbon changeover, the majority of legal scholars still stuck to analyzing the distribution and (limits to the) exercise of competences. Other studies, predominantly conducted by political scientists, seem to omit a decisive longitudinal complication, by not incorporating the persistent duality between the Union and the Community, the recent resolution thereof, and its external ramifications.[53] Once that the EU undertook to intensify its linkages with other international actors, it has made an ever-greater inroad on their rulebooks, e.g. by securing full membership

49 Herman Van Rompuy, 'Address to the 66th United Nations General Assembly General Debate', 22 September 2011, EUCO 78/11, p. 4.

50 Richard Rosecranze, 'The European Union: A New Type of International Actor', in: Jan Zielonka (ed.), *Paradoxes of European Foreign Policy*, The Hague: Kluwer Law International 1998, p. 22. See also Joseph Nye, *Soft Power: The Means to Success in World Politics*, New York: Public Affairs 2004, pp. 73–99.

51 Manners, *supra* n. 1, p. 239 and p. 252.

52 Ibid., p. 241.

53 E.g. Spyros Blavoukos and Dimitris Bourantonis (eds.), *The EU Presence in International Organizations*, Abingdon: Routledge 2011; Robert Kissack, *Pursuing Effective Multilateralism. The European Union, International Organisations and the Politics of Decision Making*, Basingstoke: Palgrave Macmillan 2010.

to some organizations, therewith prying open the door for others to join as well.[54]

The Union's rise and transformation from an economic to a normative political player has also had an inexorable political impact, the profundity of which has not been gauged satisfactorily either. Ostensibly missing is thus a survey of what the EU has accomplished, and of the perceptions of its accomplishments in the eyes of others – taking into account the complexity of the legal framework, its evolution over time, and the contemporary state of play. With the intent of progressing on the earlier frames of analyses, this is exactly what the current volume sets out to do, inquiring into the Union's impact, recognition and acceptance in a coherent, refined and systematic manner. This collating of a heterogeneous set of standpoints from the 'global arena' (to put it in slightly martial terms) should allow for a fair balance to be struck between views from the outside looking in, and from the inside looking out. Ultimately, this holistic approach is expected to provide us with insight into, what we tentatively dub, the Union's 'emerging international identity'.

5. Identifying Identities

As remarked above, the internal competences of the EU have gone through a long period of flux, and even in the post-Lisbon era, their central tenets remain ill-defined. In comparison, the concept of 'international identity' constitutes a concept with parameters that might be considered even less fixed.[55] The preamble of the TEU obliquely makes mention of the term, outlining that it is bound to be reinforced by the implementation of the CFSP and the progressive framing of a common defense policy.[56] Interestingly, in the Maastricht version, the international identity was

54 Cf. Hoffmeister, *supra* n. 14, p. 67. Vis-à-vis the Council of Europe, the Union has pursued a most unusual trajectory, further detailed in the contribution by Streinz to this volume (Chapter 5).

55 Amongst legal scholars and political scientists, there does exist consensus with regard to the 'actorness' of the EU, but no agreement on how this quality should be defined and measured. See, with further references, Aurel Sari, 'Between Legalisation and Organisational Development: Explaining the Evolution of EU Competence in the Field of Foreign and Security Policy', in: Paul James Cardwell (ed.), *EU External Relations Law and Policy in the Post-Lisbon Era*, Berlin-Heidelberg: Springer 2011, p. 60–61. For socio-cultural understandings of the concept of (European) identity, see e.g. Jeffrey Checkel and Peter Katzenstein (eds.), *European Identity*, Cambridge: Cambridge University Press 2009.

56 TEU, Preamble, 11th recital.

also referred to in the TEU itself, and proclaimed as something that was yet to be "asserted on the international scene".[57] Nonetheless, already in December 1973, the Heads of State or Government of the EEC countries affirmed their determination to introduce the concept of European identity into their common foreign relations.[58] Unhelpfully, neither then nor now, any further definition was given.

Although we did note earlier that the Union's internal modus of decision-making and its external representation are different things, there exists an irrefutable linkage between its internal activity and its external identity.[59] As indicated above, an entity's international identity cannot solely be determined with reference to an internal set of rules, but depends equally on the degree of recognition of the coveted status by other players. If we would adhere to a strictly positivist understanding, the concept would denote the ability of the EU to act on the international stage and to assume legally binding obligations. The Union's identity in an international organization would then refer to its formal influence on the output of the organization concerned, including official participation in its organs, voting rights and the membership of drafting committees.[60] This conceptualization of international identity unmistakably correlates with that of international legal personality, but is broader in ambit, and more open to interdisciplinary analysis.[61]

With the EU not being a monolithic actor, contrasting positions can be taken on the precise delineation of its identity. From one vantage point, the Union can be perceived as an empty shell, its identity being purely derivative, coinciding (at most) with the sum of the individual identities of the Member States. From a second perspective, the Union and its Member States could be perceived as full equals, with a transcendental (joint) identity arising from their combined actions. Third and last, one may stick to the perception of an indissoluble whole, with Member States forming an inextricable part of the overarching structure, regardless of the

[57] TEU, Article B, par. 2. For further reflections on the significance of this divergence, viewed within the light of EU-NATO interaction, see the contribution of Larik to this volume (Chapter 3).

[58] 'Declaration on European Identity', Copenhagen, 14 December 1973, *Bull. EC* [1973] No. 12.

[59] In her contribution to this volume, focusing on EU-WTO relations (Chapter 4), Perišin even sees external identity as being conditional on internal activity.

[60] Jørgensen and Wessel, *supra* n. 18, p. 262.

[61] Cf. the definition provided by the ICJ in *Reparation for Injuries Suffered in the Service of the United Nations (Advisory Opinion)*, ICJ Reports 1949, p. 178.

erstwhile Community/Union duality.[62] Naturally, these abstract takes on identity leave unaddressed the question of how the competences are formally distributed, and which offices are meant to take care of the EU's representation (High Representative, European Council President, etc.).[63] To be sure, the legal issues are important, and must definitely not be ignored. At the same time, we should not confine ourselves to a one-sided 'law in the books' methodology, if only because it offers little clarity with regard to the concept of international identity. The latter, we contend, is better exposed by assessing the Union's *modus operandi* in reality, and taking the law in action into account. In certain international forums, for instance, the delivering of a common EU position by the Council Presidency on behalf of the Member States might convey the impression that the latter lack (or have lost) the power to act autonomously. This shows how, irrespective of the doctrine of pre-emption, particular factual circumstances might well spark an external perception of competence transfer, thereby amplifying the identity of the former to the detriment of the latter.[64]

In sum, a strict positivist understanding of identity would not adequately conceptualize the informal structures through which the Union participates in international organizations, since the concept is inherently multifaceted. At its most hazy, it defines 'the relationship between the EU and the rest of the world'. More substantially, it encompasses all the means and forms, both tangible and intangible, through which the EU manifests itself at the international level. Overall, identity is a question of standpoint, so that capturing the entirety calls for the inclusion of different standpoints.[65] For that reason, in this volume, we undertake to review the Union's role and performance within the framework of various organizations, reflecting on the most pertinent rules and practices. Even then,

---

62 Cf. Armin von Bogdandy, 'The Legal Case for Unity: The European Union as a Single Organization with a Single Legal System', (1999) 36 *Common Market Law Review*, p. 887.

63 Hereby, the greater the number of committees of an international organization, the greater the conundrum is, due to the various EU actors having to coordinate ever more intensely. This is vividly illustrated in the contribution by Takács and Verschaeve to this volume, focusing on the interplay between the EU and the OECD (Chapter 8).

64 Assuming that the observers attach value to the distinction in the first place (i.e. in the first or second scenario just sketched).

65 Ian Manners and Richard Whitman, 'Towards Identifying the International Identity of the European Union: A Framework for Analysis of the EU's Network Relationships' (1998) 21 *Journal of European Integration*, pp. 237–8; see also Ian Manners and Richard Whitman, 'The "Difference Engine": Constructing and Representing the International Identity of the European Union (2003) 10 *Journal of European Public Policy*, p. 231; Massimiliano Andretta and Nicole Doerr, 'Imagining Europe: Internal and External Non-State Actors at the European Crossroads' (2007) 12 *European Foreign Affairs Review*, p. 385.

catching the whole image must prove illusory; but musing on its status, functioning and representation within these contexts should enable us to trace the main contours nevertheless.

6. Structure of the Inquiry

If in the early 1990s, the determination was committed to paper to assert the Union's identity on the international scene, this in itself did not diminish the potential for confusion: after all, the E(E)C had been around for much longer, with its external relations patchwork leaving every room for Member States to hinder or obstruct the emergence of structural common positions. A grand tidying-up exercise was nearly twenty years in waiting, but finally pulled off at the end of 2009. Though in certain respects, the transition is not yet fully completed, much of the dust has started to settle, making it possible to probe the repercussions for its profile in international legal traffic. All the same, in order to acquire a complete picture, the examination necessarily has to be sustained and diachronic, also taking into view the preceding maneuvers and involvements of the Community.[66]

The EU maintains official relations with a rich variety of international organizations, with its most intensive participation in their work taking the form of either full membership or observer status. Our objective is to cover a representative selection, which includes the United Nations, the North Atlantic Treaty Organization, the World Trade Organization, the Organization for Economic Co-Operation and Development, the Council of Europe, the Hague Conference on Private International Law, the International Labour Organization, and the International Monetary Fund. For one thing, this provides an adequate mix between older and younger organizations. Additionally, it incorporates both the general and the specialized, as well as environments in which the EU is either a full member, observer, or holds (as such) no status at all. Since it does not participate in the work of the selected organizations with equal intensity or for an equally long period, the chosen line-up appears reasonably balanced, is expected to yield significant results, and allows for a sound comparative analysis.

---

[66] Cf. astoundingly misguided remarks such as in Hedley Bull, 'Civilian Power Europe: A Contradiction in Terms?', (1982) 21 *Journal of Common Market Studies*, p. 151: "'Europe' is not an actor in international affairs, and does not seem likely to become one."

In consecutive chapters, the participation of the Union in each of these organizations will be reviewed from an outside-in and/or an inside-out perspective. As said, the studies take a holistic approach, investigating both the EU's position and the relevant perception(s) thereof. Each of the contributions can be regarded as an attempt at critical and systematic stocktaking, aiming to sketch the interaction from multiple angles, with reference to the relevant legal rules, official documents and other sources.[67]

The individual chapters adhere to a similar methodological setup, exploring a same set of questions. They generally start off with a discussion of the internal EU competences and measures in the policy area of the respective international organization. However, as remarked, the Union's recognition in a particular environment is unlikely to depend solely upon the division of competences between the EU and its Member States.[68] Besides the (vertical) dynamics between the Union institutions and the Member States, there is the (horizontal) dynamic between the EU and its international partners. It can be expected that there exists a traceable legal, political or economic incentive for the respective international organization (and its other members) to facilitate the participation of the Union in the work of that organization; otherwise it would not have been allowed to participate at all. Therefore, some of the underlying paradigms require further exploration, inquiring e.g. into the precise relationship between the policy objectives of the organization concerned and the pertinent competences of the EU, whether the Union's participation is complementary to the pursuit of the internal objectives of either of them, and how important and effective the collaboration between the two actors has turned out to be so far.

After or alongside this sketch of the wider context, the individual chapters engage in an analysis of the formal status of the Union and (if applicable) the residual role left for the Member States. Naturally, it makes a crucial difference whether the EU enjoys the status of a full member, whether it merely holds an observer status, or has no formal position whatsoever. In the first scenario, it will be interesting to establish whether the participation of the Member States has been integrally replaced by the membership of the Union. If there is a residual role left for the Member

[67] Inspired by Armin von Bogdandy, Philipp Dann and Matthias Goldmann, 'Developing the Publicness of Public International Law: Towards a Legal Framework for Global Governance Activities', (2011) 9 *German Law Journal*, p. 1398.

[68] Jørgensen and Wessel *supra* n. 18, p. 285.

States, a pertinent question will be how the division of competences between the EU and its Member States has been addressed within the frame of the organization, and in particular, how the international partners are informed about the precise delimitation of competences. In the event that the Union enjoys no formal position whatsoever, it becomes highly useful to ascertain whether any legal or practical obstacles prevent (or prevented) the Union from joining in any official capacity, or whether a possible 'stand-off approach' was perhaps the result of a conscious choice. Therefore, if the international organization only accords the Union limited formal recognition, leading questions are inter alia: are there any informal arrangements acknowledging the international identity of the Union? How and to what extent is the constitutional relation between the Union and its Member States accommodated within the structure of the organization concerned? Do the existing dynamics testify to a smooth interplay or not?

The analyses combine insights from theory and practice, but naturally cannot hope to cover every aspect. Furthermore, while the contributors form a mix of insiders and outsiders, their perceptions are not empirically tested against a larger audience. A concluding chapter attempts nonetheless to juxtapose the different experiences, underline common trends and recurring patterns, and formulate some general conclusions with regard to the Union's emerging international identity.

7. Some Provisional Assumptions

From the outset, it is expected that the viability of an emerging international identity depends on the specific setting. Rather than possessing a single international *habitus*, the Union's profile in the global legal arena may be singularly chameleonic, changing and adjusting in accordance with the needs and the possibilities of each particular environment. For instance, as will be pointed out, the Hague Conference on Private International Law has taken quite a receptive approach towards the EU. Traditionally, the latter's Member States have dominated the harmonization efforts pursued within the sphere of the Conference. However, the introduction of a legal basis in the Treaty of Amsterdam (1999), empowering the Union to adopt measures relating to judicial cooperation in civil matters, constituted a serious threat to the Conference's pertinence. It responded by actively recruiting the membership of non-European countries. Moreover, its statutes were amended to allow for the accession of a regional economic integration organization (REIO). The EU itself leapt at the chance, by acceding in 2007. The Hague Conventions that were adopted more recently within the Conference contain a specific clause allowing for ratification by a REIO, and provide for a special 'disconnection clause' regulating the application of the Convention with the internal rules of the REIO. This accommodating approach of the Hague Conference towards the EU was one born out of necessity, as the harmonization efforts relating to private international law within the Union seriously threatened to undermine the work of the Hague Conference. Thus, the broad(er) recognition of the international identity of the Union within the Hague Conference appeared to be vital for the organization's future existence.[69] Ultimately, this could turn out to be a relevant paradigm in other settings as well.

In contrast, a more reluctant approach might be assumed within conglomerates such as the United Nations, where the political stakes are significantly higher. Hitherto, the exercise by the EU of its internal competences has had no direct effect on the functioning of the UN. While the Union currently holds an enhanced observer status, attempts to upscale its package of rights have only recently been successful, after repeatedly encountering resistance from other international partners. Even today, despite energetic efforts both on- and off-stage, the common positions upheld and promoted by the EU are not invariably hailed with immediate support in either the Security Council or the General Assembly – although vice versa, most UN measures have been unquestionably adhered to within the European legal order.[70] These contrasting trends make one pause whether the conception of a Union 'identity' within the framework of the United Nations can claim any true credibility. Obviously, the dedicated chapter in this volume endeavors to shed light on this issue, and underpin or disprove our preliminary assumptions.[71]

Considering the post-Lisbon proliferation of offices with external tasks or ambitions, issues of representation are certain to arise. Despite the evaporation of the Community, the friction is not expected to have abated all that much, since it did not lead to a decrease in the total number of

---

69 For further discussion, see the contribution of Kuipers to this volume (Chapter 7).

70 At least by the EU legislature and the executive; as the *Kadi*-saga illustrates, the judiciary is (once again) a different matter.

71 See the contribution of De Baere and Paasivirta to this volume (Chapter 2).

actors, or an amalgamation of CFSP and non-CFSP procedures.[72] Rather, the half-hearted replacement of the rotating European Council Presidency by a permanent chair, and the upgrading of the position of the High Representative, added extra stakeholders to the fray. Whenever the Union is a full member of an organization, it may be represented by the Commission or the HR, pushing the other EU institutions to the background. They can also take the floor on behalf of the Member States, in case the latter are parties as well. Absent the Commission or HR however, the Member State holding the rotating Council Presidency may act in three distinct capacities: as the mouthpiece of the Union, on the basis of a common position agreed within that framework; on behalf of the collective Member States; or rather as voicing the interests of the individual country at stake. Consequently, even today, international organizations might not always know whom to address, nor in what capacity the addressee answers.[73] Unavoidably then, in organizations dealing with a subject-matter that fall within shared competence, the Union's international identity is likely to be less forthcoming. By the same token, substantial internal friction is likely to excite dito external friction. Yet, as observed, this need not be a hard and fast rule, since third parties may still believe to be confronted with an indissoluble whole, as long as the Union and its Member States keep managing to toe a straight line.

Finally, we cannot afford to neglect the ruptures created by the sovereign debt crisis, a scourge that could eventually knock away the foundations from under the whole supranational architecture. Even in a more optimistic scenario, it is bound to have implications for the ways in which the Union relates to the world.[74] As the crisis already erupted several years ago, these implications should be eminently visible. On the one hand, the fault lines within the Eurozone look set to obtain greater visibility in organizations where the Member States continue to partake individually, i.e. not where the EU holds an exclusive competence. This should, predictably, result in an increasingly fragmented image. On the other hand, the crisis has simultaneously brought the (majority of) countries closer together, to an extent actually bolstering their resolve. Thus, in

---

[72] Apart from the merger of the treaty-making procedures (formerly Art. 24 TEU and Art. 300 TEC).

[73] Cf. Govaere, Capiau and Vermeersch, *supra* n. 40, p. 162.

[74] Malcolm Evans and Panos Koutrakos, 'Introduction', in: Malcolm Evans and Panos Koutrakos (eds.), *Policy Interconnections between the EU and the Rest of the World*, Oxford: Hart Publishing 2011, p. 8.

forums such as the OECD and the IMF, where the Union is not a party in its own right, the emergence of an impregnable united front cannot be excluded out of hand either.

8. Conclusion: Minding the Gap

All in all, it does not appear too far-fetched to posit that the legal proclamation of an autonomous identity is but one thing, and its recognition by other international actors quite something else. Looking through the eyes of the latter requires embarking on an expedition from a highly practical perspective, which should make it possible to ascertain whether there exists a gap between the judicially prescribed unity on the one hand, and the prevailing realities in the global arena on the other. Last, but by no means least, this inquiry should enable us to assert whether the EU is chiefly regarded as a simple derivative, something more than the sum of its parts – or an entity that is genuinely in possession of an international identity of its own.

CHAPTER TWO

IDENTITY AND DIFFERENCE: THE EU AND THE UN AS PART OF EACH OTHER

Geert De Baere and Esa Paasivirta

1. Introduction

Much like the EU, the UN was conceived in the aftermath of World War II,[1] with the clear objective never to allow a similar cataclysmic event to happen again. Though both are rather different international organizations, the ever-expanding range of issues that come within the purview of EU law engender an increasing amount of connection points at different levels.[2] The Union is quite unambiguous as regards the importance it attaches to the UN. As the European Security Strategy puts it: "The fundamental framework for international relations is the United Nations Charter."[3] The EU, including its Member States, is also the single largest financial contributor to the UN system. The twenty-seven EU Member States fund 38% of the UN's regular budget, more than 40% of UN peacekeeping operations, and about 50% of all UN members' contributions to UN funds and programmes.[4]

It is therefore not surprising that the UN features prominently in the constituent Treaties of the EU. Article 3(5) TEU, which is placed within the common provisions of the EU Treaty, provides that the EU is to

[1] See, for example, Paul Kennedy, *The Parliament of Man. The Past Present, and Future of the United Nations*, New York: Vintage Books 2006, pp. 3–47; cf. Giandomenico Majone, *Europe as the Would-be World Power. The EU at Fifty*, Cambridge: Cambridge University Press 2009, p. 202.

[2] Koen Lenaerts and Eddy De Smijter, 'The United Nations and the European Union: Living Apart Together', in: Karel Wellens (ed.), *International Law: Theory and Practice. Essays in Honour of Eric Suy*, The Hague-Boston-London: Martinus Nijhoff Publishers 1998, pp. 439–458, p. 439; Jan Wouters, Frank Hoffmeister and Tom Ruys, 'Introduction', in: Jan Wouters, Frank Hoffmeister and Tom Ruys (eds.), *The United Nations and the European Union: An Ever Stronger Partnership*, The Hague: T.M.C. Asser Press 2006, p. 1.

[3] *A Secure Europe in a Better World. European Security Strategy*, Brussels, 12 December 2003, p. 9.

[4] See 'About the EU at the UN', available at <http://www.eu-un.europa.eu/articles/en/article_9389_en.htm>.

contribute to the "strict observance and the development of international law, including respect for the principles of the United Nations Charter". With respect to the EU's external action, Article 21(1) TEU provides that the Union's action on the international scene is to be "guided by the principles which have inspired its own creation, development and enlargement, and which it seeks to advance in the wider world", which include "respect for the principles of the United Nations Charter and international law", and obliges the Union to "promote multilateral solutions to common problems, in particular in the framework of the United Nations". Article 21(2)(c) TEU further provides for the Union to define and pursue common policies and actions, and to work for a high degree of cooperation in all fields of international relations, in order to preserve peace, prevent conflicts and strengthen international security, in accordance with, inter alia, the purposes and principles of the UN Charter. Article 34 TEU outlines certain rules on Member State participation in the UN Security Council (UNSC), to which we will return below.

Article 42 TEU provides for the Common Security and Defence Policy (CSDP) to be conducted in accordance with the UN Charter. In particular, Article 42(1) TEU provides that the Union may use CSDP capacity "on missions outside the Union for peace-keeping, conflict prevention and strengthening international security in accordance with the principles of the United Nations Charter". Article 42(7) TEU then provides that if "a Member State is the victim of armed aggression on its territory, the other Member States shall have towards it an obligation of aid and assistance by all the means in their power, in accordance with Article 51 of the United Nations Charter". The eleventh recital in the preamble to the TEU explicitly connects the development of the CSDP, and the potential establishment of a common defense in accordance with Article 42 TEU, to the emergence of the Union's international identity. The progressive development of the CSDP is intended to reinforce "the European identity and its independence in order to promote peace, security and progress in Europe and in the world". That identity, as Article 42 TEU itself makes abundantly clear, inherently includes the respect for the principles of the United Nations Charter.

The TFEU contains a certain number of references to the UN Charter as well. The seventh recital in the preamble notes the intention of the Member States "to confirm the solidarity which binds Europe and the overseas countries and desiring to ensure the development of their prosperity, in accordance with the principles of the Charter of the United Nations". Within the context of development cooperation, Article 208(2) TFEU provides that the EU and its Member States are to "comply with the commitments and take account of the objectives they have approved in the context of the United Nations and other competent international organisations". Article 214(7) TFEU further provides that the EU is to "ensure that its humanitarian aid operations are coordinated and consistent with those of international organisations and bodies, in particular those forming part of the United Nations system". Finally, Article 220(1) TFEU obliges the EU to "establish all appropriate forms of cooperation with the organs of the United Nations and its specialised agencies".

In a sense, these extensive Treaty references reflect on the part of the EU a constitutional attitude towards the UN system, rather than an instrumental attitude grounded in traditional foreign policy objectives. That attitude, or so we would argue, forms an inherent part of the Union's emerging international identity. The present chapter focuses mainly on how this attitude is reflected in the role played by the EU in its cooperation with the UN.

In that regard, it should be kept in mind that the EU's global role does not exist in a vacuum. The international organizations (IOs) in which the EU wishes to play a role have their own institutions and membership structures. The EU too has its past, and its Member States have a history of participating in the UN as its members. When assessing the position of the EU within the UN, it is therefore important to distinguish carefully between the international legal dimension on the one hand, and the EU law dimension on the other hand.[5] We shall therefore commence with a short overview of the rules governing EU external representation, followed by an exploration of the Union's internal coordination processes. Moving to the UN level, the chapter then analyses the drivers, structures, and constraints involved in EU cooperation with the United Nations, which is followed by an examination of the Union's status and its participation within the UN. It should be noted that we will not address in detail the implementation by the EU of UN obligations which, especially in the

[5] Cf. Frank Hoffmeister and Pieter-Jan Kuijper, 'The Status of the European Union at the United Nations: Institutional Ambiguities and Political Realities', in: Jan Wouters, Frank Hoffmeister and Tom Ruys (eds.), *The United Nations and the European Union: An Ever Stronger Partnership*, The Hague: T.M.C. Asser Press 2006, p. 10; Knud Erik Jørgensen and Ramses Wessel, 'The position of the European Union in (other) International Organizations: Confronting Legal and Political Approaches', in: Panos Koutrakos (ed.), *European Foreign Policy. Legal and Political Perspectives*, Cheltenham: Edward Elgar 2011, p. 264.

light of the ongoing *Kadi* saga,[6] merits a separate treatment that exceeds the scope of this chapter.[7]

2. EU External Representation and Internal Coordination

As far as the EU rules are concerned, it is important to recall that the internal decision-making of the EU and its external representation are different things. This implies, for example, that it is not because one institution is responsible for external representation, for example the Commission, that the same institution also decides on the policy line to be taken in external forums. It is a question of the difference between message and messenger, which follows from Articles 16 and 17 TEU. Article 16 TEU contains an institutional description of the tasks of the Council, and provides for it to exercise legislative and budgetary functions jointly with the Parliament, and to carry out policy-making and coordinating functions as laid down in the Treaties. Article 17 provides a similar institutional description of the Commission, and lays down its basic functions. In this respect, Article 17 TEU provides that, "with the exception of the Common Foreign and Security Policy and other cases provided for in the Treaties, the Commission is to ensure the Union's external representation". In the Common Foreign and Security Policy (CFSP), the EU representation is ensured by the High Representative of the Union for Foreign Affairs and Security Policy (Article 18(2) TEU) and, "at his level and in that capacity", by the President of the European Council, without prejudice to the powers of the High Representative (Article 15(6) TEU).

---

[6] Case T-315/01, *Yassin Abdullah Kadi* v *Council and Commission*, [2005] ECR II-33649; Case T-301/01, *Ahmed Ali Yusuf and Al Barakaat International Foundation* v *Council and Commission*, [2005] ECR II-3533; Joined Cases C-402/05 P and C-415/05 P, *Yassin Abdullah Kadi and Al Barakaat International Foundation* v *Council and Commission*, [2008] ECR I-6351; Case T-85/09, *Yassin Abdullah Kadi* v *Commission*, [2010] ECR II-5177; Case C-584/10 P, *Commission* v *Yassin Abdullah Kadi*, [2011] OJ C72/9, pending; Case C-593/10 P, *Council* v *Kadi*, [2011] OJ C72/9, pending; Case C-595/10 P, *United Kingdom* v *Yassin Abdullah Kadi*, [2011] OJ C72/10, pending. In his Opinion of 19 March 2013 in Joined Cases C-584/10 P, C-593/10 P, and C-595/10 P, A-G Bot proposes that the Court should set aside the judgment of the General Court in Case T-85/09 and dismiss the action brought by Mr. Kadi.

[7] For further discussion, see e.g. Daniel Halberstam and Eric Stein, 'The United Nations, the European Union, and the King of Sweden: Economic Sanctions and Individual Rights in a Plural World Order', (2009) 46 *Common Market Law Review*, p. 13; Gráinne de Búrca, 'The ECJ and the International Legal Order: A Re-Evaluation', in: Gráinne de Búrca and J.H.H. Weiler (eds.), *The Worlds of European Constitutionalism*, Cambridge: Cambridge University Press 2012, p. 105.

There exists a delicate balance between Articles 16 and 17 TEU, which requires distinguishing between different situations in international meetings. On the one hand, there are situations where the EU position is well-known, for instance due to EU legislation or earlier EU statements or Council conclusions. In these cases, the Commission (or the High Representative) can express the EU position without necessarily having to resort to further internal procedures. On the other hand, there are situations where the Union's position is not known, i.e. when the Union does not have a position (or fully developed position). In this case, there is no EU position to be represented on the external scene. It is quite another matter if, for instance, the Commission has expressed a view during the internal debate of the Union, which has however not been adopted as the EU position for external purposes. In that case, one falls back on Article 16(1) TEU, which assigns to the Council the policy-making functions, and would thus require the Council to endorse (or amend) the position that the Commission has proposed.[8] Thus, while the EU representation is entrusted to the Commission and the High Representative (leaving the President of the European Council to one side for a moment), the balance with the policy-making functions of the Council is essential to ensure that the institutional arrangements are efficient, and that they operate in a manner that generates trust between the institutions.

Before the entry into force of the Lisbon Treaty, the Commission represented EU positions concerning the first pillar, that is to say 'Community' matters, to the extent permitted by the UN rules and practices, while the Council Presidency represented the Union in other cases, mostly pertaining to the CFSP. From time to time, both institutions switched seats in the middle of a UN meeting if the competence changed from the first to the second pillar, or vice versa.[9]

However, the Lisbon Treaty removed all explicit references in the Treaties to the role of the Council Presidency in the external representation of the EU. The new Treaty rules (Articles 17 and 27(2) TEU) set a clear framework: the external representation of the EU is ensured by the High

---

[8] Esa Paasivirta, 'The EU's External Representation after Lisbon: New Rule, a New Era?', in: Panos Koutrakos (ed.), *The European Union's External Relations a Year after Lisbon*, The Hague: CLEER Working Papers 2011/3, p. 42.

[9] Maximilian B. Rasch, *The European Union at the United Nations. The Functioning and Coherence of EU External Representation in a State-Centric Environment* (Studies in EU External Relations: 1), Leiden/Boston: Martinus Nijhoff Publishers 2008, pp. 108–109 and p. 112; Pedro Antonio Serrano de Haro, 'Participation of the EU in the work of the UN: General Assembly Resolution 65/276', *CLEER Working Papers* 2012/4, pp. 8–9.

Representative in the CFSP area, and by the Commission in other external relations matters. This is an important change, especially in CFSP matters, as well as a confirmation of the Commission's external role in other matters.

While the Lisbon Treaty thus leaves the Presidency without a formal role in the external representation of the Union, the Member States retain their sovereignty to conduct their own foreign relations, subject to the rules of the Treaty. In principle, this gives them room in the area of shared competences. These shared competences fall outside the CFSP activities and include areas such as the environment, energy and internal market, where the Member States retain competence unless the Union has already exercised its competence. The Member States are in principle free to determine their own representation when acting outside the Union institutional framework, so long as they respect the principle of loyal cooperation or sincere cooperation as laid down in Article 4(3) TEU.

Generally, the attention in defining external representation post-Lisbon has shifted from the CFSP to the notion of shared competences. While the Lisbon Treaty in general sets out a clear framework for Union representation (the Commission, the High Representative, or the EU Delegations) the area of shared competences leaves certain issues open. As is provided in Article 2(2) TFEU, when the Treaties confer on the Union a competence shared with the Member States in a specific area, the Union and the Member States may legislate and adopt legally binding acts in that area. It is specified that the Member States exercise their competence "to the extent that the Union has not exercised its competence". Article 2(2) is a reflexive rule, in the sense that it ties Member States competences to EU legislation that evolves over time. In practice, it may be difficult to draw a clear line, as it often requires a detailed examination of the relevant EU legislation. While most competences are shared to start with, as is clear from the list of shared competences in Article 4 TFEU, once there is EU legislation in place the Member States are precluded from acting on their own, and the area becomes subject to exclusive Union competence (Article 3(2) TFEU).[10] Certain differences of view have been reported with

[10] This has been a source of some unease on the part of the Member States, which was already apparent during the negotiations culminating in the Lisbon Treaty, and which caused them to attach Protocol No. 25 on the exercise of shared competence to the EU and TFEU Treaties. Its Sole Article provides that, with reference to Article 2(2) TFEU, "when the Union has taken action in a certain area, the scope of this exercise of competence only covers those elements governed by the Union act in question and therefore does not cover the whole area". Given that the Treaties are not readily to be divided up in areas,

regard to external representation in the areas of shared competences.[11] Some Member States tend to argue that the representation by EU actors (in particular the Commission and EU Delegations) is confined to areas within its exclusive competence. The wording of Article 17 TEU does not make a difference as to the nature of the competence (exclusive or shared), however. Nor does it follow from the Treaty rules that representation falls on the rotating Presidency, as pre-Lisbon practice might suggest. In this connection, it may be noted that some controversies have also arisen with regard to so-called hybrid Council decisions authorizing the negotiation and signing of international agreements. Such decisions combine, on the one hand, a regular Council decision (under Article 218 TFEU) and, on the other hand, an inter-governmental decision ('Representatives of the Governments meeting within the Council'). That combination, which would also result in regular qualified majority voting in the Council being turned into unanimity, has now been challenged by the Commission, which is seeking annulment of such hybrid acts in cases which are currently pending before the Court of Justice.[12]

The agendas of UN meetings cover a wide variety of issues which regularly involve matters falling within the (non-CFSP) shared competences areas. In that case, loyal cooperation between the EU actors and the Member States is necessary in order to maintain unity in the external representation of the Union.[13] That also requires practical arrangements to permit the EU to address the issues at stake in a manner which is both fitting and efficient for the external context, and respectful of the internal competences. In practice, a number of statements are made "on behalf of the EU and its Member States".

---

and that the concept of "area" of competence in the case-law of the Court of Justice is not fully clear, the Protocol provides limited clarification, if any. Cf. Geert De Baere, 'The Basics of EU External Relations Law: An Overview of the Post-Lisbon Constitutional Framework for Developing the External Dimensions of EU Asylum and Migration Policy', in: Marleen Maes, Marie-Claire Foblets and Philippe De Bruycker (eds.), *External Dimensions of European Migration and Asylum Law and Policy*, Brussels: Bruylant 2011, p. 136.

[11] See *The EU External Representation in the Area of Shared Competences*, Warsaw: The Polish Institute of International Affairs 2012, pp. 7, 18.

[12] ECJ, Case C-28/12, *Commission* v *Council*, [2012] OJ C73/23, pending; Case C-114/12, *Commission* v *Council*, [2012] OJ C138/5, pending. The use of such a hybrid act was also proposed within the framework of the negotiations on a legally binding instrument on mercury within the framework of the United Nations Environment Programme (UNEP): see Geert De Baere, '*Mercury Rising*: The European Union and the International Negotiations for a Globally Binding Instrument on Mercury', (2012) 37 *European Law Review*, pp. 650–655.

[13] See ECJ, Case C-246/07, *Commission* v *Sweden*, [2010] ECR I-3317, par. 73, and the case-law cited there.

Given the division of competences and the institutional context just described, the Union and its Member States have developed a sophisticated process to coordinate their views in order to reach an EU position within the UN. That process has its origins in the coordination of the Benelux countries in the UN General Assembly (UNGA) that started already in the late 1940s, and was further developed with the establishment of the European Political Cooperation in 1970.[14] Over the years since, the Community/Union has been active in the UN, the coordination process has intensified, and become entrenched in the diplomatic practice of EU Member States.[15]

That coordination takes place both in Brussels and in New York (or Geneva). Finalization of the EU interventions takes place in New York, with significant input by Member States, on the basis of positions taken in Brussels within the Council pursuant to Article 16 TEU.[16] In that regard, the Political and Security Committee (Article 38 TEU) plays an important interlocutory role with respect to CFSP issues, and various Council Working Groups are of significant importance to EU action within the UN.[17] For example, the Working Group on the UN (CONUN) is responsible for UN institutional and horizontal issues, while EU positions within the Third Committee are coordinated in Brussels within the Council Working Group responsible for Human Rights Policy (COHOM).[18]

Since the Treaty of Lisbon's entry into force on 1 December 2009, the European Commission Delegation and EU Council Liaison Office have merged into the European Union Delegation, under the authority of the High Representative for Foreign Affairs and Security Policy, and representing the EU in both the CFSP field as well as in other matters.[19]

---

[14] Rasch, *supra* n. 9, p. 30 and p. 60; Davide Zaru and Charles-Michel Geurts, 'Legal Framework for EU Participation in Global Human Rights Governance', in: Jan Wouters et al. (eds.), *The European Union and Multilateral Governance. Assessing EU Participation in United Nations Human Rights and Environmental Fora*, Basingstoke: Palgrave Macmillan 2012, p. 54.

[15] Jan Wouters, Frank Hoffmeister and Tom Ruys, 'Epilogue: the UN and the EU – The Road to Partnership', in: Jan Wouters, Frank Hoffmeister and Tom Ruys (eds.), *The United Nations and the European Union: An Ever Stronger Partnership*, The Hague: T.M.C. Asser Press 2006, p. 385.

[16] Rasch, *supra* n. 9, p. 30.

[17] *The EU External Representation in the Area of Shared Competences*, *supra* n. 11, p. 11.

[18] Sudeshna Basu, 'The European Union in the Human Rights Council', in: Jan Wouters, et al. (eds.), *The European Union and Multilateral Governance. Assessing EU Participation in United Nations Human Rights and Environmental Fora*, Basingstoke: Palgrave Macmillan 2012, pp. 89–91.

[19] 'About the EU at the UN', *supra* n. 4.

The EU Delegation is now also in charge of coordination. Furthermore, the European External Action Service (EEAS) has progressively taken up the chairmanship of the relevant EU meetings in Brussels, so that coordination in New York mirrors that in Brussels.[20]

The question is whether extensive internal EU coordination and EU outreach are fully compatible. It has been argued by some that the coordination process is too time-consuming, and hence, in fact part, of the problem with respect to an effective and efficient Union representation at the UN.[21] The Maastricht Treaty's establishment of the CFSP introduced a provision in the TEU that provides for coordinated Union action in international organizations (now Article 34), which eventually sparked a culture of EU cohesion at the UN, founded on intensive common preparation, and ingrained in the habits of EU diplomats in New York. An inevitable side-effect has indeed been that the achievement of EU common positions has become more time-consuming than the eventual projection of that position within the UN,[22] and that the Union's position is not easily amenable to negotiation.[23] For example, during the negotiations of a UNGA Resolution on a moratorium on the use of the death penalty, the EU's negotiating position became a matter of controversy between the nine non-EU co-authors, on the one hand, and the EU and its Member States, on the other. As the former were not prepared to accept the EU position, the Portuguese Presidency was eventually given more leeway to negotiate a practicable deal with the other co-authors.[24] Nevertheless, the rapidly

---

20 Emanuele Giaufret, 'The EU in the UNGA Third Committee', in: Jan Wouters et al. (eds.), *The European Union and Multilateral Governance. Assessing EU Participation in United Nations Human Rights and Environmental Fora*, Basingstoke: Palgrave Macmillan 2012, p. 73. See in general on Brussels-based meetings chaired by the EEAS and on EU Delegations in multilateral settings: Jan Wouters et al., *The Organisation and Functioning of the European External Action Service: Achievements, Challenges and Opportunities*, Brussels: European Parliament, Directorate-General for External Policies of the Union, Directorate B, Policy Department 2013, pp. 37–45 and pp. 77–80.

21 Rasch, *supra* n. 9, p. 309.

22 Esa Paasivirta and Dominic Porter, 'EU Coordination at the UN General Assembly and ECOSOC: A View From Brussels, A View From New York', in: Jan Wouters, Frank Hoffmeister and Tom Ruys (eds.), *The United Nations and the European Union: An Ever Stronger Partnership*, The Hague: T.M.C. Asser Press 2006, pp. 47–48.

23 See in general, with respect to mixed EU-Member State action, Geert De Baere, *Constitutional Principles of EU External Relations*, Oxford: Oxford University Press 2008, p. 238.

24 Robert Kissack, 'The EU in the Negotiations of a UN General Assembly Resolution on a Moratorium on the Use of the Death Penalty', in: Jan Wouters et al. (eds.), *The European Union and Multilateral Governance. Assessing EU Participation in United Nations Human Rights and Environmental Fora*, Basingstoke: Palgrave Macmillan 2012, p. 107.

evolving negotiation positions of third countries may imply that the EU comes too late to influence the decision-making process in a meaningful way.[25] It has been noted furthermore that the intense coordination processes leave less room for informal lobbying and limited possibility for pro-active policy development.[26] The coordination process, which inevitably involves compromises, may also result in statements that are not found to be persuasive.[27]

However, the net result of such intensive coordination is that there is a common EU position on almost 95% of resolutions,[28] and that the EU votes unanimously on four out of five UNGA resolutions that are the subject of a vote, while split votes are mostly confined to politically or ethically sensitive issues.[29] Of course, votes in which the EU is unable to agree on a common line occur from time to time. In its 2003 communication ('The European Union and the United Nations: The Choice of Multilateralism'), the Commission warned that while "in the past the practical implications of such split votes have generally been marginal, their impact on the EU's credibility is disproportionate – particularly in cases where there are established CFSP Common Positions on the issues in question".[30]

Nevertheless, it is important to bear in mind that coherence of the EU's action in a specific UN body is not dependent on the EU coordination process alone, but at least as much on the institutional culture of the UN body in question. It has been pointed out, for example, that the fact that the EU acts very coherently with regard to development cooperation is largely driven by the consensus-oriented decision-making culture of the UN body in question.[31] Conversely, within the UNGA, the EU's internal coordination is quite successful, yet the Union often remains in a minority position.[32]

3. Drivers, Structures, and Constraints of EU Presence at the UN

One may wonder why the EU wants to be present at the UN at all. The simple answer is that many EU policies and competences are impacted

---

[25] Communication from the Commission to the Council and the European Parliament, 'The European Union and the United Nations: The choice of multilateralism', COM(2003) 526 final, p. 21.

[26] Rasch, *supra* n. 9, p. 32 and p. 309.

[27] Jørgensen and Wessel, *supra* n. 5, pp. 282–283.

[28] COM(2003) 526 final, p. 16.

[29] Wouters, Hoffmeister and Ruys, *supra* n. 15, pp. 385–386.

[30] COM(2003) 526 final, p. 4.

[31] Rasch, *supra* n. 9, p. 142.

[32] Jørgensen and Wessel, *supra* n. 5, p. 283.

upon by matters decided at the UN level, for example with respect to climate change, maritime policies, and counter–terrorism. Furthermore, the desire for EU participation is particularly strong in areas that reflect its own values.[33] As the Union's actions in areas within the scope of UN activity have increased, the need for upgrading the status of the EU in the various UN bodies has become more acute.[34]

Many international organizations dating from before the establishment of the European Communities have no provision in their constitutions to accommodate other international organizations wishing to become members. The UN is perhaps the paradigmatic example of that genus. The only way for the Union to join such an international organization would be to persuade the existing members to amend the constitution of the organization (in the case of the UN, in accordance with the onerous procedure of Article 108 of the UN Charter) in order to enable other international organizations to become members. Should that be successful, the Union and the Member States become members of the relevant international organizations alongside each other. A well-known example of such a construction is the Food and Agricultural Organization of the United Nations (FAO).[35] The FAO constitutional provisions, in combination with the Union's complex vertical and horizontal division of competences, were almost destined to create prohibitive difficulties, the discussion of which

---

[33] Sudeshna Basu, et al., 'The European Union's Participation in the United Nations Human Rights and Environmental Governance: Key Concepts and Major Challenges', in: Jan Wouters et al. (eds.), *The European Union and Multilateral Governance. Assessing EU Participation in United Nations Human Rights and Environmental Fora*, Basingstoke: Palgrave Macmillan 2012, p. 4.

[34] Wouters, Hoffmeister and Ruys, *supra* n. 15, p. 386.

[35] The FAO admitted the EEC as a member, alongside its Member States, by decision of 26 November 1991, taken under Art II(3) and (5) FAO Constitution: ECJ, Case C-25/94, *Commission* v. *Council*, [1996] ECR I-1469, par. 2. On EC membership of the FAO, see further Jörn Sack, 'The European Community's Membership of International Organizations', (1995) 32 *Common Market Law Review*, pp. 1243–1247. Specifically on the exercise of voting rights within the FAO, Joni Heliskoski, 'Internal Struggle for International Presence: The Exercise of Voting Rights Within the FAO', in: Alan Dashwood and Christophe Hillion (eds.), *The General Law of E.C. External Relations*, London: Sweet & Maxwell 2000, pp. 79–99; see also Article II(5) FAO Constitution; ECJ, Case C-25/94, *Commission v Council*, [1996] ECR I-1469, par. 3; XLI(2)–(3) FAO General Rules of the Organization. For more details on the participation of the Community/Union and the Member States in the FAO, see Panos Koutrakos, *EU International Relations Law*, Oxford/Portland: Hart Publishing 2006, pp. 168–172; Jørgen Mærsk Pedersen, 'FAO-EU Cooperation: An Ever Stronger Partnership', in: Jan Wouters, Frank Hoffmeister and Tom Ruys (eds.), *The United Nations and the European Union: An Ever Stronger Partnership*, The Hague: T.M.C. Asser Press 2006, pp. 63–91.

exceeds the scope of this chapter.[36] As with the FAO, any international organization of which both the Union and the Member States are parties will have to determine whether both the Union and the Member States get voting rights and, if so, how these are to be exercised.[37]

True to its 1946 legacy, the UN is a state-oriented system. That is reflected in Article 4(1) of the UN Charter, which reserves membership to "all other peace-loving states".[38] Membership is also geographically organized. All actors are part of a regional group,[39] which structures the system: each have their own consultations. In essence, the UN is premised on the protection of the sovereign equality of states as one of the basic organizing principles of the international legal order, even though it does involve blocs and regional groups in its decision-making processes.[40] However, the EU is a political group rather than just a geographical group, and in fact, its Member States fall under three regional groups at the UN: the Western European and Others Group (WEOG), the Eastern European Group, and one Member State, i.e. Cyprus, falls under the Asian Group. Because the Union does not fit within a single regional group, EU officials are somewhat displaced in this group system.

There is also a constraint that stems from history. The EU participation in the work of international organizations always starts from a 'clean slate' situation: it does not have a past of participating in IOs, while in most organizations, the Member States have a history as independent actors. As the EU enters an IO, it requires adjustment of daily practices on the part of

---

[36] See Sack, *supra* n. 35, pp. 1243–1247; *The EU External Representation in the Area of Shared Competences, supra*, n. 11, pp. 15–24. Cf. Joni Heliskoski, *Mixed Agreements as a Technique for Organizing the International Relations of the European Community and its Member States*, The Hague: Kluwer Law International 2001, pp. 105–110, who argues that the exercise of the right to vote by either the Union or the Member States is also bound to have implications on the vertical division of competences in abstracto, or in other words in other cases relating to the same subject-matter. On the Arrangement of the Commission and the Council regarding the exercise of membership rights of the FAO, see De Baere, *supra* n. 23, p. 255.

[37] See, for example, as regards the Stockholm Convention on Persistent Organic Pollutants: Case C-246/07, *Commission* v *Sweden*, [2010] ECR I-3317, on which further Geert De Baere, '"O, Where is Faith? O, Where is Loyalty?" Some Thoughts on the Duty of Loyal Co-operation and the Union's External Environmental Competences in the Light of the *PFOS* Case', (2011) 36 *European Law Review*, pp. 405–419.

[38] On which, see further Thomas Grant, *Admission to the United Nations, Charter Article 4 and the Rise of Universal Organization*, Leiden/Boston: Martinus Nijhoff Publishers 2009.

[39] See <http://www.un.org/Depts/DGACM/RegionalGroups.shtml>.

[40] Katie Laatikainen and Karen Smith (eds.), *The European Union at the United Nations: Intersecting Multilateralisms*, London: Palgrave Macmillan 2006, p. 3.

the Member States. Smaller Member States, which do not usually have the requisite diplomatic resources, mostly welcome the EU's role in international forums in general and in the UN in particular, while larger Member States with elaborate and developed diplomatic machineries are in a different position. How the Member States view the EU's presence in international organizations also depends on the organization in question. For example, there are a large number of regional fisheries organizations, and the EU alone is usually a member of them. That is of course an exception. In most other contexts, it is still difficult to imagine that the EU would entirely replace the Member States, keeping in mind that, amongst other things, it is important to keep them engaged. EU membership in the WTO and the FAO suggests that full EU membership in international organization results from well-established competences and clear operational needs.

Finally, there can be a pushback from non-EU States. The Union's presence can be perceived as additional influence from the EU on top of the Member States, which is sensitive in particular as regards voting rights. This normally requires adjustment so that either the EU or the Member States vote, but not both.[41] Furthermore, within the Human Rights Council, the EU is faced with the prevalent regional bloc mentality and the strong presence of the Organization of the Islamic Conference (OIC) and the African Group.[42] Nevertheless, cases such as the Human Rights Council's Special Session on Darfur and the EU's participation in the negotiations on the moratorium on the death penalty appear to indicate that the particular political constellation is in the end decisive on the EU's potential for significantly impacting on the decision-making process, rather than the legal and institutional architecture of the relevant UN forum.[43]

4. The EU's Status and Participation

Though the Union cannot become a member of the UN, it has since early-on endeavored to exert influence on UN decision-making. To that end,

[41] However, the particular context needs to assessed on a case-by-case basis. For instance, the situation appears quite different in the case of internationally established funds where the financing originates from the EU itself as well as from the Member States, both having approved it separately according to their own budgetary procedures.

[42] Basu, *supra* n. 18, p. 97.

[43] Hans Bruyninckx, et al., 'The Position(s) of the EU in the UN System: The Examples of Human Rights and Environmental Governance', in: Jan Wouters et al. (eds.), *The European Union and Multilateral Governance. Assessing EU Participation in United Nations Human Rights and Environmental Fora*, Basingstoke: Palgrave Macmillan 2012, p. 257.

the Commission established in 1964 an information office in New York in order to foster relations with third states within the UN framework.[44] On 11 October 1974, the UNGA requested the UN Secretary-General "to invite the European Economic Community to participate in the sessions and work of the General Assembly in the capacity of observer",[45] making it the first non-state actor to enjoy permanent observer status at the UN.[46] That status applies as much to the UNGA's committees and sub-committees as it does to the plenary.[47] Likewise, the EU has an observer status at the ECOSOC,[48] including in most of its functional commissions, as well as in UN subsidiary organs.[49] It is also a full participant at the Commission on Sustainable Development,[50] and has been invited to participate in the Peacebuilding Commission as an "institutional donor"[51] and a "relevant international organization".[52] The Union made full use of this possibility and, through a significant investment of time and effort, both in internal coordination and in liaising with other actors in the UNGA, has become one of the key actors.[53]

The EU therefore profits from different forms of participation and status depending on the UN body. The UN's work can broadly be divided into two segments: on the one hand the UNGA and ECOSOC, and on the other hand the UNSC.[54] The EU is an observer in the UNGA, while the UNSC

44 Rasch, *supra* n. 9, p. 105.

45 Status of the European Economic Community in the General Assembly, UN Doc. A/RES/3208(XXIX). Compare Art 12(2) Constitution of the International Labour Organization (ILO): "The International Labour Organization may make appropriate arrangements for the representatives of public international organizations to participate without vote in its deliberations." For further details on the Union's position in the ILO, see the contribution of Delarue to this volume.

46 Zaru and Geurts, *supra* n. 14, p. 57.

47 Hoffmeister and Kuijper, *supra* n. 5, p. 18.

48 By virtue of Rule 79 of the Rules of Procedure of the Economic and Social Council, UN Doc. E/5715/Rev.2: "Representatives of intergovernmental organizations accorded permanent observer status by the General Assembly and of other intergovernmental organizations designated on an ad hoc or continuing basis by the Council on the recommendation of the Bureau, may participate, without the right to vote, in the deliberation of the Council on questions within the scope of the activities of the organization."

49 Rasch, *supra* n. 9, p. 106.

50 ECOSOC Decision 1995/201, 'Full Participation of the European Community in the Commission on Sustainable Development'.

51 'The Peacebuilding Commission', UN Doc. A/RES/60/180, point 9.

52 A/RES/60/180, point 7(b).

53 See Jan Wouters, 'The European Union as an Actor Within the United Nations General Assembly', in: Vincent Kronenberger (ed.), *The European Union and the International Legal Order: Discord or Harmony?*, The Hague: T.M.C. Asser Press 2001, pp. 375–404.

54 Paasivirta and Porter, *supra* n. 22, p. 36.

does not have observers. Furthermore, the UNGA has different grades of status: observer, enhanced observer, and member,[55] and it has about 80 observer organizations. However, neither the UN Charter nor the UNGA Rules of Procedure specifically mention observers, leaving their status to be determined through UNGA practice.

Within the UNSC, the EU can currently exercise considerable influence through the presence of its Member States that are UNSC members, either as permanent members (UK and France) or on a rotating basis. Pursuant to Article 34(2) TEU, they are under an obligation to "concert and keep the other Member States and the High Representative fully informed", and in the execution of their functions, they are to defend the positions and the interests of the Union, without prejudice to their responsibilities under the provisions of the UN Charter. Finally, since Lisbon, the third subparagraph of Article 34(2) TEU provides that when the Union has defined a position on a subject that is on the UNSC agenda, those Member States which sit on the UNSC are to request that "the High Representative be invited to present the Union's position". In that context, Rule 39 of the UNSC's Provisional Rules of Procedure provides for it to invite "members of the Secretariat or other persons, whom it considers competent for the purpose, to supply it with information or to give other assistance in examining matters within its competence". The representative of the EU has also issued statements in the UNSC on a fairly regular basis in its public sessions.[56] The coordination by the EU Member States regarding the UNSC matters has been significantly increased over the years. However, it is well-known that the EU does not have a common view on the on-going UN consultations on the Security Council reform, particularly on the issue of membership in an enlarged UNSC.[57] The reason lies presumably in the high visibility of UNSC action and the prestige it entails.

Within the UNGA, it should be borne in mind that much of the preparatory work takes place in informal meetings. As a general rule, the more formal the session, the more difficult it is for non-members to take part in the process. Only a fraction of the time spent on meetings within the UN is spent in official or formal settings, and practically all UN resolutions

---

55 Cf. Hoffmeister and Kuijper, *supra* n. 5, p. 14.

56 See, for a recent example, '27 June 2012, New York – Statement on behalf of the European Union by H.E. Mr. Thomas Mayr-Harting, Head of the Delegation of the European Union to the United Nations, at the Security Council Debate on the situation in Afghanistan (UNAMA)', available at <http://www.eu-un.europa.eu/articles/en/article_12359_en.htm>.

57 http://www.un.org/News/briefings/docs/2011/111201_SC_Reform.doc.htm.

are prepared by way of informal consultations. Strictly legally speaking, informal meetings are not UN meetings, though they are frequently held in a UN meeting room and in the presence of the Secretariat.[58] There are, however, no procedural rules, and the participants can speak freely rather than making formal statements. Once a resolution moves from an informal setting to the UNGA, the EU has been experiencing difficulties in having its voice heard. Formal sessions are of course important for visibility, and rank matters in the UN world. The Heads of State and Government speak at the UNGA general debate and set out the UNGA agenda for the forthcoming session, and speaking there is a matter of pride and status. In the past, the EU managed to make its voice heard through the Council Presidency, which was by far the most important EU actor within the UN framework. The Presidency represented the EU most visibly by giving statements in formal UN meetings, a practice instituted by the Italian Presidency in 1975, and taken up by the British Presidency in 1981.[59] However, as mentioned above, since the entry into force of the Lisbon Treaty, the Council Presidency does not have a formal role anymore in the external representation of the EU, which was taken over by the EU actors, i.e. the permanent President of the European Council, the High Representative, the Commission, and the EU Delegation. However, the fact that the EU actors do not represent individual countries but the Union was a risk factor in the state-centered UN world. As a key EU negotiator, Mr. Serrano de Haro, has pointed out, in that sense the Union's goal post Lisbon was not so much to seek a stronger position at the UN, but a status equivalent to the existing one, with its representatives under its proper arrangements rather than those of the EU Member State holding the Council Presidency.[60]

With that goal in mind, the Union tabled a draft resolution in August 2010 intended to grant it enhanced participation rights in the UNGA.[61] However, on 14 September 2010, just days after the EU had successfully negotiated the adoption of a resolution on Kosovo,[62] which underscored

[58] Paasivirta and Porter, *supra* n. 22, p. 37.

[59] Rasch, *supra* n. 9, pp. 35 and 40.

[60] Serrano de Haro, *supra* n. 9, pp. 15–16.

[61] 'Participation of the European Union in the work of the United Nations', UN Doc. A/64/L.67.

[62] 'Request for an advisory opinion of the International Court of Justice on whether the unilateral declaration of independence of Kosovo is in accordance with international law', UN Doc. A/RES/64/298, which welcomed "the readiness of the European Union to facilitate a process of dialogue between the parties; the process of dialogue in itself would

the Union's capacity to build consensus within the UNGA,[63] the Union was diplomatically rebuffed by a counter-resolution proposing the deferral of the resolution tabled by the Union on its participation in the work of the UN. From the EU side, "the EU's debacle at the UN", as Jean-Claude Piris (the former Chief Legal Counsel of the EU Council) put it, was rather disturbing, though the trouble was overcome soon after.[64]

Indeed, on 3 May 2011, at its 88th plenary meeting, the UNGA adopted Resolution 65/276, 'Participation of the European Union in the work of the United Nations'.[65] The Resolution applies to the participation of the representatives of the EU, in its capacity as observer, in the sessions and work of the UNGA and its committees and working groups, in international meetings and conferences convened under the auspices of the Assembly and in UN conferences.[66] It remains to be seen what impact the Resolution will have in other UN bodies, such as the Human Rights Council, or specialized agencies, such as the World Health Organization, which act under their own rules.[67] Nevertheless, it sets a recognized model and one would expect it to influence arrangements elsewhere. The right to co-sponsor resolutions and decisions was consciously never included in the EU negotiation position, as they were viewed as too closely linked to voting rights, reserved to UN members.[68] Conversely, the request to include in the Resolution the right to raise points of order was dropped by the EU at the end of the negotiation process to secure an uncontroverted adoption of the Resolution.[69] The importance of that concession is also underscored in the UN Secretary-General's Note.[70]

---

be a factor for peace, security and stability in the region, and that dialogue would be to promote cooperation, achieve progress on the path to the European Union and improve the lives of the people" (point 2).

63 Michael Emerson and Jan Wouters, *The EU's Diplomatic Debacle at the UN. What Else and What Next?*, Centre for European Policy Studies (CEPS) Commentary, 1 October 2010, p. 3.

64 Jean-Claude Piris, *The Future of Europe. Towards a Two-Speed EU?*, Cambridge: Cambridge University Press 2012, p. 4.

65 UN Doc. A/RES/65/276.

66 A/RES/65/276, point 2.

67 Jan Wouters, Jed Odermatt and Thomas Ramopoulos, *The Status of the European Union at the United Nations after the General Assembly Resolution of 3 May 2011*, Leuven: Leuven Centre for Global Governance Studies 2011, pp. 4–5.

68 This is reflected in A/RES/65/276, Annex, point 3.

69 Serrano de Haro, *supra* n. 9, p. 16 and 32.

70 'Participation of the European Union in the work of the United Nations. Note by the Secretary-General', UN Doc. A/65/856, point 12.

Resolution 65/276 takes account of UN practice and constraints, rather than proposing revolutionary steps.[71] Indeed, the 'enhanced observer status' granted by the Resolution builds on earlier instances of granting the Union a similar status, for example at the 1992 Rio Summit and the 2002 Johannesburg Summit, as well as at the annual sessions of the ECOSOC functional Commission on Sustainable Development.[72] Within the UNGA, the seating order of the Community had been adjusted on earlier occasions to place it before observers but after all states, for example in meetings of the UN Ad Hoc Working Group on Biodiversity in Areas beyond National Jurisdiction and the United Nations Open-ended Informal Consultative Process on Oceans and the Law of the Sea (UNICPOLOS).[73]

It has been lamented that the UNGA Resolution as adopted on 3 May 2011 bears little resemblance to the draft of August 2010, and that it was "utterly de-Europeanized".[74] Indeed, the final resolution contains no explicit references to the Lisbon Treaty. A number of UN members stressed in the course of the negotiation of the Resolution that the Lisbon Treaty was, in accordance with the long-established principle of international law *pacta tertiis nec nocent nec prosunt*,[75] neither binding for third states nor for the UN.[76] The EU Presidency at the time (Hungary) emphasized when introducing the Resolution before the UNGA that the new draft specifically addressed the request from several UNGA members to remove references to the Lisbon Treaty and to focus the draft squarely on the UN.[77]

---

[71] Cf. Hoffmeister and Kuijper, *supra* n. 5, p. 34, already noting "a trend to upgrade the observer status of the European Community to that of a full participant throughout the entire UN System"; and Giaufret, *supra* n. 20, p. 83.

[72] Cf. in general Jochen Jesinghaus, 'EU-UN Cooperation for Sustainable Development', in: Jan Wouters, Frank Hoffmeister and Tom Ruys (eds.), *The United Nations and the European Union: An Ever Stronger Partnership*, The Hague: T.M.C. Asser Press 2006, pp. 195–210; Karoline Van den Brande, 'The European Union in the Commission on Sustainable Development', in: Jan Wouters et al. (eds.), *The European Union and Multilateral Governance. Assessing EU Participation in United Nations Human Rights and Environmental Fora*, Basingstoke: Palgrave Macmillan 2012, pp. 171–190; Simon Lightfoot, 'The EU in the World Summit on Sustainable Development', in: Jan Wouters et al. (eds.), *The European Union and Multilateral Governance. Assessing EU Participation in United Nations Human Rights and Environmental Fora*, Basingstoke: Palgrave Macmillan 2012, pp. 232–250.

[73] Paasivirta and Porter, *supra* n. 22, p. 46.

[74] Wouters, Odermatt and Ramopoulos, *supra* n. 67, p. 3.

[75] Recalled by the ECJ in Case C-386/08, *Brita*, [2010] ECR I-1289, par. 44–45.

[76] Serrano de Haro, *supra* n. 9, p. 24.

[77] General Assembly, Sixty-fifth session, Official Records of the 88th plenary meeting, Tuesday, 3 May 2011, 10 a.m., New York, UN Doc. A/65/PV.88, p. 4.

However, the key substance of the Lisbon Treaty is there. The Resolution now notes (seventh recital):

> that the States members of the European Union have entrusted the external representation of the European Union, previously performed by the representatives of the member State holding the rotating Presidency of the Council of the European Union, to the following institutional representatives: the President of the European Council, the High Representative of the Union for Foreign Affairs and Security Policy, the European Commission, and European Union delegations, which have assumed the role of acting on behalf of the European Union in the exercise of the competences conferred by its member States.

The UN members thereby give effect to the EU Treaty reforms.

One of the important achievements of Resolution 65/276 is no doubt that EU representatives are to be allowed "to be inscribed on the list of speakers among representatives of major groups, in order to make interventions".[78] That facilitates the passing of EU messages and serves the Union's visibility as well. The EU representatives may therefore intervene in the debate with representatives of major groups, normally ahead of representatives of individual Member States, instead of at the end of the list of speakers as in the past.[79] Furthermore, the EU representatives are to be invited to participate in the general debate of the UNGA; permitted to have EU communications relating to the sessions and work of the UNGA and to the sessions and work of all international meetings and conferences convened under the auspices of the Assembly and of UN conferences, circulated directly, and without intermediary, as documents of the Assembly, meeting or conference; permitted to present proposals and amendments orally as agreed by the EU Member States; and allowed to exercise the right of reply regarding EU positions as decided by the presiding officer.[80] The EU representatives are also to be "ensured seating among the observers".[81]

There have been some exceedingly critical comments on Resolution 65/276, emphasizing the meager results and the harm done by the difficult

---

[78] A/RES/65/276, Annex, point 1(a); and UN Doc. A/65/856, point 5.

[79] Serrano de Haro, *supra* n. 9, p. 29, hailing this as "one of the major achievements of the Resolution". See contra: Wouters, Odermatt and Ramopoulos, *supra* n. 67, p. 3, arguing that UNGA practice is for its President to determine the exact order of speakers, and that in practice this implies that the EU delegation will have to negotiate each summer with the office of the UNGA President in order to secure a speaking slot.

[80] A/RES/65/276, Annex, point 1(b) to (e).

[81] A/RES/65/276, Annex, point 2.

negotiation process.[82] It is of course correct that the Resolution is a modest step forward, and certainly does not fix everything. Even so, it arguably provides a good basis to proceed, its impact depending on its practical implementation, and it may serve as source of inspiration beyond the UNGA confines. The first signs in that regard appear to be hopeful.[83] One immediately visible example was, of course, the address by Mr. Herman Van Rompuy, President of the European Council, to the UNGA on 22 September 2011, immediately following the British Prime Minister, Mr. David Cameron.[84] It marked the first time that a non-state representative intervened in the General Debate.[85]

The question of how 'special' the EU is to justify being treated differently from other regional organizations in the UN system loomed large during the debates leading up to the adoption of Resolution 65/276. Clearly, by UN standards, the Union is an atypical organization, a regional integration organization characterized by strong supranational features and wide-ranging and deep integration. The Resolution (sixth recital) alludes to that specificity, by recalling that the European Union is a "party to many instruments concluded under the auspices of the United Nations", and an observer or participant in the work of several specialized agencies and bodies of the United Nations.[86] That reflects the EU's actor capacity, most clearly seen in the fact that it regularly participates in international treaties and conventions alongside States. Many UN members stated that other international organizations could be granted modalities such as those sought by the EU,[87] and paragraph 3 of the Resolution contemplates the possibility of granting enhanced participatory rights to other international organizations. The Arab Group pointed to the League of Arab States, and the representative of the Caribbean Community (CARICOM) was active on behalf of his organization in offering rather particular interpretations

82 See Bruyninckx, Wouters, Basu and Schunz, *supra* n. 43, pp. 279–280; Wouters, Odermatt and Ramopoulos, *supra* n. 67, p. 4.

83 Serrano de Haro, *supra* n. 9, pp. 32–33.

84 General Assembly, Sixty-sixth session, 15th plenary meeting, Thursday, 22 September 2011, 11 a.m., New York, UN Doc. A/66/PV.15, pp. 27–30. For an analysis of part of Mr. Van Rompuy's message (in particular on the responsibility to protect), see Geert De Baere, 'The European Union and the Responsibility to Protect', in: Bart Van Vooren, Steven Blockmans and Jan Wouters (eds.), *The EU's Role in Global Governance. The Legal Dimension*, Oxford: Oxford University Press 2013, pp. 95–109

85 Serrano de Haro, *supra* n. 9, p. 32.

86 A/RES/65/276, sixth recital in the preamble. Cf. Serrano de Haro, *supra* n. 9, p. 25.

87 A/65/PV.88, p. 4.

of which actors could represent the EU. CARICOM's long interpretative declaration prompted the EU Presidency of the Council to raise a point of order and to reject in rather terse terms such unilateral interpretations as unhelpful.[88]

At any rate, in UN circles, the EU is often viewed as a cohesive group of certain UN Member States rather than an actor in and of itself. Within the Third Committee, for example, the Union is principally perceived as the expression of the political will of its Member States.[89] To some extent this is also still reflected in Resolution 65/276, which permits EU representatives to "present proposals and amendments orally *as agreed by the States members* of the European Union; such proposals and amendments shall be put to a vote only *at the request of a Member State*".[90]

5. Conclusion

So, how does the European Union fare within the United Nations? The *tour d'horizon* offered above does not permit to draw far-reaching conclusions. The EU's coordination process is part of the daily practice of European diplomats. Coordinated EU positions contribute to a smooth functioning of the UN and ensure that the Union's Member States feel less need to dilute or qualify those positions. The EU's positions are therefore viewed as mostly balanced and well thought-out, which exercises a natural pull from third States to join them.[91]

The Union's well-established habit of coordination could probably be deployed more effectively, including for purposes of outreach towards other UN members and by further developing burden-sharing in that respect under the guidance of the EU Delegation. The adoption of Resolution 65/276 by the UNGA is an important step forward in that regard, and helpful for delivering a common message with improved visibility. It is as clear an illustration as can be of the EU's incrementally emerging international identity, which in turn, as was argued above, is inherently tied to the principles of the UN Charter.

---

88 A/65/PV.88, p. 13. Nevertheless, CARICOM reaffirmed its interpretation of the Resolution in the 'Letter dated 9 May 2011 from the Permanent Representative of the Bahamas to the United Nations addressed to the Secretary-General', UN Doc. A/65/834.

89 Giaufret, *supra* n. 20, p. 71.

90 A/RES/65/276, Annex, point 1(d) (emphases added).

91 Rasch, *supra* n. 9, p. 32; Jørgensen and Wessel, *supra* n. 5, p. 283.

Nevertheless, it must not be forgotten that while there is a close link between status and influence, the former does not guarantee the latter. Important though the Union's status in the various UN bodies may be for its international identity, it must be kept in mind that the strength of its influence within the UN is determined first and foremost by the strength of the EU position to be put forward.

CHAPTER THREE

ARMA FERO, ERGO SUM? THE EUROPEAN UNION, NATO AND THE QUEST FOR 'EUROPEAN IDENTITY'

Joris Larik

1. Introduction

The emergence of a security and defense policy of the European Union, and the questions it raises for the relationship between the Union and the North Atlantic Treaty Organization, have always been closely linked to the question of the 'identity' of the EU on the international stage. Already in the Single European Act of 1986, the Member States concluded "that closer co-operation on questions of European security would contribute in an essential way to the development of a European *identity* in external policy matters".[1] Subsequently, the Treaty on European Union, signed in Maastricht in 1992, stipulated as one of the objectives of the newly established Union "to assert its *identity* on the international scene", which was to be achieved "*in particular* through the implementation of a common foreign and security policy including the progressive framing of a common defense policy, which might lead to a common defense".[2] In 2009, the preamble of the TEU as amended by the Lisbon Treaty continues to express the resolve of the Member States to implement a Common Foreign and Security Policy (CFSP), including a Common Security and Defense Policy (CSDP), "*thereby* reinforcing the European *identity*".[3] Against this backdrop of evolving Treaty language, it seems that once the European Union as a polity starts to become active in the area of security, it reaches a new level of self-consciousness – a more palpable kind

[1] Art 30(6)(a) Single European Act [1987] OJ L 169/1 (SEA) (emphasis added).

[2] Art. 2(1) TEU (pre-Lisbon; emphases added). In the course of this chapter, references to the EU Treaties will be made in the following way: The Treaties, as amended by the Lisbon Treaty, in force as of 1 December 2009, will be designated as Treaty on European Union (TEU) and Treaty on the Functioning of the European Union (TFEU). For reasons of simplicity, references to the pre-Lisbon Treaties will be made in the form of the Treaties as amended by the Nice Treaty, and designated as the Treaty on European Union (TEU (pre-Lisbon)) and the Treaty establishing the European Community (TEC).

[3] Eleventh recital of the preamble, TEU (emphases added).

of international existence. To (ab)use René Descartes' famous axiom, the underlying sentiment could be termed: The Union bears arms, therefore I am – arma fero, ergo sum.

This kind of soul-searching that preoccupied the Union as well as those who study it was warranted by the fact the European *Union* was a new initiative to take European integration beyond the allegedly 'low politics' of economic integration,[4] and put it on a more ambitious, political track. According to Bretherton and Vogler, "the lack of access to military capabilities was central to discourses on EU identity either for those wishing to disparage or, indeed, to celebrate its pacifistic nature".[5] Consequently, once the Union equipped itself with such capabilities, old narratives such as Europe being a 'civilian power' were put in question.[6] A vivid academic discussion was prompted subsequently about the nature of the EU as a global player, ranging from heralding the coming of an 'ethical power'[7] to cautioning against the prospect of 'militarizing' a project that used to be inherently civilian and pacifistic.[8]

These upheavals of course did not take place in a political, institutional or legal vacuum. By expanding its activities into these new areas, the Union came into contact with institutions that already occupied these fields. After all, the North Atlantic Treaty Organization (NATO), and in its shadow the Western European Union (WEU), had been charged with providing security to Western Europe for decades before the Maastricht Treaty was signed. Also in the transatlantic dimension of security and defense policy, the quest for a European identity was evident. This is well captured in the term devised for the ill-fated project for a European pillar

---

[4] To use the term famously coined by Stanley Hoffmann, *The European Sisyphus: Essays on Europe, 1964–1994*, Boulder: Westview Press 1995.

[5] Charlotte Bretherton and John Vogler, *The European Union as a Global Actor*, Abingdon: Routledge 2006, p. 190.

[6] Seminally François Duchêne, 'Europe's role in world peace', in: Richard Mayne (ed.), *Europe Tomorrow: Sixteen Europeans Look Ahead*, London: Fontana 1972, pp. 32–47; see on the initial difficulties of integration theories to cope with this development, Hanna Ojanen, 'The EU and Nato: Two Competing Models for a Common Defence Policy', (2006) 44 *Journal of Common Market Studies*, pp. 57–76.

[7] See for an introduction to the concept e.g. Lisbeth Aggestam, 'Introduction: Ethical Power Europe?', (2008) 84 *International Affairs*, pp. 1–11.

[8] See for a rather sceptical perspective e.g. Ian Manners, 'Normative Power Europe Reconsidered: Beyond the Crossroads', (2006) 13 *Journal of European Public Policy*, pp. 182–199. In addition, there were also voices doubting that the EU would manage to live up to these ambitions in the first place, see Robert Kagan, *Of Paradise and Power: America and Europe in the New World Order*, New York: Knopf 2003.

embedded within NATO, viz. the 'European Security and Defence *Identity*' (ESDI).[9]

The EU-NATO relationship is thus particularly well suited for scrutinizing the Union's 'international identity' through the interaction with another international organization. Both do indeed share many things: both organizations have their headquarters in Brussels, and both sealed their latest grand conceptual overhaul in Lisbon, with the Lisbon Treaty[10] and the 2010 Strategic Concept[11] respectively. Twenty-two European countries are members of both organizations. All EU members except Cyprus are part of NATO's Partnership for Peace (PfP) programme. Both have been key institutions in the post-war European architecture for more than half a century. Yet, comparing their historic trajectories and the legal norms that define them reveals that there is much that sets them apart.

Generally, the relations between the EU and NATO have already captivated the sustained interest of international relations scholars for many years.[12] The resulting literature forms part of a wider discussion of transatlantic relations, the organization of European security, the continuing relevance and function of NATO in the post-Cold War world, as well as

---

[9] NATO, Final Communiqué of the Ministerial Meeting of the North Atlantic Council, Press Communiqué M-NAC-1(96)63, 3 June 1996, <http://www.nato.int/docu/pr/1996/p96-063e.htm> (emphasis added).

[10] Treaty of Lisbon amending the Treaty on European Union and the Treaty establishing the European Community, signed at Lisbon, 13 December 2007 [2007] OJ C 306/1.

[11] NATO, 'Strategic Concept for the Defence and Security of the Members of the North Atlantic Treaty Organization, adopted by Heads of State and Government at the NATO Summit in Lisbon, 19–20 November 2010' (NSC 2010).

[12] As testimony, see the various collections such as Jolyon Howorth and John Keeler (eds.), *Defending Europe: The EU, NATO and the Quest for European Autonomy*, Basingstoke: Palgrave Macmillan 2003; Hall Gardner (ed.), *NATO and the European Union: New World, New Europe, New Threats*, Aldershot: Ashgate 2004; Johannes Varwick (ed.), *Die Beziehungen zwischen NATO und EU: Partnerschaft, Konkurrenz, Rivalität?*, Opladen: Budrich 2005; or individual monographs and articles such as Paul Cornish and Geoffrey Edwards, 'Beyond the EU/NATO dichotomy: the beginnings of a European strategic culture', (2001) 77 *International Affairs*, pp. 587–603; Ojanen, *supra* n. 6; James Sperling, 'The European Union and NATO: Subordinate partner, cooperative pillar, competing pole?', in: Spyros Blavoukos and Dimitris Bourantonis (eds.), *The EU Presence in International Organizations*, London: Routledge 2011, pp. 33–60 ; Simon Smith, 'EU-NATO cooperation: a case of institutional fatigue?', (2011) 20 *European Security*, pp. 243–264; Nina Græger and Kristin Haugevik, 'The EU's Performance with and within NATO: Assessing Objectives, Outcomes and Organisational Practices', (2011) 33 *Journal of European Integration*, pp. 743–757. See also a previous piece by the present author, Joris Larik, 'Kennedy's "two pillars" revisited: Does the ESDP make the EU and the US two equal partners in NATO?', (2009) 14 *European Foreign Affairs Review*, pp. 289–304.

the role of the EU as an international actor in its own right.[13] However, while the literature on the legal aspects of security and defense policy of the EU has thrived as well,[14] we find few contributions addressing the relationship between the Union and the Alliance as a matter of law.[15]

As this chapter will argue, despite mutual affirmations of their importance, the European Union has not only come to incorporate security and defense policy into its ambit of competences, but has put itself on a track to become a fully-fledged security policy actor, arguably surpassing NATO. At the same time, the relevance of NATO has declined, and it is left with the choice either to branch out or accept a residual yet not insignificant role in transatlantic relations. These contrary organizational histories left a strong legal imprint, which allows for a number of observations of the Union's international identity, albeit *not through* NATO, but rather through the hallmarks of its own legal order and its relations with NATO. Essentially, it shows that the EU has risen to become both an ambitious international actor with virtually all-encompassing competence in the area of external relations as well as a constitutionalized community. While security and defense policy remain sensitive 'high politics', in which the Member States retain a strong say as well as autonomous policies of their own, this has not prevented this rise; neither has the continued existence of NATO or the superpower status of the United States. To elaborate on these observations, the paper is structured in two main sections. The first will address the field of defense and security policy, focusing on the major shifts in the international system and how both the EU and

---

[13] The concepts of 'actorness' and 'identity' are indeed intertwined, with the latter linking "the Union's presence, and understandings about its capabilities, in constructing expectations concerning EU practices"; see Bretherton and Vogler, *supra* n. 5, p. 6.

[14] See, seminally, Ramses Wessel, *The European Union's Foreign and Security Policy: A Legal Institutional Perspective*, The Hague: Kluwer Law International 1999; more recently Martin Trybus and Nigel White (eds.), *European Security Law*, Oxford: Oxford University Press 2007; Anne Cammilleri-Subrenat, *Le droit de la politique européenne de sécurité et de défense dans le cadre du traité de Lisbonne*, Paris: Lavoisier 2010; Frederik Naert, *International Law Aspects of the EU's Security and Defence Policy, with a Particular Focus on the Law of Armed Conflict and Human Rights*, Antwerp: Intersentia 2011. Also the principal textbooks on EU external relations law dedicate chapters to the CFSP/CSDP, see Piet Eeckhout, *EU External Relations Law*, Oxford: Oxford University Press 2011, Chapters 5 and 11; Panos Koutrakos, *EU International Relations Law*, Oxford: Hart Publishing 2006, Chapters 11 and 13.

[15] See as notable exceptions the extensive treatise by Martin Reichard, *The EU-NATO Relationship: A Legal and Political Perspective*, Aldershot: Ashgate 2006; and Simon Duke, 'The EU, NATO and the Treaty of Lisbon: Still Divided Within a Common City', in: Paul James Cardwell (ed.), *EU External Relations Law and Policy in the Post-Lisbon Era*, Berlin: Springer 2012, pp. 335–355.

NATO have reacted to them. Against this backdrop, the second section will turn to the legal interaction between the two organizations. A conclusion will sum up the findings.

2. The Evolution of NATO and the EU over Time

When appraising the relationship between the EU and NATO, it is worthwhile to take a look back at where both have come from and how they developed in the course of time in a changing international context. Both have their origins in the aftermath of the Second World War and the looming Cold War. The relations between the two can be divided roughly into three periods: one of neat complementarity, followed by one of upheaval and uncertainty, and finally an emerging one marked by the quest of the EU for comprehensive international actorness.[16]

As a preliminary point, it should be underlined that unlike other areas of EU external relations, defense and security policy was not born out of the need to externalize following the development of common internal rules. Rather, with the Maastricht Treaty, internal and external security entered the scene at the same time, and both initially in a strong intergovernmental fashion. Later on, the so-called 'third pillar' (at first known as 'Justice and Home Affairs') was 'communitarized' and now figures among competences governed by the TFEU.[17] Nevertheless, also in the post-Lisbon TEU, it is stressed that the Union is to respect the "essential State functions, including ensuring the territorial integrity of the State, maintaining law and order and safeguarding national security" and that the latter "remains the sole responsibility of each Member State".[18] Also with regard to foreign and security policy, the Member States continue to stress

---

16 These three periods correspond roughly to the three periods identified by Günter Burghardt for the bilateral EU-US relationship, Günter Burghardt, 'The EU's transatlantic relationship', in: Alan Dashwood and Marc Maresceau (eds.), *Law and Practice of EU External Relations: Salient Features of a Changing Landscape*, Cambridge: Cambridge University Press 2008, pp. 376–397. For a more fine-tuned division of periods from 1999 to 2009, see Daniel Keohane, 'EU and NATO', in: Giovanni Grevi, Damien Helly and Daniel Keohane (eds.), *European Security and Defence Policy: The First 10 Years (1999–2009)*, Paris: EUISS 2009, pp. 127–138.

17 This area in turn is gaining an external dimension of its own; see e.g. Florian Trauner and Helena Carrapiço, 'The External Dimension of EU Justice and Home Affairs after the Lisbon Treaty: Analysing the Dynamics of Expansion and Diversification', (2012) 17 *European Foreign Affairs Review*, pp. 1–18.

18 Art. 4(2) TEU; also Art. 276 TFEU on the restricted jurisdiction of the Court of Justice in this area.

their prerogatives, which they made clear in two declarations attached to the Treaties.[19] Thus, anything touching upon security, be it of an internal or external character, remains a sensitive issue over which the Member States are adamant to retain control.

2.1 *Neat Complementarity: Transatlantic Defense – A European Common Market*

The first and longest period ranges roughly from the founding of NATO to the fall of the Berlin Wall half a century later. NATO was founded in 1949 by virtue of the Washington Treaty[20] as an alliance set up to defend Western Europe from a Soviet attack.[21] With regard to other international commitments of its members, the treaty claims precedence,[22] a feature that Reichard terms "NATO primacy".[23] NATO has continued to exist on the basis of this Treaty, with its membership growing over time significantly from twelve founding members to twenty-eight at the time of writing.

If we turn to the evolution of the European Union, in this period we find no fewer than four precursor organizations that would later be absorbed into what is now the EU. These include the three European Communities, i.e. the European Coal and Steel Community, founded in 1952 following the Schuman Declaration, and subsequently the European Atomic Energy Community as well as the European Economic Community in 1957, all by the original six members. In addition, by expanding the Brussels Treaty of 1948, the Western European Union was established in 1954 as a defensive pact among the six Communities members and the United Kingdom.

Taken all together,[24] this multitude of international organizations form part of what has been termed the 'transatlantic bargain' in the post-war

---

[19] See also Declarations No. 13 and 14 concerning the Common Foreign and Security Policy attached to the Treaties.

[20] The North Atlantic Treaty, Washington D.C., 4 April 1949 (NAT).

[21] See in detail on the historic origins of the treaty Timothy Ireland, *Creating the Entangling Alliance: The Origins of the North Atlantic Treaty Organization*, Westport: Greenwood Press 1981; and Ellen Hallams, *The United States and NATO since 9/11: The Transatlantic Alliance Renewed*, Abingdon: Routledge 2010, Chapter 1 on "The Origins of the Transatlantic Community".

[22] Art. 8 NAT. The treaty in turn respects the primacy of the Charter of the United Nations, Art. 7 NAT.

[23] Reichard, *supra* n. 15, p. 148. This is not to be confused with the idea of primacy of EU law over national law, a point which will be elaborated on section 3.2.

[24] For the sake of completeness, one would also have to bear in mind the Organization for European Economic Cooperation (OEEC, now Organization for Economic Cooperation and Development (OECD)), charged with coordinating the distribution of economic

world. This entailed, in a nutshell, "that the United States would contribute to the defense of Europe and to Europe's economic recovery from the war if the Europeans would organize themselves to help defend against the Soviet threat and use economic aid efficiently".[25]

While economic recovery and integration progressed in Western Europe and the idea of a common market as the centerpiece of the economic community advanced, defense integration faltered. This was epitomized by the failure of the establishment of a European Defence Community (EDC) in the 1950s. This led to a so-called 'revised' transatlantic bargain, in which defense issues were the exclusive domain of NATO, which in turn relied heavily on American nuclear deterrence.[26] The WEU, as a substitute to the EDC, took a back seat subordinate to NATO.[27] Consequently, a neat division of labor emerged between NATO as the organization charged with military defense matters of Europe on the one, and the European Communities on the other hand being preoccupied with economic integration.[28]

In this first period, "in the shadow of the Cold War and under the protection of NATO"[29] the identity of the European Communities grew as a primarily economic club, shying away from the 'high politics' of defense and international security. This identity was reinforced a contrario through this division of tasks with NATO. For the Soviet Union, the European Communities literally did not exist, as the former refused to recognize them until as late as 1989.[30]

---

assistance from the United States in the framework of the Marshall Plan. See further on this organization the contribution by Tamara Takács and Joren Verschaeve to this volume (Chapter 8).

25 Stanley Sloan, *NATO, the European Union, and the Atlantic Community: The Transatlantic Bargain Challenged*, second edition, Lanham: Rowman & Littlefield 2005, p. 1.

26 Id., Chapter 3.

27 Gustav Schmidt, 'Getting the Balance Right: NATO and the Evolution of EC/EU Integration, Security and Defence Policy' in *idem* (ed.), *A History of NATO: The First Fifty Years*, Volume 2, Basingstoke: Palgrave Macmillan 2001, pp. 3–28, p. 11.

28 One could also add the Council of Europe and its European Court of Human Rights as the third complement of this arrangement, being in charge of human rights protection in Europe. See further on this particular organization the contribution by Thomas Streinz to this volume (Chapter 5).

29 Bretherton and Vogler, *supra* n. 5, p. 212.

30 This refusal only ended with the conclusion in 1989 of the Agreement between the European Economic Community and the European Atomic Energy Community and the Union of Soviet Socialist Republics on trade and commercial and economic cooperation [1990] OJ L 68/3.

2.2 *In Search of New Identities in the 'New World Order'*

With the end of the Cold War, the first phase of the EU–NATO relationship comes to an end and a period of upheaval begins, in which both organizations had to redefine their roles in the proverbial 'new world order'.[31] As NATO moved away from a focus on territorial defense and the European Communities moved away from their focus on economic integration, both came to enter the field of international security writ large. The questions that this raised to both, however, were very different at the outset. As far as NATO was concerned, given that its original raison d'être had vanished with the demise of the Soviet Union and the Warsaw Pact, it indeed faced an existential crisis, as voices were raised that it had become obsolete and it, too, ought to vanish.[32] To avert getting 'out of business', it embarked on a process of transformation, thereby acquiring a role beyond that of territorial defense.

NATO adopted two further strategic concepts in 1991 and 1999, which reflected this change of role.[33] It exercised its new, 'out of area', non-collective defense tasks first in the Balkans through intervention into the Bosnian civil war, as well as later in Kosovo. In these cases, the European Union and its predecessors were absent. Calls for a European-led intervention in the Balkans wars – the "hour of Europe"[34] – were left unheeded. Following the terrorist attacks of 9/11,[35] it also took on a role in the so-called 'War on Terror', notably by taking over the International Security

[31] George H.W. Bush, President of the United States, 'Address Before a Joint Session of Congress, Washington D.C., 11 September 1990', available at: <http://millercenter.org/scripps/archive/speeches/detail/3425>.

[32] See Reinhard Meier-Walser, 'Die Entwicklung der NATO 1990–2004', in: Johannes Varwick (ed.), *Die Beziehungen zwischen NATO und EU: Partnerschaft, Konkurrenz, Rivalität?*, Opladen: Budrich 2005, pp. 25–44, pp. 25–27.

[33] NATO, 'The Alliance's New Strategic Concept, agreed by the Heads of State and Government participating in the Meeting of the North Atlantic Council, 7 November 1991 – 8 November 1991', available at <http://www.nato.int/cps/en/natolive/official_texts_23847.htm>; and NATO, 'The Alliance's Strategic Concept, approved by the Heads of State and Government participating in the meeting of the North Atlantic Council in Washington D.C., 24 April 1999', available at: <http://www.nato.int/cps/en/natolive/official_texts_27433.htm>.

[34] To recall the (in)famous expression by Luxembourgish foreign minister Jacques Poos in 1991, quoted in Jolyon Howorth and John Keeler, 'The EU, NATO and the Quest for European Autonomy', in: Jolyon Howorth and John Keeler (eds.), *Defending Europe: The EU, NATO and the Quest for European Autonomy*, Basingstoke: Palgrave Macmillan 2003, pp. 3–21, p. 7.

[35] This was also the first time that Art. 5 of the North Atlantic Treaty on collective defence was invoked, resulting in surveillance of US airspace in the framework of operation *Eagle Assist*.

Assistance Force (ISAF) in Afghanistan and by conducting related counterterrorism operations.[36]

Especially on the formerly Eastern bloc countries, it retained an undiminished force of attraction. Many former Warsaw pact countries, as well as the Baltic States, which had been occupied and incorporated into the Soviet Union itself, became NATO members in two waves of enlargement, in 1999 and 2004 respectively.[37] Later on, also the countries of the Western Balkans, including those of the former Yugoslavia, joined the queue for membership. These countries, at the same time, aspire to EU membership, which has led to a similar enlargement of the Union.

During this same turbulent period, also the European Communities embarked on reinventing themselves. In contrast to NATO, however, the question was not to abolish them unless a new raison d'être was found. Instead, over the course of two decades, the goals and competences of the European institutions were progressively expanded, far beyond economic integration and international trade. An early hint at this development was given already in the 1980s with the Stuttgart Declaration on European Union[38] and the later Single European Act (SEA). This codified and consolidated a practice known as European Political Cooperation (EPC), through which the EC Member States coordinated their foreign policies. This expansion of the tasks of what would become the EU went straight to the core of the question of its identity. This is made explicit already in the SEA itself, in which the Member States pledged to cooperate more closely not only on matters of foreign policy, but also specifically on security matters. As was stressed already in the introduction, this "would contribute in an essential way to the development of a European identity in external policy matters".[39] However, the Act is prudent in underlining also that these new commitments are not to "impede closer co-operation in the field of security between certain of the High Contracting Parties within the framework of the Western European Union or the Atlantic Alliance".[40]

---

[36] See further Hallams, *supra* n. 21, Chapter 7 on "NATO's Transformation".

[37] See on the latter in particular NATO, Prague Summit Declaration, issued by the Heads of State and Government participating in the meeting of the North Atlantic Council in Prague on 21 November 2002, Press Release (2002)127, 21 November 2002; see further Frank Schimmelfennig, *The EU, NATO and Integration of Europe: Rules and Rhetoric*, Cambridge: Cambridge University Press 2003, pp. 37–51.

[38] European Council, Solemn Declaration on European Union, Stuttgart 19 June 1983, reproduced from the Bulletin of the European Communities, No. 6/1983, pp. 24–29.

[39] Art 30(6)(a) SEA.

[40] Art 30(6)(c) SEA.

Thus, the Member States of the Communities still paid heed to 'NATO primacy'.

This question of identity was reiterated in the watershed Maastricht Treaty of 1992, which formally founded the European Union. By adding two intergovernmental pillars to what had thus far been the *supra*national Communities, it equipped the Union with its own Common Foreign and Security Policy (CFSP), including what was then known as the European Security and Defence Policy (ESDP, later CSDP). It took a number of years, however, before the ESDP came of age. After the unsuccessful initiative of a "European Security and Defence Identity" within NATO and supervised by the WEU, a breakthrough within the EU was reached through the Anglo-French understanding at Saint-Malo in 1998.[41] A year later, it was decided to incorporate the WEU into the EU altogether.[42]

In practice, after the humble beginnings of operation *Concordia* in Macedonia in 2003, in rapid succession more than two dozen civilian and military missions have been carried out in the framework of the ESDP around the world.[43] In these operations, almost all EU Member States, including NATO and non-NATO members, have regularly participated. The exceptions are Denmark, which due to its CSDP opt-out does not participate in military operations,[44] as well as Malta and Cyprus. Moreover, non-EU countries have contributed to such operations, in some cases even NATO members. A telling example for this is the Norwegian participation in the CSDP anti-piracy operation *Atalanta*. While not a member of the EU (and not aspiring to become one), this NATO member has contributed ships to the CSDP anti-piracy operation, but thus far not to the concurrent NATO operations.[45]

---

[41] British-French Summit, St-Malo, 3–4 December 1998, 'Joint Declaration on European Defence', reproduced in: Institute for Security Studies, Western European Union, *From Nice to St-Malo, European Defence: Core Documents*, compiled by Maartje Rutten, Chaillot Paper No. 47 (May 2001), pp. 8–9.

[42] European Council, 'Presidency Conclusions – Cologne European Council', 3 and 4 June 1999, Annex III; see further Cammilleri-Subrenat, *supra* n. 14, pp. 206–210; and earlier Ramses Wessel, 'The EU as Black Widow: Devouring the WEU to Give Birth to a European Security and Defence Policy' in Vincent Kronenberger (ed.), *The EU and the International Legal Order: Discord or Harmony?* (The Hague: T.M.C. Asser Press 2001), pp. 405–434.

[43] See in detail the various chapters on ESDP/CSDP operations in Giovanni Grevi, Damien Helly and Daniel Keohane (eds.), *supra* n. 16.

[44] Denmark can and does contribute to civilian CSDP missions. On its opt-out see further section 3.1.

[45] EU NAVFOR Somalia, 'Norwegian Frigate Joins EU NAVFOR', press release, 3 August 2009, available at: <http://eunavfor.eu/norwegian-frigate-joins-eu-navfor/>. See generally

In addition, it should not go unnoticed that in terms of bilateral cooperation, the EU and the United States have concluded a Framework Agreement on the participation of the US in EU crisis management operations in 2011.[46] Under the terms of this agreement, the United States may contribute civilian personnel, units, and assets (which the agreement calls the 'US contingent') to EU crisis management operations.[47] It is a CFSP agreement concluded by the EU without its Member States.[48] It contains no reference to NATO whatsoever.

As both organizations started to expand their ambit of competences and ambitions into the field of international security, the relationship between the two became increasingly more complex. For the United States, this represented both a risk and an opportunity. On the one hand, as successive American administrations had called throughout the Cold War and thereafter for more commitment from the European Allies and more equitable 'burden sharing',[49] the new ESDP could be used to enhance Europe's contributions to the alliance. On the other, an autonomous ESDP at the very least posed the risk of unnecessarily duplicating functions and thus wasting resources. In addition, decoupled from NATO, the ESDP might evolve in ways inconsistent with US interests, or even develop into a counterweight to American power.[50] Also for the more Atlanticist members of the EU, these prospects were worrisome. Hence, mechanisms had to be devised to balance the development of an autonomous ESDP with maintaining 'NATO primacy'.

This came about, following lengthy negotiations, in the form of the so-called 'Berlin Plus' arrangement between the two organizations, which

---

on Norway's active participation in the CSDP, Christophe Hillion, 'Integrating an Outsider: An EU Perspective on Relations with Norway' (2011) 16 *European Foreign Affairs Review*, pp. 505–506. Norway has, however, contributed aircraft to the NATO operation.

[46] Framework Agreement between the United States of America and the European Union on the participation of the United States of America in European Union crisis management operations, [2011] OJ L 143/1.

[47] Id., Art. 2(2).

[48] The legal basis of the agreement is Art. 37 TEU juncto Art. 218(5) and (6) TFEU.

[49] See in detail Gustav Lindström, *EU-US Burdensharing: Who Does What?*, Chaillot Paper No. 82 (September 2005).

[50] Together with the discrimination of non-EU allies, duplication and decoupling form Madeleine Albright's proverbial 'three D's', see Reichard, *supra* n. 15, pp. 153–162; Jolyon Howorth, *Security and Defence Policy in the European Union*, Basingstoke: Palgrave Macmillan 2007, pp. 135–146.

was finalized in 2003.[51] It enables access of the European Union to NATO planning, using a NATO European command option for CSDP operations as well as the use of NATO assets and capabilities.[52] It still forms the most formalized relationship between the two.

2.3 *NATO and the EU post-Lisbon*

A third phase can be seen emerging in the EU–NATO relationship with the entry into force of the Lisbon Treaty. This is not to say that either organization has consolidated its role and international identity. While this remains an on-going process, in recent years another jump has been made on the part of the EU to 'assert itself' even more strongly and fully on the international scene. As Reichard sums it up, while till the mid-1990s NATO was the "pre-eminent" security actor in Europe, a decade later "the EU is moving centre stage".[53] The EU Treaties now outline a comprehensive and more assertive foreign and security policy, and also codify mutual defense commitments among the EU Member States. At the same time, NATO is left drifting, preoccupied predominantly with Afghanistan and with an unclear future ahead.

This new phase was foreshadowed by one of the most serious rifts in transatlantic relations, viz. the Iraq crisis of 2002/03. The United States under the George W. Bush administration opted for unilateral action backed by a mixed 'coalition of the willing', which also pitted EU Member States supporting or opposing the intervention against each other.[54] Consequently, both NATO and the European Union remained firmly on the back seat in this particular crisis. Only after the war was over, both engaged in minor training operations there (operation *EUJUST LEX-Iraq* and operation *NATO Training Mission-Iraq* respectively).

The efforts made subsequently to mend these European and transatlantic dissensions helped to set in motion a process which would ultimately culminate in the Lisbon Treaty. As the first important indication of rapprochement, under the direction of EU High Representative Javier

---

[51] Reichard, *supra* n. 15, pp. 273–288; Matthias Dembinski, 'Die Beziehungen zwischen NATO und EU von "Berlin" zu "Berlin Plus": Konzepte und Konfliktlinien', in: Johannes Varwick (ed.), *Die Beziehungen zwischen NATO und EU: Partnerschaft, Konkurrenz, Rivalität?*, Opladen: Budrich 2005, pp. 61–80.

[52] Council of the European Union, 'Background on EU-NATO permanent arrangements (Berlin +)', available at: <http://www.consilium.europa.eu/uedocs/cmsUpload/03-11-11%20Berlin%20Plus%20press%20note%20BL.pdf>.

[53] Reichard, *supra* n 15, p. 356.

[54] See Hallams, *supra* n. 40, pp. 85–104.

Solana, the European Council adopted the European Security Strategy (ESS) before the end of 2003. Even though criticized by some commentators as not really representing a 'real' national-style security strategy,[55] it nonetheless represents a first coherent outline of the European Union as an actor in the area of international security writ large. It explicitly stresses the importance of the transatlantic relationship as "irreplaceable", with the EU and US having the potential of forming "a formidable force for good in the world".[56] NATO, it asserts further, "is an important expression of this relationship".[57] However, it also underlines that "no single country is able to tackle today's complex problems on its own".[58] In addition, important nuances in the ESS as compared to its American counterpart at the time[59] were the stronger emphases on multilateralism ('effective multilateralism', as the EU likes to call it) and the so-called 'comprehensive approach' to security challenges, i.e. an approach not only relying on military strength ('shock and awe') but also on long-term engagement employing military as well as civilian capabilities.

Here we see already a sign of the relative shifts between the two organizations. While the transatlantic alliance is acknowledged, in so many words the ESS makes clear that it is an important aspect of EU foreign policy, but only *one* among many. Furthermore and crucially, it is the Union itself which declares to become active across the entire spectrum, something NATO at no point aspired to.

While the ESS is a policy document, these wide-ranging global ambitions found their legal expression at the Convention on the Future of Europe, which took place in 2002–2003 and eventually produced the draft Treaty Establishing a Constitution for Europe.[60] This project was ill-fated and ultimately abandoned, at least in terms of the constitutional 'label'.

---

55 Asle Toje, 'The European Security Strategy: A Critical Appraisal', (2005) 10 *European Foreign Affairs Review*, pp. 117–133.

56 European Council, *A Secure Europe in a Better World, European Security Strategy*, Brussels, 12 December 2003, at 13 (ESS). See also *Report on the Implementation of the European Security Strategy: Providing Security in a Changing World*, Brussels, S407/08, 11 December 2008.

57 ESS, p. 9. Note also the reference to the historic importance of the United States and NATO in European security, p. 1.

58 ESS, p. 1.

59 President of the United States of America, 'The National Security Strategy of the United States of America', Washington D.C., 16 March 2006; further Larik, *supra* n. 12, pp. 294–297. For the current national security strategy see President of the United States of America, 'National Security Strategy', Washington D.C., May 2010.

60 Treaty establishing a Constitution for Europe [2004] OJ C 310/1 (CT).

Nevertheless, most of the ideas of a stronger and more assertive Union on the global stage – also in the area of security and defense – voiced at the Convention and codified into the Draft Constitutional Treaty[61] would later find their way into the text of the Lisbon Treaty.[62] These ambitions are be realized through a revamped institutional framework. Innovations here include a reinforced and double-hatted High Representative (even though stripped off the title 'foreign minister'), a European External Action Service (EEAS), the setting up of a European Defense Agency to promote cooperation in the area of armaments (already set up as an agency in 2004)[63] and permanent structured cooperation among the Member States.[64] Moreover, the EU, after first having incorporated the WEU as its defense arm, eventually absorbed this international organization entirely in 2011, with the latter officially disbanding itself.[65]

With the entry into force of the Lisbon Treaty on 1 December 2009, all these elements have become part and parcel of EU primary law. To which extent, however, the Union will be able to live up to these ambitions, is indeed still an open question. Setting up the new diplomatic arm of the Union, the EEAS, has gone rather sluggishly, with many legal issues on its powers and competences remaining to be settled.[66] Equally, utilization of the new option of permanent structured cooperation is also still wanting.[67] In addition, while CSDP operation have proliferated from 2003

---

[61] See e.g. Secretariat of the European Convention, *Speeches delivered at the inaugural meeting of the Convention on 28 February 2002*, Brussels, 5 March 2002, CONV 4/02, Annex 4: 'Introductory Speech by President V. Giscard d'Estaing to the Convention on the Future of Europe', p. 16; Arts. I-3(4) and III-292 CT and Arts. III-309 to III-313 CT on the CSDP.

[62] Arts. 3(5) and 21 TEU; Arts. 42–46 TEU on the CSDP.

[63] Council of the European Union, Joint Action 2004/551/CFSP of 12 July 2004 on the establishment of the European Defence Agency [2004] OJ L 245/17.

[64] For a concise overview see Jean-Claude Piris, *The Lisbon Treaty: A Legal and Political Analysis*, Cambridge: Cambridge University Press 2010, pp. 273–275; further Christine Kaddous, 'External Action under the Lisbon Treaty', in: Ingolf Pernice and Evgeni Tanchev (eds.), *Ceci n'est pas une Constitution – Constitutionalisation without a Constitution?* Baden-Baden: Nomos 2009, pp. 173–189.

[65] See Western European Union, 'Statement of the Presidency of the Permanent Council of the WEU on behalf of the High Contracting Parties to the Modified Brussels Treaty – Belgium, France, Germany, Greece, Italy, Luxembourg, The Netherlands, Portugal, Spain and the United Kingdom', Brussels, 31 March 2010.

[66] For the legal uncertainties surrounding the EEAS as a sui generis organ, see Bart Van Vooren, 'A legal-institutional perspective on the European Union External Action Service', (2011) 48 *Common Market Law Review*, pp. 475–502; for an assessment of the first year of EEAS practice see Steven Blockmans, 'The European External Action Service one year on: First signs of strengths and weaknesses', *CLEER Working Paper* 2012/2.

[67] Note also Protocol 10 on Permanent Structured Cooperation attached to the Treaties. Arguing for an indirect use of this option, see Sven Biscop and Jo Coelmont, 'CSDP and the

to 2008, culminating in the launch of the first aero-naval operation of the EU in the fight against Somali pirates (operation *EU NAVFOR Atalanta*) in late 2008, no other operations have been launched under the CSDP ever since. This has prompted Duke to speak of a "crisis of confidence in CSDP" today.[68]

While the EU has been expanding its global ambitions and institutional machinery, and followed up with a burst of different operations around the world, the same cannot be said by any measure about NATO. The Alliance remains largely preoccupied with its operation in Afghanistan. Apart from this and the aforementioned training mission in Iraq, NATO still keeps peacekeepers in Kosovo and supports the EU in Bosnia via the 'Berlin Plus' mechanism. In parallel to the EU, it maintains an anti-piracy operation off the coast of Somalia (operation *Ocean Shield*). This in particular seems to be a case of duplication, necessitating the allocation of resources for EU–NATO–US coordination.[69]

However, in 2011 during the Libyan civil war, it was in the framework of NATO that Western nations intervened (operation *Unified Protector*), and not the European Union.[70] The two organizations existed here next to one another, as frameworks from among which states could choose, and here NATO came to be preferred by those EU Member States that wanted to act swiftly, i.e. France and the United Kingdom in this case. This does not reflect the assertions from the new NATO Strategic Concept, which after all calls for an "active and effective European Union" as "a unique and essential partner for NATO".[71] Moreover, the side-lining of the European Union in this context was perceived as a huge setback not only for the CSDP but for EU foreign policy as a whole. An editorial in Le Monde of 31 March 2011, poetically declaring the CSDP dead and buried in the sands of Libya, opined that "[t]he disunity is total and particularly striking when it is a question of deciding on war".[72] The Union, for various reasons of internal divisions, including Germany's reluctant stance in this

---

"Ghent Framework": The Indirect Approach to Permanent Structured Cooperation', (2011) 16 *European Foreign Affairs Review*, pp. 149–167.

[68] Duke, *supra* n. 15, p. 343.

[69] See Hallams, *supra* n. 21, pp. 66–84. The European Union has also launched a CDSP police operation in Afghanistan (*EUPOL Afghanistan*).

[70] See Anand Menon, 'European Defence Policy from Lisbon to Libya', (2011) 53 *Survival*, pp. 75–90.

[71] NSC 2010, *supra* n. 11, p. 2, par. 32.

[72] As quoted and translated by Menon, *supra* n. 70, p. 76.

crisis, failed to pick up arms. Thus, for many observers, it ceased to exist altogether as an actor.[73]

As a matter of general trajectory, commentators observe that the EU is on track to be leaving behind NATO. For Sven Biscop, whereas "NATO can contribute, it is not equipped to take the lead", the EU together with the United States "are the true, comprehensive foreign policy actors in Europe and North America".[74] More cautiously, Simon Duke concludes that "if the treaty-based aspirations are realised, the EU will have potential to address a far wider range of foreign policy and security challenges than NATO."[75] In sum, uncertainties surrounding the future performance of both organizations remain. On the one hand, despite all prophecies of the demise of NATO, it is still quite obviously 'in business', as illustrated most clearly in Afghanistan as well as on Europe's southern doorstep. On the other, in view of the global ambitions of the Lisbon Treaty, it remains open to which extent the Union will be able to live up to them, not least in times of internal turmoil of the Eurozone crisis.[76]

Notwithstanding these uncertainties, in terms of identity the EU has clearly surpassed NATO. For better or worse, while NATO contents itself with continuing to secure the "common defense and security" of its members and occasional international crisis management,[77] the EU claims nothing less than to "promote an international system based on stronger multilateral cooperation and good global governance"[78] in each and every way. However, as the case of Libya shows, the actorness of the EU can quickly vanish into thin air if it falters in the area of security and defense.

[73] The EU did eventually agree on a military operation in Libya. However, this came at too late a stage, and was never activated. See Council Decision 2011/210/CFSP of 1 April 2011 on a European Union military operation in support of humanitarian assistance operations in response to the crisis situation in Libya (EUFOR Libya) [2011] OJ L 89/17.

[74] Sven Biscop, *From Lisbon to Lisbon: Squaring the Circle of EU and NATO Future Roles*, EGMONT Secuirty Policy Brief No. 16, January 2011, p. 2.

[75] Duke *supra* n. 15, p. 354.

[76] Note that austerity and spending cuts already start to permeate the discourse on European defense policy, see e.g. Biscop and Coelmont, *supra* n. 67; also Giovanni Faleg and Alessandro Giovannini, *The EU between Pooling & Sharing and Smart Defence: Making a virtue of necessity?* CEPS Special Report May 2012.

[77] NSC 2010, *supra* n. 11, p. 4.

[78] Art. 21(2)(h) TEU.

3. The EU and NATO: Sisters-in-law?

As was outlined in the preceding section, the relationship between the EU and NATO has shifted in the course of history from a neat distinction of functions in post-war Europe, via a period of uncertainty, to a situation in which at least the ambitions of the Union as a global player are politically comprehensive, while NATO remains limited to its "core business"[79] of common defense as well as global crisis management. This evolution also finds its expression in the legal relationship between the two organizations.

As a preliminary matter, given that we find ourselves here in the sovereignty sensitive, 'high politics' area of security, too strong a legal dimension may not be expected in the first place. In view of the "inherently limited function of legal rules in the area of security and defense policy",[80] this is not the type of external policy where judicialized dispute settlement is common, as opposed to, for instance, trade or human rights.[81] Keeping this in mind, it is a priori unsurprising that soft arrangements rather than hard treaty law govern the relationship between both.

Nonetheless, we do find law that defines this relationship in two principal aspects. On the one hand, the Union, in its Treaties as well as in the soft arrangements between the two organizations, indeed continues to acknowledge in principle 'NATO primacy'. On the other, in the EU context, a rather strong reliance on law also in the area of the CSDP can be detected, which in turn shapes the relationship between the two organizations and their member states. In addition, through the connection between the internal market and armaments policy, also an EU-internal dimension can be seen emerging.

3.1 *A Transatlantic Nod from the EU*

As a point of departure, it should be stressed that the Union is not, and cannot be, a member of NATO. Thus, the EU does not enjoy a formal status in the sense of being a member or even observer at NATO. The North

---

[79] Biscop, *supra* n. 74, p. 1.

[80] Panos Koutrakos, 'The Role of Law in Common Security and Defence Policy: Functions, Limitations and Perceptions', in: id. (ed.), *European Foreign Policy: Legal and Political Perspectives*, Cheltenham: Edward Elgar 2011, p. 256.

[81] See the contributions by Tamara Perišin and Thomas Streinz to this volume (Chapters 4 and 5).

Atlantic Treaty does only allow states to become members.[82] The Union itself is thus not subject to the obligations under the NAT, in contrast to those of its Member States which are NATO allies.

Nonetheless, as was referred to earlier, a claim to 'NATO primacy' exists in Article 8 of the NAT, which states that:

> Each Party declares that none of the international engagements now in force between it and any other of the Parties or any third State is in conflict with the provisions of this Treaty, and undertakes not to enter into any international engagement in conflict with this Treaty.

Consequently, those Allies which would go on to participate in European integration were under an obligation to ensure that the Treaties governing the European institutions, or any other 'engagement' in this area, would not be at odds with the NAT. In times of neat complementarity, conflicts were rather unlikely. Once the EU entered into the field of security and defense policy, however, the question to which extent this 'primacy' can be maintained becomes salient.

The ESDI, as the European pillar within NATO, would have been a clear expression of such primacy, but it did not come about. The resulting ESDP, which was to be the autonomous defense capability of the EU, in turn did underline its compatibility with NATO.[83] The breakthrough in implementing the ESDP, the Franco-British Saint-Malo Summit, already catered to NATO obligations. While the two nations agreed that "the Union must have the capacity for autonomous action",[84] they asserted in the same breath that collective defense commitments under WEU and NATO must be maintained and that the obligations under NATO are to be respected. In this way, the Union and its Member States gave a 'transatlantic nod' in order to dispel American and other Allies' suspicions of the ESDP.

Also after the Lisbon reform the Treaties continue to accommodate the fact that many EU Member States are also members of NATO. Generally, EU primary law now vows to respect the "national identities, inherent in their fundamental structures, political and constitutional"[85] of the

---

[82] More precisely, "any other European State in a position to further the principles of this Treaty and to contribute to the security of the North Atlantic area" can be invited to join NATO (Art. 10 NAT).

[83] For the situation pre-Lisbon, see Heike Krieger, 'Common European Defence: Competition or Compatibility with NATO', in: Martin Trybus and Nigel White (eds.), *European Security Law*, Oxford: Oxford University Press 2007, pp. 174–197, pp. 192–194; and Reichard, *supra* n. 15, pp. 148–149.

[84] Saint-Malo Declaration, *supra* n. 41, p. 8 .

[85] Art. 4(2) TEU.

Member States. The accommodation in EU primary law of the Atlanticist attitudes and concerns of some members can be seen as a specific expression of such respect.[86] Article 42 TEU on the CSDP states that this policy

> shall respect the obligations of certain Member States, which see their common defence realized in the North Atlantic Treaty Organization (NATO), under the North Atlantic Treaty and be compatible with the common security and defence policy established within that framework.[87]

In this context, it should be noted that the position of neutral Member States is accommodated in the Treaties as well. The provision cited above also states that the CDSP will not "prejudice the specific character of the security and defence policy of certain Member States",[88] which means their neutrality. Overall, relations between Member States which are NATO allies and other EU members (Austria, Cyprus, Finland, Ireland, Malta and Sweden) have not caused particular friction in the EU-NATO relationship.[89] Arguably, this is due to the way the CSDP works, i.e. providing ample flexibility and a large degree of control to the Member States.[90] As we have seen, virtually all Member States participate in CSDP operations, neutrals as well as allies, once such operations could be agreed upon at EU level.

Two exceptions apply here. First, Denmark opted out of the CSDP altogether ever since the so-called 'Edinburgh Decision' of 1992. However, according to Protocol 22 attached to the Treaties, "Denmark will not prevent the other Member States from further developing their cooperation in this area".[91] Danish approval is not necessary to establish unanimity

---

86 The scope of 'constitutional identity' as a ground for invoking derogations from obligations under EU law, however, is rather limited. See in detail Armin von Bogdandy and Stephan Schill, 'Overcoming Absolute Primacy: Respect for National Identity under the Lisbon Treaty', (2011) 48 *Common Market Law Review*, pp. 1417–1454.

87 Art. 42(2), second subparagraph TEU. The new mutual assistance clause reiterates this concern (Art. 42(7), second subparagraph TEU), as do Protocol 10 on Permanent Structured Cooperation and Protocol 11 on Art. 42 of the Treaty on European Union attached to the Treaties.

88 Art. 42(2), second subparagraph TEU.

89 This is not to say that neutrality is not an important domestic political topic in these countries. See further Nicole Alecu de Flers, *EU Foreign Policy and the Europeanization of Neutral States: Comparing Irish and Austrian foreign policy*, Abingdon: Routledge 2012.

90 While the Member States "shall make civilian and military capabilities available to the Union for the implementation" of the CSDP (Art. 42(3) TEU), there is no mechanism to force them to do so. Generally, decisions in the area of CSDP are taken unanimously (Art. 42(4) TEU).

91 Protocol No. 22 annexed to the Lisbon Treaty on the Position of Denmark, Art. 5(1).

within the Council to take decisions in this area.[92] Thus, for instance, Denmark does not contribute to operation *Atalanta* launched by the EU, but instead commits warships to NATO's operation *Ocean Shield* in the same area and with a similar mandate. The second problematic case is the so-called 'Cyprus question', which has complicated the efforts to operationalize the EU–NATO relationship.

These efforts, as we have seen, did not yield a formal international agreement between the two organizations. Instead, what exists between them is the 'Berlin Plus' arrangement. It is officially a 'Declaration', with the detailed content of this arrangement remaining classified. This puts in question its legal value, in particular its character as an international agreement.[93] It took three years to negotiate this arrangement, which is not least due to the 'Cyprus question', viz. tensions between Greece (member of both the EU and NATO) and Turkey (member of NATO and officially an EU candidate country) over Cyprus (EU member since 2004 but outside of NATO and the PfP).[94] Related to 'primacy', there remains the contentious idea of a 'right of first refusal' by NATO. Already in the Saint-Malo Declaration, it was stated that the Union should be able to take action "where the Alliance as a whole is not engaged".[95] This formulation was subsequently incorporated in the 'Berlin Plus' arrangement as well as EU documents.[96] Whether it means that the EU cannot engage in crises where NATO is not already present or rather where NATO does not choose to be present is a matter of controversy. Thus far, NATO has never claimed it in practice.[97]

Subsequently, 'Berlin Plus' has only been drawn upon on two early occasions, operation *Concordia* in Macedonia and operation *Althea* in Bosnia. Given the time and efforts it took to finalize the arrangement, it has been observed that it "only remained relevant for less than 20 months".[98] Misgivings due to the 'Cyprus question', in particular Cyprus blocking Turkish participation in the CSDP and Turkey blocking Cypriot participation in

---

92 Id., Art. 5(2).

93 Reichard, *supra* n. 15, pp. 288–300.

94 Reichard, *supra* n. 15, pp. 283–288.

95 Saint-Malo Declaration, *supra* n. 41, p. 8.

96 'EU-NATO Declaration on ESDP', Press Release (2002) 142, 16 December 2002, available at: <http://www.nato.int/docu/pr/2002/p02-142e.htm>; see also already European Council, Presidency Conclusions, Helsinki European Council of 10 and 11 December 1999, par. 27.

97 See Reichard, *supra* n. 15, pp. 162–170.

98 Erwan Lagadec, *Transatlantic Relations in the 21st Century: Europe, America and the Rise of the Rest*, Abingdon: Routledge 2012, p. 118.

NATO/PfP, continue to impede its being utilized, or any more meaningful form of EU–NATO cooperation for that matter.[99] Against this backdrop, cooperation between EU and NATO under this framework has been the object of criticisms as being ineffective and unsatisfactory.[100]

In sum, acknowledging that 'NATO primacy' in principle and generally stressing the importance of the Transatlantic Alliance could be seen as an integral part of the Union's identity as an international actor. However, it seems to be of little practical relevance. As the Libyan example shows, while there remain situations in which NATO is chosen over the EU, this occurs rather de facto rather than as a matter of law.

3.2 *European Identity beyond NATO*

Beyond nodding to the importance of the transatlantic relationship, the EU Treaties, especially after the Lisbon reform, contain much more that is of relevance in determining the Union's identity as an international actor through security policy. Today, the shifting relationship between the two, in which the Union's ambitions by far surpass those of NATO, are plainly expressed in the Treaties. By including this in the overall system of Union primary law, this also introduces a stronger legal dimension – one which is absent from NATO. Apart from substantive obligations under the EU Treaties, the Union's institutional framework serves to lend more credence to these commitments. While retaining an intergovernmental character at large, defense policy is also linked to the supranational rules of the internal market via the still developing area of armaments cooperation.

As a point of departure here, the claim to primacy of Article 8 NAT meets as its EU counterpart the principle of 'primacy' of Union law.[101] At first glance, these may seem as diametrically opposed claims. However, they operate in quite different ways, with the primacy of EU law running deeper and producing more tangible effects. The NAT is undoubtedly an agreement setting up an international organization. Compliance with the

---

99 See Smith, *supra* n. 12, p. 247.

100 For Simon Duke, EU–NATO relations "remain ill-defined and lack much meaningful substance". Duke, *supra* n. 15, p. 354; also Smith, *supra* n. 12; Howorth, *supra* n. 51, pp. 173–177; and Asle Toje, *The EU, NATO and European Defence – A Slow Train Coming*, EUISS Occasional Paper (December 2008).

101 This principle is not codified in the EU Treaties until the present day. However, it is referred to, as well as the 'well settled case law' of the EU Court of Justice thereon, in Declaration No. 17 Concerning Primacy attached to the Treaties. This case law started, as is well-known, with the judgment of the Court of Justice in Case 6/64 *Costa* v *ENEL* [1964] ECR (English special edition) 585.

NAT is governed by international law. The case of the EU is not so simple. In the course of time, it has acquired what many consider 'constitutional' features.[102] One important such feature is that EU law claims precedence over any form of the national law of its Member States, rending the latter inapplicable to the extent that it is inconsistent with the former.[103]

Importantly, this includes in principle also international agreements concluded by the Member States, unless covered by the protection afforded by Article 351 TFEU (formerly Article 307 TEC). This Article, while respecting the rights and obligations under prior international agreements concluded by Union Member States with third parties,[104] obliges them at the same time to "take all appropriate steps to eliminate the incompatibilities established."[105] Consequently, EU Member States adhering to NATO are under a duty to eliminate incompatibilities which might arise between their obligations under the Treaties and the NAT.

The fact that we find ourselves in the 'high politics' of security policy here does not serve as an excuse not to comply with other obligations under Union law. The Court stressed this is the *Centro-Com* case. While confirming that "Member States have indeed retained their competence in the field of foreign and security policy",[106] the Court underlines that, nonetheless, "the powers retained by the Member States must be exercised in a manner consistent with [then] Community law".[107] This also entails that the basic foundations of the constitutional order of the Union, including fundamental rights protection, cannot be undermined by international commitments, including those in the pursuit of international

[102] The Court of Justice famously labeled the Treaties 'the basic constitutional charter' of the then Community in Case 294/83 *Parti écologiste 'Les Verts'* v *Parliament*, [1986] ECR 01339, par. 23; arguing for the "constitutionalization" of EU foreign affairs, including the CSDP, see Daniel Thym, 'The Intergovernmental Constitution of the EU's Foreign, Security & Defence Executive', (2011) 7 *European Constitutional Law Review*, pp. 453–480, pp. 477–478; and generally Paul Craig, 'Constitutions, Constitutionalism, and the European Union', (2001) 7 *European Law Journal*, pp. 125–150.

[103] According to the Court of Justice, this includes also constitutional law of the Member States: see Case 11/70, *Internationale Handelsgesellschaft*, [1970] ECR 1125, par. 3. See in detail on this subject, for instance, Robert Schütze, *European Constitutional Law*, Cambridge: Cambridge University Press 2012, Chapter 10 on "Supremacy and Preemption".

[104] Art. 351(1) TFEU.

[105] Art. 351(2) TFEU. It thus protects the obligations towards third parties rather than the rights of EU Member States under these agreements: see ECJ, Case 10/61, *Commission v Italy*, [1962] ECR (English special edition) 1.

[106] ECJ, Case C-124/95, *The Queen, ex parte Centro-Com Srl* v *HM Treasury and Bank of England*, [1997] ECR I-81, par. 24.

[107] Ibid., par. 25.

security. In contrast to NATO, in the case of the Union, we find a court willing to rule on such questions.[108]

Beyond the question of primacy, the post-Lisbon Treaties impose a number of important substantive obligations on the Member States. The pre-Lisbon Treaties still rather vaguely called for the EU "to assert its identity on the international scene, in particular through" the CFSP and CSDP.[109] Under the current Treaties, expressing the global ambitions of the Union, the wish to become a security actor is more clearly visible. Among the general objectives of EU external action,[110] the Union is to "safeguard its values, fundamental interests, security, independence and integrity"[111] and "preserve peace, prevent conflicts and strengthen international security".[112] With particular regard to the CSDP, the Petersberg tasks, originally devised by the WEU, have been expanded through the Lisbon reform. In addition to humanitarian and rescue tasks, peacekeeping tasks and tasks of combat forces in crisis management, including peacemaking,[113] these tasks now include also joint disarmament operations, military advice and assistance tasks, conflict prevention and post-conflict stabilization, which all may also be used to contribute to the fight against terrorism.[114]

Two further substantive obligations stand out concerning the Union as a security actor. First, the Treaties now also contain a so-called solidarity clause. It obliges the Union and its Member States to "act jointly in a spirit of solidarity if a Member State is the object of a terrorist attack or the victim of a natural or man-made disaster".[115] Secondly, the EU Treaties post-Lisbon also move towards the traditional core task of NATO, viz. common defense, with a new mutual assistance clause, which reads:

> If a Member State is the victim of armed aggression on its territory, the other Member States shall have towards it an obligation of aid and assistance by

---

108 In particular Joined cases C-402/05 P and C-415/05 P, *Kadi and Al Barakaat* v *Council and Commission* [2008] ECR I-06351; further Nikolaos Lavranos, 'Protecting European Law from International Law', (2010) 15 *European Foreign Affairs Review*, pp. 265–282.

109 Art. 2(1) TEU (pre-Lisbon). The objectives specific to the CFSP were elaborated on further in Art. 11 TEU (pre-Lisbon), and have to a significant extent inspired what is now Art. 21 TEU.

110 On the legal effects of such objectives see Joris Larik, 'Shaping the International Order as a Union Objective and the Dynamic Internationalisation of Constitutional Law', *CLEER Working Paper* 2011/05.

111 Art. 21(2)(a) TEU.

112 Art. 21(2)(c) TEU.

113 As included already in Art. 17(2) TEU (pre-Lisbon).

114 Art. 43(1) TEU.

115 Art. 222(1) TEU.

> all the means in their power, in accordance with Article 51 of the United Nations Charter. This shall not prejudice the specific character of the security and defence policy of certain Member States.[116]

This reproduces largely, albeit not exactly, Article V of the WEU Treaty.[117] Two caveats, in addition to the compatibility requirement with NATO, apply here. It should be noted, first, that it is only the Member States which are called upon here to lend assistance to *each other*. The Union and its institutions, however, do not appear here, as they do by contrast in the solidarity clause. Secondly, even though this makes the Union a mutual defense arrangement among the Member States, this should not be confused with the creation of a 'common defense' or a 'military alliance' *à la* NATO or WEU.[118] The Treaties only keep the door ajar for this option in the future.[119] A 'common defense', including in particular nuclear deterrence that could be provided by the two Member States possessing such capabilities (France and the United Kingdom), is not present at EU level. This remains thus the sole domain of NATO. In this vein, the new Strategic Concept does not fail to recall that the "supreme guarantee of the security of the Allies is provided by the strategic nuclear forces of the Alliance, particularly those of the United States".[120] Thus far it could be said that common defense is not part of the Union's identity.

Such substantive objectives and obligations have to be understood within their institutional context. While the legal nature of the CFSP/CSDP was questionable in the early phase after the Maastricht Treaty and in view of the peculiar pillar-structure that it brought about,[121] it has become more consolidated over the years. Now, with the Lisbon Treaty in force, the CFSP is part and parcel of the integrated Union structure.

---

116 Art. 42(7), first subparagraph TEU.

117 Art. V Modified Brussels Treaty: "If any of the High Contracting Parties should be the object of an armed attack in Europe, the other High Contracting Parties will, in accordance with the provisions of Article 51 of the Charter of the United Nations, afford the Party so attacked all the military and other aid and assistance in their power."

118 Piris, *supra* n. 64, p. 275, and Koutrakos, *supra* n. 80, pp. 237–240, who both note, however, the political significance of the provision.

119 Art. 42(2), first subparagraph TEU, which states ambiguously: "The common security and defence policy shall include the progressive framing of a common Union defence policy. This will lead to a common defence, when the European Council, acting unanimously, so decides."

120 NSC 2010, *supra* n. 11, p. 14, par. 18.

121 For a shrewd assessment of the intricacies of this structure see Christoph Herrmann, 'Much Ado About Pluto? The "Unity of the European Union Legal Order" Revisited', in: Marise Cremona and Bruno de Witte (eds.), *EU Foreign Relations Law: Constitutional Fundamentals*, Oxford: Hart Publishing 2008, pp. 19–51.

Nevertheless, despite the formal disappearance of the pillars, "specific rules and procedures" continue to apply in this policy area.[122] CFSP, and the CSDP as an "integral part"[123] of it, hence retain a strong intergovernmental character, which is best illustrated by the a priori exclusion of jurisdiction of the Court of Justice from this field.[124] The breadth of CFSP, as covering "all areas of foreign policy and all questions relating to the Union's security, including the progressive framing of a common defence policy",[125] is contrasted with the ill-defined nature of this competence. This is reflected by the fact that the competences catalogues of the TFEU put the CFSP as a case apart. The extent to which former Community law principles apply, remains thus open to question.[126]

However, it was already mentioned that Member States remain bound by EU law obligations even when acting in the domain of foreign and security policy. In addition, the Court retains the power to rule on cases concerning the proper legal basis of Union measures with a view to ensuring that CFSP and non-CFSP competences do encroach upon each other.[127] Furthermore, under the Treaties, the Member States are under the so-called 'duty of sincere cooperation',[128] violations of which are justiciable.[129] In the area of the CFSP, this duty is reiterated in strong terms:

> The Member States shall support the Union's external and security policy actively and unreservedly in a spirit of loyalty and mutual solidarity and shall comply with the Union's action in this area.

---

122 Art. 24(1), second subparagraph TEU. See further Peter van Elsuwege, 'EU external action after the collapse of the pillar structure. In search of a new balance between delimitation and consistency', (2010) 47 *Common Market Law Review*, pp. 987–1019.

123 Art. 42(1) TEU.

124 Art. 24(1), second subparagraph TEU juncto Art. 275(1) TFEU.

125 Art. 21(1), first subparagraph TEU.

126 Some consensus seems to exists that the CFSP/CSDP is neither exclusive nor pre-emptive, see Aurel Sari, 'Between Legalization and Organizational Development: Explaining the Evolution of EU Competence in the Field of Foreign Policy', in: Paul James Cardwell (ed.), *EU External Relations Law and Policy in the Post-Lisbon Era*, The Hague: T.M.C. Asser Press, pp. 59–95; Marise Cremona, 'Defining competence in EU external relations: lessons from the Treaty reform process', in: Alan Dashwood and Marc Maresceau (eds.), *Law and Practice of EU External Relations: Salient Features of a Changing Landscape*, Cambridge: Cambridge University Press 2008, pp. 63–67; and Eeckhout, *supra* n. 14, p. 171.

127 Art. 40 TEU; see for a discussion of the pertinent case law on this issue, Bart Van Vooren, 'The Small Arms Judgment in an Age of Constitutional Turmoil', (2009) 14 *European Foreign Affairs Review*, pp. 231–248.

128 Art. 4(3) TEU.

129 On the case law of the Court of Justice in this regard, see Andrés Delgado Casteleiro and Joris Larik, 'The Duty to Remain Silent: Limitless Loyalty in EU External Relations?', (2011) 36 *European Law Review*, pp. 522–539.

> The Member States shall work together to enhance and develop their mutual political solidarity. They shall refrain from any action which is contrary to the interests of the Union or likely to impair its effectiveness as a cohesive force in international relations.[130]

There is no cogent reason why the duty of cooperation as such should not also apply in the area of CFSP/CSDP.[131] Since the general provision on the duty of sincere cooperation obliges the Member States to "refrain from any measure which could jeopardize the attainment of the Union's objectives",[132] i.e. *all* of the Union's objectives, it might be argued that the Court would have jurisdiction to enforce this duty also in the area of CFSP/CSDP.[133] However, when arguing along the lines that still CFSP-specific objectives exist among the external action objectives of the EU,[134] the exclusion of the jurisdiction of the Court from the CFSP would also apply to them. Consequently, the exceptions to this exclusion specifically mentioned in the Treaties would thus be deemed exhaustive.[135]

In any event, both Union institutions and the Member States are legally bound to the pursuit of these objectives and to cooperate with each other to achieve them. As "trustees of the Union interest",[136] the Member States are made to partake in international actions on behalf of the Union, asserting further a shared EU identity.

As a final point, a link can be seen emerging between the initial 'core business' of the Union, or rather its predecessors, the Communities, and its more recently emerging identity as a security actor. This is the link between the efforts for better coordination of armaments policy and the rules of the internal market. It became clear early on in the history of

---

130 Art. 24(3) TEU, second and third subparagraph.

131 Christophe Hillion and Ramses Wessel, 'Restraining External Competences of EU Member States under CFSP', in: Marise Cremona and Bruno de Witte (eds.), *EU Foreign Relations Law: Constitutional Fundamentals*, pp. 79–121.

132 Art. 4(3), third subparagraph TEU.

133 Arguing in this direction, Hillion and Wessel, *supra* n. 131, pp. 108–112.

134 Alan Dashwood, 'Article 47 TEU and the Relationship between First and Second Pillar Competences', in: Alan Dashwood and Marc Maresceau (eds.), *Law and Practice of EU External Relations: Salient Features of a Changing Landscape*, Cambridge: Cambridge University Press 2008, pp. 70–103.

135 These are the already mentioned monitoring of the borderline between CFSP and non-CFSP competences (Art. 40 TEU), as well as jurisdiction over restrictive measures against natural or legal persons (Art. 275(2) TFEU).

136 To borrow the term from Marise Cremona, 'Member States as Trustees of the Union Interest: participating in international agreements on behalf of the European Union', in: Anthony Arnull et al. (eds.), *A Constitutional Order of States: Essays in European Law in Honour of Alan Dashwood*, Oxford: Hart Publishing 2011, pp. 435–457.

the CSDP that the Union would need "credible military forces"[137] in order to live up to the new tasks it had set itself. Especially after the need to rely on the United States and NATO in the Balkan conflicts of the 1990s, shortcomings in this regard became apparent. Consequently, the Union set itself ambitious 'headline goals'[138] and elaborated 'capability action plans' and 'capability improvement charts' to remedy them.[139]

With a view to improving capabilities, institutionally, an increasingly important role was to be played by the European Defense Agency. Under the post-Lisbon TEU, it

> shall identify operational requirements, shall promote measures to satisfy those requirements, shall contribute to identifying and, where appropriate, implementing any measure needed to strengthen the industrial and technological base of the defence sector, shall participate in defining a European capabilities and armaments policy, and shall assist the Council in evaluating the improvement of military capabilities.[140]

In its endeavors to foster a European Defense Technological and Industrial Base operating in a European Defense Equipment Market, it encountered the difficult issue of security exceptions to the rules of the internal market.[141] Traditionally, the Member States have based themselves on what is now Article 346 TFEU (ex-Article 296 TEC) in order to prevent an automatic opening of their armaments industries to the internal market. Under this provision, a Member State does not have to supply information "the disclosure of which it considers contrary to the essential interests of its security"[142] and is free to take measures that it deems "necessary for the protection of the essential interests of its security which are connected

137 Saint-Malo Declaration, *supra* n. 41, p. 8.

138 First, the Helsinki Headline Goal of 1999, set for 2003, European Council, Presidency Conclusions, Helsinki European Council of 10 and 11 December 1999, Annex 2 to Annex IV; then, the Headline Goal 2010, approved by General Affairs and External Relations Council on 17 May 2004, endorsed by the European Council of 17 and 18 June 2004.

139 See Council of the European Union, Development of Military Capabilities, Updated: January 2011, Military capabilities/8, available at: <http://www.consilium.europa.eu/media/1222506/110106%20updated%20factsheet%20capacites%20militaires%20-%20version%208_en.pdf>.

140 Art. 42(3), second subparagraph TEU; see also European Defence Agency, An Initial Long-Term Vision for European Defence Capability and Capacity Needs, 3 October 2006.

141 See on these difficulties and the various earlier attempts to improve European cooperation in the field of armaments, Aris Georgopoulos, 'The European Armaments Policy: A *conditio sine qua non* for the European Security and Defence Policy?', in: Martin Trybus and Nigel White (eds.), *European Security Law*, Oxford: Oxford University Press 2007, pp. 198–222.

142 Art. 346(1)(a) TFEU.

with the production of or trade in arms, munitions and war material".[143] At the same time, the article states that "such measures shall not adversely affect the conditions of competition in the internal market regarding products which are not intended for specifically military purposes".[144]

However, the broad interpretation of this exception by the Member States has been contested more recently in the case law of the Court of Justice and by the Commission.[145] Subsequently, the Commission has put forward a number of legislative proposals (the so-called 'defense package'), which resulted in the adoption in 2009 of directives concerning both intra-EU transfers of defense products and procurement rules in this area.[146] These rather recent developments remind us that the Union has not shed its original identity as a project of economic integration with the internal market as its centerpiece. Furthermore, despite the overall intergovernmental character of the CSDP, the character of the Union as a "community based on the rule of law"[147] re-enters the picture through legislative attempts and judicial clarification in the area of defense equipment. These, again, are elements lacking in the context of NATO.

4. Conclusion

In this chapter, the relations between the EU and NATO have been assessed from the vantage point of what they can tell us about the identity of the Union on the international stage. Both organizations share more than half a century of history, most of which was centered on the European continent, but which has acquired during the past two decades an increasingly global outlook. As we have seen, the relationship between the two has shifted significantly over time. While initially they complemented each other functionally, the end of the Cold War brought about a period

[143] Art. 346(1)(b) TFEU.

[144] Art. 346(1)(b) TFEU.

[145] See, respectively, ECJ, Case C-337/05, *Commission* v *Italy*, [2008] ECR I-02173; and European Commission, Interpretative Communication on the application of Article 296 of the Treaty in the field of defence procurement, 7 December 2006, COM(2006) 779 final; further Koutrakos, *supra* n. 14, pp. 245–258.

[146] Directive 2009/43/EC of the European Parliament and of the Council of 6 May 2009 simplifying terms and conditions of transfers of defence-related products within the Community [2009] OJ L 146/1; Directive 2009/81/EC of the European Parliament and of the Council of 13 July 2009 on the coordination of procedures for the award of certain works contracts, supply contracts and service contracts by contracting authorities or entities in the fields of defence and security [2009] OJ L 216/76.

[147] ECJ, Case 294/83 *Parti écologiste 'Les Verts'* v *Parliament*, [1986] ECR 01339, par. 23.

of reorientation for both. While NATO managed to stay in business as a defense and international crisis management organization, the Union's ambitions have become decidedly higher and more comprehensive. It has certainly not lived up to all of them, but in any event has surpassed NATO on its way to become a global actor in its own right across all areas of foreign policy.

In terms of the identity of the Union through interaction with other international organizations, this has been a case apart for two related reasons: first, the fact that this concerns the sovereignty-sensitive area of security and defense, where secrecy and intergovernmentalism are the hallmarks, which often overshadow legal rules and deny judicial intervention; second, the fact that the EU has never been a member of NATO. We can thus hardly speak of the shaping of an EU identity *through* NATO, not to mention *through the law* that would bind the two.

Rather, it is what distinguishes the two organizations that allows us to reflect on the Union; and one of the principal differences between them is the stronger reliance on law in the framework of the Union. The integrative force of law, in turn, shapes the identity of the Union also in the area of CSDP. In this respect, the wording of the pre-Lisbon preamble of the TEU that the Union would assert its international identity "in particular" through CFSP and CSDP was misleading for two reasons. First, at all times the Union has respected the commitment of its Member States to NATO, not least by providing an EU primary law foundation for accommodating NATO membership. What the Treaties tell us with this is that Atlanticism is decidedly not at odds with the CSDP or the Union's identity. Secondly, contrary to the perceptions that international identity goes hand in hand with bearing arms, it was argued here that the fact that the Union started to bear arms did not in itself create its particular identity. Instead, that it did so and yet remained a community based on the rule of law with a deeply integrated economy, yet flexible enough to respect also the identities of its Member States, is what truly defines its identity. Therefore, the new formulation of the TEU preamble stating that further implementation of the CFSP/CSDP means "thereby *reinforcing* the European identity and its independence in order to promote peace, security and progress in Europe and in the world" is doubtlessly more appropriate.

CHAPTER FOUR

EU IDENTITY FROM THE PERSPECTIVE OF THE WTO – THE SPILLOVER EFFECTS OF THE UNION'S INTERNAL MARKET IN THE INTERNATIONAL TRADING ARENA

*Tamara Perišin**

1. Introduction

The European Union's identity from the perspective of the World Trade Organization is influenced by a complex interaction of many factors. This identity has institutional and substantive aspects.

The institutional aspects of the Union's international identity as seen by the WTO (discussed below in part 2) relate to the fact that both the EU and all of its Member States are WTO members. A historical overview clarifies how this institutional arrangement came into being. It explains that the Union's identity in international trade gradually evolved as a consequence of the fact that, with each Treaty amendment, the Member States conferred upon the EU (i.e. each of its predecessor organizations) more competences in this field.

More substantive aspects of the EU's identity in the WTO (discussed in part 3) are connected to the external effects of the internal market. The EU is a WTO-legal regional trading block, but despite being legal, only some of its measures contribute to external trade, while others create obstacles to it. The WTO's view of the EU thus also depends on whether the latter internally takes into account these external effects and the compliance of its measures with WTO rules. There is a cross-correlation between how the WTO perceives the Union and how the EU takes WTO law into account.[1] Two case studies (one in the field of animal welfare,

---

* The author wishes to thank Tamara Ćapeta, John Morijn, Siniša Rodin, Stephen Weatherill and Derrick Wyatt for useful discussions on issues raised in this paper or for comments on earlier drafts. Special thanks to Marise Cremona for the invitation to present this paper at the EUI-CLEER joint conference 'Trade Liberalisation and Standardisation', Florence, and to the participants of this conference. The opinions expressed in this paper are the author's.

[1] For a detailed analysis of WTO law from an EU perspective, see Brigite Egelund Olsen, Michael Steinicke and Karsten Engsig Sørensen (eds.), *WTO Law from a European Perspective*, The Hague: Kluwer Law International 2012.

another on the environmental effects of air transport) mean to shed light on whether the EU institutions take WTO law into account, and whether their approach has been changing. The final substantive aspect of the EU's identity in the WTO derives from its actions in the dispute settlement process. Particularly relevant here are cases where the EU is the respondent, as it then has to justify to the world its internal measures, i.e. its internal choices and identity.

2. Institutional aspects of the Union's identity in the WTO

2.1 *Institutional Arrangements and the Setting-up of the GATT*

It is well known that the first steps in setting up the global trading system predate European integration. For in 1947, when the General Agreement on Tariffs and Trade (GATT) was established, neither the EU nor its predecessor organizations existed. The original parties to the GATT were only the states themselves. All six countries which later initiated the European integration process (Belgium, France, Germany, Italy, the Netherlands and Luxemburg) were also original parties to the GATT.

2.2 *Institutional Arrangements and the Setting-up of the WTO*

Since the establishment of the GATT in 1947, until the time the Uruguay Round was negotiated in the 1980s and 1990s, the political and economic situation in Western Europe changed dramatically. The European Community had become a powerful supranational organization, with its own legal personality and competences in the external sphere. The European Court of Justice was thus asked to give an opinion on who should become a WTO member and a party to the agreements under the WTO umbrella – the EC, the European Coal and Steel Community (ECSC), the European Atomic Energy Community (EURATOM), and/or the Member States.

In its Opinion 1/94, the ECJ gave an interpretation of what was then Article 113 TEC (Article 133 TEC post-Amsterdam; currently Article 207 TFEU). This was an interpretation of the division of competences in external trade which was relevant for WTO membership.[2] The Court held that in the field of Common Commercial Policy, Article 113 TEC gave the Community exclusive competence for concluding all multilateral agreements

---

[2] Opinion 1/94, *Competence of the Community to conclude international agreements concerning services and the protection of intellectual property*, [1994] ECR I-5267.

on trade in goods.[3] This covered not only the GATT, but also, among others, the agreements on Technical Barriers to Trade (TBT) and the Application of Sanitary and Phytosanitary Measures (SPS).

Concerning competence to enter into international agreements on trade in services, the Court considered that it was necessary to differentiate between the four modes of provision of services envisaged by the General Agreement on Trade in Services (GATS). The relevant criterion for distinguishing between the modes was whether or not a mode entailed the movement of persons. On the one hand, concerning the provision of services which do not include the movement of persons ("cross-border supply"), the ECJ held that the Community enjoyed competence on the basis of Article 113 TEC. On the other hand, as regards the provision of services where there is movement of persons ("consumption abroad", "commercial presence", "presence of natural persons"), these were not covered by Article 113 TEC.[4] However, the Community did have competence to regulate the latter three modes of services provision internally as regards movement of Member States' nationals and the treatment of third country nationals. If the EU had exercised this internal competence, it would also have acquired implied exclusive external competence on those matters. The ECJ held that had the EC "included in its internal legislative acts provisions relating to the treatment of nationals of non-member countries or expressly conferred on its institutions powers to negotiate with non-member countries[,] it (...) [would have acquired] exclusive external competence in the spheres covered by those acts"; however, the EC had not exercised its internal competence in all service sectors, so there was no implied exclusive external competence in those fields.[5] The Court confirmed that "an internal power to harmonize which has not been exercised in a specific field cannot confer exclusive external competence in that field on the Community".[6]

The special regime of transport services is also worth mentioning here.[7] These services were not covered by Article 113 TEC. This provision was the legal basis solely for the adoption of certain embargoes on the suspension of transport services. These embargoes related primarily to the export and import of products, but "they could not have been effective if it had not

[3] Ibid., par. 22–34.
[4] Ibid., par. 44–47.
[5] Ibid., par. 90–97.
[6] Ibid., par. 88.
[7] Ibid., par. 48–53.

been decided at the same time to suspend transport services".[8] Transport services were primarily covered by the 'Transport' Title of the Treaty. That field, just like the field of non-transport services, was not fully regulated internally, so there was no exclusive external power of the Community. For all these reasons, the Court concluded that the EC and the Member States shared competence for concluding the GATS.[9]

As regards TRIPs, the ECJ distinguished between two aspects of that agreement. On the one hand, the Court held that the section of TRIPs which related to border measures aimed at enforcement of intellectual property rights fell within the CCP, and could be regulated by an international agreement on the basis of Article 113 TEC. On the other hand, other areas of TRIPs were not sufficiently connected to the movement of goods to be regulated by an international agreement on the basis of Article 113 TEC.[10] Furthermore, other internal competences in the field of intellectual property did exist (ex Articles 100, 100a, 235 TEC). Again, however, these powers had not been fully exercised, so that they did not create an exclusive external power for concluding the TRIPs agreement. Consequently, this meant that the EC and its Member States were jointly competent to conclude it.[11]

The fact that the Community had exclusive competence for international agreements on goods, while competence for international agreements on services and intellectual property was shared did not mean that both the EC and the Member States were supposed to negotiate and conclude agreements and be in charge of their fulfillment. If the Member States and the EC were engaged in constant discussion over their division of competence, "[t]he Community's unity of action vis-à-vis the rest of the world [would] (...) be undermined and its negotiating power greatly weakened".[12] The ECJ thus held that as regards agreements for which "it is apparent that the subject-matter (...) falls in part within the competence of the Community and in part within that of the Member States, it is essential to ensure close cooperation". According to the ECJ, this "obligation to cooperate flows from the requirement of unity in international representation of the Community", and it thus applies "both in the process of negotiation and conclusion and in the fulfillment of the commitments

---

8 Ibid., par. 51.
9 Ibid., par. 77–98.
10 Ibid., par. 55–71.
11 Ibid., par. 99–105.
12 Ibid., par. 106.

entered into".[13] The duty of cooperation also has special importance in WTO dispute settlement, especially in connection to the remedy of retaliation; this remedy would be less efficient for the EC if it could retaliate only in the field of goods, but not in the field of services or intellectual property.[14]

It is due to Opinion 1/94 that both the Community and the Member States became original members of the WTO in 1995.[15] However, the WTO Agreement explicitly states that the EC represents all of its Member States and has "a number of votes equal to the number of (...) [its] Member States".[16] This means that, within the Community internally, Member States might have had different opinions on trade issues, but externally the EC had a unified position and could place all its votes in favor of that position. This gave the EC, and later the EU, significant power in the WTO. The unified position of the EC/EU in the WTO is particularly visible in the dispute settlement process. The EC/EU could act as claimant even when only one or some of its Member States had an interest in challenging a third country's measure. Similarly, the EC/EU could find itself in the position of a respondent not only when a challenged measure was adopted by its institutions, but also when it was adopted by a single Member State (e.g. in *EC – Asbestos*).[17]

2.3 *Institutional Arrangements after the Treaty of Lisbon*

Since the establishment of the WTO, the competences of the Community gradually increased with successive Treaty amendments (e.g. for concluding agreements on all modes of service supply and commercial aspects of intellectual property). The EC became exclusively competent in more fields of external trade, but there are still areas of WTO law over which Member States retain some competence (e.g. transport services).[18]

---

[13] Ibid., par. 108.

[14] Ibid., par. 109.

[15] Art. XI of the Agreement Establishing the World Trade Organization (hereinafter referred to as the WTO Agreement).

[16] Art. IX:1 WTO Agreement.

[17] *European Communities – Measures Affecting Asbestos and Asbestos-Containing Products*, Report of the Panel, WT/DS135/R, 18 September 2000; *European Communities – Measures Affecting Asbestos and Asbestos-Containing Products*, Report of the Appellate Body, WT/DS135/AB/R, 12 March 2001.

[18] On the evolution of competences in the field of the CCP, see Rafael Leal-Arcas, 'Exclusive or Shared Competence in the Common Commercial Policy: From Amsterdam to Nice', (2003) 30 *Legal Issues of Economic Integration*, p. 3; Marise Cremona, 'Balancing Union and Member State Interests: Opinion 1/2008, Choice of Legal Base and the

The latest amendments embodied in the Treaty of Lisbon have given the Union legal personality, so that the role of the EC within the WTO has now been taken up by the EU. Thus far, this has not caused any substantive change. Article 3(1)(e) TFEU now explicitly mentions the CCP as one of the Union's exclusive competences (as was already established by the ECJ in Opinion 1/75).[19] The new Article 207 TFEU (replacing Article 133 TEC post-Amsterdam, ex Article 113 TEC) provides a legal basis for

> the conclusion of tariff and trade agreements relating to trade in goods and services, and the commercial aspects of intellectual property, foreign direct investment, the achievement of uniformity in measures of liberalization, export policy and measures to protect trade such as those to be taken in the event of dumping or subsidies.

The Treaty of Lisbon also increased the role of the European Parliament in the CCP. For "measures defining the framework for implementing" the CCP, the ordinary legislative procedure applies, which gives the EP the power to co-decide issues with the Council (previously called the co-decision procedure). For negotiating and concluding international agreements, Article 218 TFEU calls for the consent of, or consultations with, the European Parliament, depending on the type of agreement which is being concluded. While in the EU, the increased powers of the European Parliament are generally perceived as a positive development leading to more democratic decision-making, it remains to be seen whether the same will be true in the CCP. Below, it will be shown that the European Parliament is frequently indifferent to the external effects of EU measures which are the core of the CCP. It is still not clear whether or how this new role in the CCP will sensitize the European Parliament to external trade issues.

3. Substantive aspects of the Union's identity in the WTO

3.1 *External Trade Effects of the Internal Market*

The Union's identity in the global arena as perceived by other international actors depends on what the Union does internally. Consequently, in the field of international trade, the EU's identity is affected by the Union's internal market rules.

Common Commercial Policy Under the Treaty of Lisbon', (2010) 35 *European Law Review* 5, p. 678; Opinion 1/2008, *Creation of a unified patent litigation system*, [2009] ECR I-11129.

[19] Opinion 1/75, *Draft Understanding on a Local Cost Standard* [1975] ECR 1355.

3.1.1 *The EU as a WTO-Legal Regional Block*

From the perspective of the WTO, the EU internal market constitutes a regional trading block (RTB). RTBs are deviations from the most favored nation principle (MFN). They typically cause trade diversion in the sense that the globally most efficient producer is discriminated against in relation to the less efficient producer from within the RTB. However, RTBs are explicitly permitted by the GATT and the GATS. Article XXIV GATT allows WTO members to form two types of RTBs: customs union and free trade areas, as well as interim agreements necessary for the formation of the two mentioned types of RTBs. Similarly, Article V GATS allows WTO members to enter into an agreement that would liberalize trade in services between them to a greater extent than under the WTO regime. The idea behind allowing RTBs can be understood from the Understanding on Article XXIV GATT, which is a part of GATT 1994.[20] Its preamble recognizes that RTBs have contributed to the "expansion of world trade".[21]

The EU has similarly argued that it contributes not only to its own internal trade, but also to world trade. The Union's official documents frequently emphasize its commitment to world trade, especially through the WTO. For example, the EU's 2011 report issued in connection to the trade policy review states that multilateral trade and the WTO "are the focus for the EU trade policy, as the EU believes that a system of global rules is the best way to ensure that trade between countries remains open and that prosperity can be widely shared".[22] Similarly, at the WTO Ministerial Conference in 2011, the EU Commissioner for trade, Mr. De Gucht, reiterated the Union's commitment to multilateral world trade. He stated that protectionism remains a threat to the world economy and that WTO members need to do more. In his view, the biggest challenge is to unblock the Doha Round, and progress in Doha negotiations in the opening up of markets is crucial for maintaining the centrality of the multilateral trading system. He claimed that some progress had been made, but that more needed to be done in connection to trade facilitation and non-tariff barriers, and that it was important to focus on areas which are of interest to both developing and developed countries. Commissioner De Gucht also

---

[20] *Understanding on the Interpretation of Article XXIV of the General Agreement on Tariffs and Trade 1994.*

[21] Ibid., Recital 3 of the Preamble.

[22] *Trade Policy Review – Report by the European Union – Revision*, WT/TPR/G/248/Rev. 1, 28 July 2011.

stressed that the WTO must continue to oversee regional trade agreements, so that they are constructed in a way to support and not undermine the multilateral system.[23] One could conclude from this that he believes that the EU is a type of RTB that supports the multilateral system, but that there are RTBs which do the opposite.

However, what is relevant for the present paper is not whether the EU thinks that it contributes to world trade, but whether this is really so, and whether other WTO members and the WTO itself might perceive this to be the case. The issue is complex because internal market measures can both facilitate and impede external trade.

3.1.2 *Internal Market Rules Facilitating External Trade*

Some studies support the claim that the EU internal market facilitates world trade by arguing that "[t]he liberalization of external trade has been at least as strong as the intra-EU liberalizing effects".[24] This would be because some mechanisms originally designed to facilitate internal trade also contribute to external trade, e.g. mutual recognition and partial/ minimum harmonization.

First, the principle of *mutual recognition* in its original form, as set up by the ECJ in *Cassis de Dijon*, provides that any product lawfully produced and marketed in one Member State must be allowed on the market of another Member State, unless the latter has a justified reason for denying access to its market.[25] The principle has been extended to other areas beyond trade in goods. For international trading partners, this means that their products and services can be marketed within the EU more easily. Once a product or service from a third country satisfies the conditions for being placed on the market in one Member State, it will have to be granted access to the market of another Member State, unless there is a justified reason for denying such access.

---

[23] Plenary Session of the WTO Ministerial Conference, December 2011, available as a webcast at <http://gaia.world-television.com/wto/2011/min11_webcast_e.htm#eec>.

[24] Chris Allen, Michael Gasiorek and Alasdair Smith, 'Trade Creation and Trade Diversion', *The Single Market Review Series, Subseries IV – Impact on Trade and Investment*, summary available at <http://ec.europa.eu/internal_market/economic-reports/docs/studies/stud12_en.pdf>; Peter Hoeller, Nathalie Girouard and Alessandra Colecchia, 'The European Union's Trade Policies and Their Economic Effects: Economics Department Working Papers No. 194', OECD, 1998; Ari Kokko, Thomas Mathä and Patrik Gustavsson Tingvall, 'Regional Integration and Trade Diversion in Europe', (2007) 26 *Integration and Trade*, p. 205.

[25] ECJ, Case 120/78, *Rewe-Zentral AG* v *Bundesmonopolverwaltung fur Branntwein*, [1979] ECR 649 (hereinafter referred to as *Cassis de Dijon*).

Second, partial harmonization, especially *minimum harmonization*, contributes to the Union's external trade. Partial harmonization primarily occurs through the 'new approach' directives which partially harmonize an area, but leave Member States some regulatory choice. Minimum harmonization sets certain standards, but allows countries to adopt stricter ones. In such a case, it is typically also necessary for the relevant directive to guarantee the free movement of goods that comply with it. This means that each Member State can impose stricter standards on its domestically produced goods, but not on imports from another Member State. This regulatory choice left to states translates into more choice for importers from third countries. These importers can first import their goods into an EU country which for them has the most convenient rules, and then, if the relevant directive guarantees the free movement of products which comply with it (as directives usually do), their goods will be in free circulation within the entire Union.

3.1.3 *Internal Market and Obstacles to External Trade*

In contrast to the described mechanisms, the EU internal market can equally present an impediment to international trade. Such impediments can be grouped into three main types.

First, 'Fortress Europe' has many *deliberate mechanisms which limit its external trade* by protecting domestic production and stimulating intra-EU trade. For example, such mechanisms are primarily external customs levied on goods from third countries. It is well known that only internal customs within the Union are prohibited, but that the EU has a common customs tariff towards third countries. WTO law does not prohibit customs, but merely requires the observation of the MFN principle and the gradual lowering of tariffs in subsequent negotiation rounds. Still, despite being WTO-legal, customs certainly cause some trade diversion and inhibit the globally optimal allocation of resources. Furthermore, the EU still has a lot of subsidies in various sectors, such as agriculture and fisheries. These are sectors which the EU has traditionally been reluctant to liberalize, although the Doha Round requires some progress.[26] However, apart from these mechanisms where the EU intentionally decides to limit its external trade, there are also areas where this can happen without necessarily being planned.

---

[26] See <http://europa.eu/pol/agr/index_en.htm>.

Thus, the second type of obstacle to external trade arises when *the EU internal process of decision-making itself creates a trade barrier.* This was the situation in the *EC – Biotech*[27] case on the placing on the EU market of genetically modified organisms (GMOs). The dispute largely arose as a consequence of the fact that EU Member States have different attitudes towards GMOs. Their disagreement led to several types of trade barriers to the movement of goods which existed at both national and EU levels, and which were all challenged within the WTO. Firstly, since the relevant EC directives and regulations in force allowed Member States to prohibit or restrict trade in biotech products which had already been approved for EU-wide marketing in accordance with relevant Community law, individual Member States used this opportunity to create many obstacles. Secondly, the EC itself stopped approving biotech products pending the adoption of its new regulatory regime, so during this period there was a *de facto* moratorium on approvals. It is interesting that even after the Panel's decision in *EC – Biotech*, which found the EC to be in breach of its WTO obligations, most EU Member States still did not intend to change their policies, despite the Commission's proposals supported by certain other Member States.[28] It is also interesting that the Council was frequently so split on the issue of biotech products that it could not reach a qualified majority either for approving or for rejecting a product.[29] This shows how the EC's 'federal' nature and its dynamics of decision-making create obstacles to trade.

As the third type of obstacles to external trade, one should note that it is not only the legislative process, but also *the legislative outcome that can cause obstacles to trade.* Harmonization can bring about rules which are more trade restrictive than the average of Member States' rules which they replace. And not only can EU rules be stricter than the average of the

---

[27] *European Communities – Measures Affecting the Approval and Marketing of Biotech Products*, Reports of the Panel, WT/DS291/R, WT/DS292/R, WT/DS293/R, 29 September 2006.

[28] For example, the Council rejected the Commission's proposals requesting Austria to lift its ban on two types of genetically modified maize. The UK, the Netherlands, the Czech Republic and Sweden voted against the rejection. See Press Release, 2773rd Council Meeting, Environment, Brussels, 18 December 2006, 16164/06 (Presse 349), provisional version, <http://www.consilium.europa.eu/ueDocs/cms_Data/docs/pressData/en/envir/92249.pdf>; and EurActiv, 'Austria Finds Backing for GMO Bans', 19 December 2006, <http://www.euractiv.com/climate-environment/austria-finds-backing-gmo-bans-news-217644>.

[29] See Press Release (provisional version) of the 2849th Council Meeting Agriculture and Fisheries, 6199/08 (Presse 33), <http://www.consilium.europa.eu/ueDocs/cms_Data/docs/pressData/en/agricult/98819.pdf>, p. 6.

Member States' rules, but they can be as strict as the strictest rule of a single one of them (often referred to as the 'regulatory peak').[30] There are many examples of restrictive EU measures. For example, the Union's very restrictive rules on tobacco labeling constitute significant obstacles to all types of tobacco trade.[31] However, the clearest examples of situations where EU rules are stricter than the average of Member States' rules, and as strict as the strictest rule of a Member State, are total bans, e.g. the ban of oral tobacco (snus) and the ban of seal products. In the case of oral tobacco, prior to EU legislation, only three Member States banned this product and it was permitted in all the other countries.[32] However, the Union legislature considered this different regime to present an obstacle to the internal movement of goods so it used its internal market competence to ban snus entirely. The ECJ upheld this use of an internal market competence in *Swedish Match*.[33] Similarly, prior to EU legislation, only two Member States (Belgium and The Netherlands) banned seal products,[34] and twenty-five Members permitted the marketing of these products. However, the EU again used its internal market competence to ban seal products throughout the Union.[35] Cases on the validity and legality of EU measures

---

[30] Alasdair R. Young, 'Incidental Fortress: The Single European Market and the World Trade', (2004) 42 *Journal of Common Market Studies*, p. 393.

[31] Directive 2001/37/EC of the European Parliament and of the Council of 5 June 2001 on the approximation of the laws, regulations and administrative provisions of the Member States concerning the manufacture, presentation and sale of tobacco products, OJ [2001] L 194, p 26. On the validity of this Directive, see Case C-491/01, *The Queen and Secretary of State for Health, ex parte: British American Tobacco Investments Ltd and Imperial Tobacco Ltd, supported by Japan Tobacco Inc. and JT International SA*, [2002] ECR I-11453 and Case C-210/03, *Swedish Match AB and Swedish Match UK Ltd* v *Secretary of State for Health*, [2004] ECR I-11893. For a comment, see Anthony Arnull *et al.*, *Wyatt & Dashwood's European Union Law, Fifth Edition*, London: Sweet & Maxwell 2006, pp. 944–952; Tamara Perišin, *Free Movement of Goods and Limits of Regulatory Autonomy in the EU and WTO*, The Hague: T.M.C. Asser Press 2008, pp. 101–109.

[32] *Swedish Match*, *supra* n. 31, par. 37.

[33] *Swedish Match*, *supra* n. 31.

[34] Loi relative à l'interdiction de fabriquer et de commercialiser des produits dérivés de phoques, 16 Mars 2007, Moniteur Belge 18 Mars 2007 <http://www.ejustice.just.fgov.be/cgi/api2.pl?lg=fr&pd=2007-04-18&numac=2007011138>; Besluit van 15 maart 2011 houdende wijziging van het Besluit aanwijzing dier- en plantensoorten Flora – en faunawet en het Besluit vrijstelling beschermde dier- en plantensoorten in verband met Europees verbod handel zeehondenproducten, Staatsblad van het Koninkrijk der Nederlanden 155, 2011, 4 <https://zoek.officielebekendmakingen.nl/stb-2011-155.pdf>.

[35] Council Regulation (EC) 1007/2009 of the European Parliament and of the Council of 16 September 2009 on trade in seal products, OJ [2009] L 286/36; Commission Regulation (EU) 737/2010 of 10 August 2010 laying down detailed rules for the implementation of Regulation (EC) 1007/2009 of the European Parliament and of the Council on trade in seal products, OJ [2010] L 216/1.

on seal products are currently pending before the ECJ and WTO Panel, respectively.[36]

There are several possible reasons why the EU rules are stricter than the average of Member States' rules. Primarily, the Treaty requires EU institutions to ensure high levels of health, safety, environmental protection and consumer protection when adopting common rules.[37] Article 114 TFEU, a frequently used legal basis for measures aiming at the establishment and functioning of the internal market, provides in its paragraph 3 that the measures proposed on this basis "will take as a base a high level of protection" of "health, safety, environmental protection and consumer protection", "taking account in particular of any new development based on scientific facts". There are also special horizontal clauses throughout the Treaty which mandate that a high level of certain values is achieved through EU legislation, and which then lead to strict and trade restrictive rules. In addition, very restrictive common rules can be a consequence of the fact that a state with more stringent rules frequently has a better bargaining position than a state with lower standards. For, "[s]o long as there is no agreement, its industry is protected from foreign competition [which does not meet equally high standards], while [the industry] (...) of its trading partners [is] hurt by being denied access to the market".[38] However, the strength of a bargaining position depends on the given voting rules and on whether products from the State with more stringent rules will be competitive in other states, bearing in mind that the cost incurred in complying with the high standards will be reflected in the price. Finally, and most importantly, the ECJ has been generous towards EU legislative institutions in delineating the boundaries of their competences. In the field of the internal market in particular, the Court has allowed the legislature to adopt measures which were only remotely (if at all) connected to the establishment and functioning of the internal market, but were at the same time intended to achieve another legitimate aim

---

[36] Currently pending EU cases are: Case C-583/11 P, *Inuit Tapiriit Kanatami and Others* v *Parliament and Council*, [2012] OJ C 58/3; Case T-526/10, *Inuit Tapiriit Kanatami and Others* v *Commission*, action brought on 9 November 2010 [2011] OJ C 13/34. Currently pending WTO disputes are: *European Communities – Measures Prohibiting the Importation and Marketing of Seal Products* (Complainant: Canada), DS400 2 November 2009; *European Communities – Measures Prohibiting the Importation and Marketing of Seal Products* (Complainant: Norway), DS401 5 November 2009.

[37] Art. 114(3) TFEU (ex 95(3) TEC); Art. 168 TFEU (ex 152 TEC); Art. 169 TFEU (ex 153 TEC); Art 191 TFEU (ex 174 TEC).

[38] Young, *supra* n. 30, p. 401 and p. 410.

for which the EU would not have the necessary regulatory competence. These are, for example, the mentioned rules on tobacco labeling[39] and on oral tobacco.[40]

All these types of obstacles to trade, regardless of whether or not they are internally legal and legitimate, have a negative effect on trade with third countries which do not have such high standards in protecting certain non-trade aims. Third countries which are WTO members then use the WTO dispute settlement mechanism to challenge EU rules in order to try to eliminate these obstacles.

3.2 *Taking WTO Law into Account in the EU's Internal Legislative or Judicial Process*

The Union's identity in the WTO is in cross-correlation with how the EU treats WTO law and the external trade effects of its rules on other WTO members. If the EU did not take WTO law or the external trade effects of its measures into account, it would be perceived to be acting unilaterally instead of multilaterally. This does not mean to say that the Union should always try to satisfy the interests of its trading partners or that it should fear WTO challenges. The EU can, in pressing matters, even deliberately use its market power to promote certain non-trade interests outside its territory by blocking the access of goods and services to its market that do not meet its standards.[41] However, unilateral action can always lead to disputes as well as to unilateral action of other WTO members. EU institutions should be aware of these possible consequences, since an informed decision-maker is in a better position to reconcile the interests of its internal trade, external trade and the protection of values (both from the perspective of domestic rationality and global efficiency).[42]

There are numerous ways in which the EU could gain information about the external effects of its measure, particularly about other WTO

39 *British American Tobacco, supra* n. 31.

40 *Swedish Match, supra* n. 31.

41 See Marise Cremona, 'The Single Market as a Global Export Brand', (2010) 21 *European Business Law Review*, p. 663.

42 Taking account of foreign views on domestic measures is important in achieving domestic rationality. For more on whether foreign interests should be taken into account in domestic decision-making, with a view to achieving global efficiency which cannot be achieved by mere domestic rationality, or whether domestically rational measures are globally efficient, see Donald H. Regan, 'What Are Trade Agreements For? – Two Conflicting Stories Told by Economists, with a Lesson for Lawyers', (2006) 9 *Journal of International Economic Law*, p. 951.

members' attitudes, even before the adoption of a measure. One way of doing this is through the Union's own process of preparing legislation when its legislature can consult various interest groups, the general public, etc. It is important to include at this stage all relevant actors, including other countries. The jurisprudence of the Appellate Body even suggests that a lack of consultation in the pre-legislation stage with certain WTO members on a non-discriminatory basis may in itself represent a violation of WTO obligations.[43] Another way of gaining information about other WTO members' positions is through institutionalized procedures in the WTO. For example, this kind of information exchange about the effects of the measure happens in the SPS committee. When a WTO member plans to adopt an SPS measure, other WTO members can express their views and concerns within the SPS committee. As Scott pointed out, "[t]he raising of such concerns [has on certain instances] operated to sensitize Members as to the external impact of their regulatory proposal (...) [and consequently] led Members to adjust their demands".[44] All this contributes to EU legislation being drafted in a WTO-consistent manner.

There is indeed a significant number of examples where EU decision-makers have analyzed a proposed or an existing measure to check its WTO compliance, in order to avoid litigation with another WTO member. Quite recently, for example, some steps were taken for the adoption of an EU ban on food products derived from cloned animals' offspring,[45] but this ban was never proposed. It seems that the Commission and the Council had concerns about its WTO compatibility,[46] although there were even disagreements between the EU institutions (which leaked out).[47]

---

[43] *United States – Import Prohibitions on Certain Shrimp and Shrimp Products*, Report of the Appellate Body, WT/DS58/AB/R, 12 October 1998, par. 167–176; *United States – Import Prohibitions on Certain Shrimp and Shrimp Products*, Recourse to Article 21.5 of the DSU by Malaysia, Report of the Appellate Body, WT/DS58/AB/RW, 22 October 2001, par. 122, 134.

[44] Joanne Scott, *The WTO Agreement on Sanitary and Phytosanitary Measures*, Oxford: Oxford University Press 2007, pp. 57–58.

[45] *Report from the Commission to the European Parliament and the Council on Animal Cloning for Food production*, Brussels, 19.10.2010, COM(2010) 585 final.

[46] Euractiv, 'EU cloning ban dispute turns to trade, consumers', 12 May 2011, <http://www.euractiv.com/cap/eu-cloning-ban-dispute-turns-tra-news-504753>; Barbara Casassus, 'Europe fails to reach deal on cloned meat', *Nature*, 29 March 2011, <http://www.nature.com/news/2011/110329/full/news.2011.192.html>; Charlie Dunmore, 'EU talks on food from cloned animals collapse', Reuters, 29 March 2011, <http://www.reuters.com/article/2011/03/29/us-eu-food-clones-idUSTRE72S1SL20110329>.

[47] 'European Parliament News: Parliament issues urgent call to regulate cloned foods', 11 May 2011, <http://www.europarl.europa.eu/news/en/pressroom/content/2011

The question now arises whether the tendency of taking external effects and WTO law into account is on the rise or decline. This chapter does not attempt to offer a complete analysis of all the EU measures affecting trade, checking whether WTO compliance was taken into account in the legislative or judicial process. However, below, we will engage in case studies in two fields – animal welfare and the environmental effects of air transport. These build upon studies conducted by de Búrca and Scott in 2000.[48] These scholars used two examples, one from each of these fields, to demonstrate the effects of the WTO on the Union's legislative and judicial decision-making (respectively). The current chapter builds on these two examples, and contrasts each of them with a newer example in the same substantive field and at the same stage of decision-making (legislative or judicial).

3.2.1 *Case Study – Animal Welfare*

The EU does not have competence to regulate on the basis of animal welfare. However, if the EU regulates an area on the basis of another competence, it has to take into account animal welfare protection.[49] Most frequently, measures adopted in the field of the internal market are the ones used to achieve a high level of protection of other interests, including animal welfare. The high level of protection of non-trade interests turns these internal market measures into *de facto obstacles to the importation of goods from outside the EU that do not meet the Union's high* standards.

Two pieces of legislation will be analyzed to assess whether the EU takes into account WTO compliance when adopting marketing bans which seek to achieve a high level of animal welfare. These are the Cosmetics Directive[50] as the older example (discussed by de Búrca and Scott),[51] and the Seal Products Regulation as the newer example. Both of these

0506IPR18894/html/Parliament-issues-urgent-call-to-regulate-cloned-foods>; EUbusiness, 'Leaked EU Council paper reveals cloned food restrictions were possible', 11 May 2011, <http://www.eubusiness.com/Members/BEUC/cloned-food-2>.

[48] Gráinne de Búrca and Joanne Scott, 'The Impact of the WTO on EU Decision-making', in: Gráinne de Búrca and Joanne Scott (eds.), *The EU and the WTO – Legal and Constitutional Issues*, Oxford: Hart Publishing 2003, p. 1, also available as Harvard Jean Monnet Working Paper 06/00, at <http://centers.law.nyu.edu/jeanmonnet/archive/papers/papers00.html>.

[49] Art. 13 TFEU and Art. 114(3) TFEU.

[50] Council Directive 76/768/EEC of 27 July 1976 on the approximation of the laws of the Member States relating to cosmetic products, OJ [1976] L 262/169.

[51] De Búrca and Scott, *supra* n. 48, pp. 6–12.

measures were adopted on the basis of internal market competence,[52] but have significant (and in the latter case dominant) external trade effects.

The older example, the Cosmetics Directive, was originally adopted in 1976 and regulated the composition, labeling and packaging of cosmetic products. Since then, the Directive has been amended several times, it was recently recast by the Cosmetics Regulation which comes into force in 2013.[53] One of the important amendments was adopted in 1993.[54] This amendment added to the list of prohibited cosmetic products "ingredients or combinations of ingredients tested on animals".[55] The entry into force of this provision was originally set for 1 January 1998, but it was postponed several times. In 2000, de Búrca and Scott's case study on the amendments of the Cosmetics Directive identified that one of the reasons for the Union legislature to postpone the entry into force of the marketing ban of products derived from animal testing was the desire of the EU regulator to make the measure WTO compliant.[56] This was not the official reason mentioned in the Directive's amendments, but it was expressed in the Commission's answers to the European Parliament.[57] The Commission stated the following:

> it is the Commission's view that it cannot unilaterally impose the Community's welfare-based production standards on third countries. For example, WTO rules do not permit the Community to prohibit imports of cosmetic products on the sole ground that they have been tested on animals, even if the Community imposes such an animal-testing ban for marketing of Community products. Rather than proceeding to an import ban of such products, the Community should focus on the creation of multilateral standards

[52] The original Cosmetics Directive was adopted on the basis of then Art. 100 TEC (now 115 TFEU). At the time of the adoption of the original Cosmetics Directive, the Article which is now 114 TFEU (Art. 95 TEC post-Amsterdam, ex Art. 100a TEC pre-Amsterdam) did not yet exist, but the Directive's amendment on animal testing discussed below was adopted precisely on that legal basis. The Seal Products Regulation was also adopted on the basis of Art. 114 TFEU.

[53] Regulation (EC) No 1223/2009 of the European Parliament and of the Council of 30 November 2009 on Cosmetic Products, OJ [2009] L 342/59. Certain parts of the Regulation have entered into force before 2013.

[54] Council Directive 93/35/EEC of 14 June 1993 amending for the sixth time Directive 76/768/EEC on the approximation of the laws of the Member States relating to cosmetic products, OJ [1993], L 151/32.

[55] The provision then became Art. 4(1)(i) Cosmetics Directive.

[56] de Búrca and Scott, *supra* n. 48, pp. 6–12.

[57] E-0949/98, 'Written Question to the Commission "Impact on animal protection of the GATT/WTO" by Mark Watts' (PSE), 30 March 1998; and 'Answer to Written Question E-0949/98 given by Sir Leon Brittan on behalf of the Commission', 7 May 1998. See on this De Búrca and Scott, *supra* n. 48, p. 8.

> for animal welfare. The Community should first try to convince its trading partners to modify their policies in the direction it thinks appropriate. Consumers in Europe should, moreover, be in a position to make an informed choice about the animal welfare aspects of the products they buy, for example through labelling schemes. Given that animal welfare is becoming increasingly relevant in terms of international trade, this issue may in the future be raised in the WTO context. The possibility of amending WTO rules to address welfare concerns more generally will be addressed in the context of the determination of the Community's negotiating objectives for the next stage of the WTO negotiations.[58]

As de Búrca and Scott explained at the time,[59] this was a very cautious move of the EU legislature. It was certainly not clear at that time (nor is it now) that a trade ban on products not complying with animal welfare standards would be contrary to WTO rules. There was, and is, plenty of room to argue that such a measure is in accordance with WTO law. This is why it is unclear whether WTO compliance was indeed a reason for postponing the entry into force of the provision, or whether there was another interest involved. De Búrca and Scott mentioned at the time (in subtle terms) that this might be comparable to the Member State action known as 'blame it on Brussels', where Member States "point to the constraints of EC membership to justify an unpopular measure adopted at home", but that in this case it was the EU itself which was hiding behind the alleged constraints of WTO membership.[60] However, what is relevant for the present purposes is that WTO compliance formed part of the political debate and it was taken into account in the legislative process.

The newer example, the Seal Products Regulation, tells a somewhat different story. In 2007, two years before the EU rules on this matter were adopted, Belgium and the Netherlands adopted legislation banning trade in seal products. This led to a Europe-wide discussion on seal hunting, reflecting on whether an EU ban was needed.[61] Canada reacted promptly to the Belgian and Dutch measures, and the same year requested

---

58 Answer to E-0949/98, *supra* n. 57.

59 De Búrca and Scott, *supra* n. 48, pp. 9–12.

60 Ibid., pp. 11–12.

61 See European Food Safety Authority, *Scientific Opinion on Animal Welfare Aspects of the Killing and Skinning of Seals* <http://www.efsa.europa.eu/EFSA/efsa_locale-1178620753812_1178671319178.htm> (08/07/2012); European Parliamentary Questions, <http://www.europarl.europa.eu/sidesSearch/sipadeMapUrl.do?PROG=QP&SORT_ORDER=DA&S_REF_QP=%25&S_RANK=%25&F_MI_TEXT=seal&MI_TEXT=seal&LEG_ID=6&L=EN>; Helena Spongenberg, 'Canada Starts Trade Dispute with the EU Over Seals', EUobserver, 27 September 2007, <http://euobserver.com/9/24853>.

consultations with the EC, which constituted the first step in a WTO challenge.[62] At the time, one might have reasonably assumed that the WTO challenge would make the EU legislature reluctant to adopt Union legislation on the matter. However, this assumption would soon be proven wrong. In 2009, Regulation 1007/2009 was adopted banning the placing of seal products on the market (with narrow exceptions for indigenous communities, marine management and importation for personal use).[63] This total ban is currently being challenged within the EU by interested individuals on the grounds that it breaches the principles of conferred competences, subsidiarity, proportionality and fundamental rights. The ban is also challenged at the WTO by Canada and Norway, given that it raises concerns about possible protectionism and other types of irrationalities, permissible justifications, necessity, etc.[64] European parliamentarians did not ask much about WTO compliance before the adoption of the Regulation.[65] Following the adoption of the Regulations and their challenges, the Commission was asked some questions concerning WTO compliance, but it merely replied that it would defend the measure.[66] It

[62] *European Communities – Certain Measures Prohibiting the Importation and Marketing of Seal Products* (*Complainant: Canada*), DS369 25 September 2007.

[63] Seal Products Regulation, *supra* n. 35.

[64] Disputes cited *supra*, n. 36. For an analysis of these disputes and the issues raised, see Tamara Perišin, 'Is the EU Seal Products Regulation a Sealed Deal? – EU and WTO Challenges', *International and Comparative Law Quarterly*, forthcoming; Robert Howse and Joanna Langille, 'Permitting Pluralism: The Seal Products Dispute and Why the WTO Should Permit Trade Restrictions Justified by Non-Instrumental Moral Values' (2012) 37 *Yale Journal of International Law* 2, p. 367; Peter L. Fitzgerald, '"Morality" May Not Be Enough to Justify the EU Seal Products Ban: Animal Welfare Meets International Trade Law' (2011) 14 *Journal of International Wildlife Law & Policy*, pp. 85–136; Ferdi de Ville, 'Explaining the Genesis of a Trade Dispute: The European Union's Seal Trade Ban', (2012) 34 *Journal of European Integration*, pp. 37–53; Laurens Ankersmit, Jessica Lawrence and Gareth Davies, 'Diverging EU and WTO Perspectives on Extraterritorial Process Regulation', *Minnesota Journal of International Law Online* (Spring 2012), available at: <http://ssrn.com/abstract=2007098>; Xinjie Luan and Julien Chaisse, 'Preliminary Comments on the WTO Seals Products Dispute: Traditional Hunting, Public Morals and Technical Barriers to Trade', (2011) 22(2) *Colorado Journal of International Environmental Law and Policy*, pp. 79–121.

[65] Two MEPs posed a question on the WTO dispute to the Commission: E-0373/08, 'Written Question to the Commission "The challenge of seal bans in the WTO" by Jens Holm (GUE/NGL) and Kartika Tamara Liotard (GUE/NGL)', 4 February 2008.

[66] For a full list of parliamentary questions on seals and WTO compliance in the 7th parliamentary term, see <http://www.europarl.europa.eu/sidesSearch/sipadeMapUrl.do?L=EN&PROG=QP&SORT_ORDER=DA&S_REF_QP=%&S_RANK=%&MI_TEXT=seal+and+wto&F_MI_TEXT=seal+and+wto&LEG_ID=7> (08/07/2012); and in particular see E-002592/2011, 'Question for written answer to the Commission "Measures against the annual commercial seal hunt in Canada" by Bart Staes (Verts/ALE)',

is true that, once a measure is challenged, no answer of the Commission recognizing WTO compliance problems is politically feasible.

What one can see from the legislative history of the Cosmetics Directive and the Seal Products Regulation is a stark difference in the attitude of the EU legislature towards WTO compliance. On the one hand, the entry into force of the marketing ban of cosmetic products and ingredients tested on animals was postponed on the ground that the measure might not be WTO compliant. In that case, the EU was excessively cautious as there was and still is plenty of room to defend that measure against any WTO challenges. On the other hand, the EU adopted the seal products ban for which there are more compelling arguments that it might not be WTO compatible.[67] Furthermore, at the time the EU seal products ban was being adopted, Canada had already submitted a WTO complaint against the EC, challenging the comparable measures of Belgium and the Netherlands.

This limited comparison of the older and newer example cannot lead to a general conclusion that the EU legislature is becoming more indifferent to WTO compliance, but it does show an interesting shift in attitude. All this affects the image of the EU as seen from the WTO: EU decision-making, which takes less account of WTO law and of the external effects of measures, can be perceived as unilateralism and can lead to disputes and retaliation.

The study also suggests that the attitude towards WTO compliance differs between EU institutions. In both instances, it seems that the Commission was aware of WTO obligations. In the case of the Cosmetics Directive, problems with WTO compliance were explicitly mentioned by the Commission in its answers to the European Parliament. In the case of the Seal Products Regulation, WTO compliance might not have been explicitly mentioned in the public documents – but the Commission's proposal for the Regulation, which one could argue was easily WTO-compliant, was very different from the finally adopted Regulation. The original Proposal for the Regulation[68] shows that the intention of the Commission was not

17 March 2011; E-003975/11, 'Question for written answer to the Commission "Seal culling in Canada" by Oreste Rossi (EFD)', 29 April 2011; 'Joint answer to written questions E-002592/11, E-003975/11 given by Mr. Potočnik on behalf of the Commission', 29 June 2011; E-003088/2012, 'Question for written answer to the Commission "CETA Agreement" by Cristiana Muscardini (PPE)', 21 March 2012; 'Answer given to written question E-003088/2012 by Mr. De Gucht on behalf of the Commission', 3 May 2012.

67 See Perišin, *supra* n. 64.

68 Proposal for a Regulation of the European Parliament and of the Council concerning trade in seals products, 2008/0160 (COD).

to introduce a 'total' ban, but a conditional one. Seal products obtained through hunting and skinning which observed certain animal welfare standards and which were properly certified and labeled would have been permissible in the EU. The conditional ban proposed by the Commission was probably in accordance with WTO rules, and would probably not have even led to a WTO challenge. However, this originally planned conditional ban was never adopted, as amendments to the proposal were added by various committees within the European Parliament.[69] In contrast to the conditional ban, the total ban (with narrow exceptions for indigenous communities, marine management and individual imports) has many weaknesses.[70] This would suggest that the Commission is more aware of, or cares more about, the EU's WTO obligations than the Parliament. This might change given the Parliament's new role in the CCP envisaged by the Lisbon Treaty. It remains to be seen whether the European Parliament will become more sensitized to external trade and WTO law. It is important for the EU to be aware that the actions of all of its institutions affect whether it is perceived as acting multilaterally, which is indeed how it wants to portray itself.

3.2.2 *Case Study – Air Transport's Environmental Effects*

Transport is an area which has significant effects on both internal and external trade, and the EU possesses special competences in this field. Transport also has significant effects on the environment, so EU rules on transport frequently seek to achieve a high level of environmental protection as well.

This case study looks at two pieces of legislation in the field of air transport which sought to achieve a high level of environmental protection, but presented obstacles to the business activities of airlines and thus led to challenges. These are the Regulation on Civil Subsonic Jet Planes,[71] as the

---

69 For a detailed analysis of the Regulation's legislative history, see de Ville, *supra* n. 64.

70 On which, see further Perišin, *supra* n. 64.

71 Council Regulation (EC) No. 925/1999 of 29 April 1999 on the registration and operation within the Community of certain types of civil subsonic jet aeroplanes which have been modified and recertificated as meeting the standards of volume I, Part II, Chapter 3 of Annex 16 to the Convention on International Civil Aviation, third edition (July 1993), OJ [1999] L 115/1. The Regulation was subsequently superseded by Directive 2002/30/EC of the European Parliament and of the Council of 26 March 2002 on the establishment of rules and procedures with regard to the introduction of noise-related operating restrictions at Community airports, OJ [2002] L 085/40.

older example used by de Búrca and Scott,[72] and the Aviation Emissions Directive as the newer example.[73] The study of both the older and the newer piece of legislation focuses not on the legislative histories (as in the previous section on animal welfare), but on the disputes.

The older example of dispute concerns the Regulation on Civil Subsonic Jet Planes, which raised the noise standard for civil subsonic jet planes so that only planes complying with the strict rules of Chapter 3 of the Chicago Convention on International Civil Aviation (CCICA) could register and operate in the EU (where previously compliance with CCICA Chapter 2 was sufficient).[74] The Regulation also imposed an additional technical requirement that re-engined planes needed to have "engines with a by-pass ratio of less than 3"[75] which was challenged by the company Omega Air before UK and Irish courts.[76] In Omega Air's view, this additional technical requirement going beyond the international standard was disproportionate and was not based on any reasons.[77] The national courts referred the questions to the ECJ concerning the validity of the Regulation, inquiring whether the mentioned provision of the Regulation breached the duty to provide reasons and the principle of proportionality, all in the light of possible rights that individuals might have under the GATT and TBT.[78] By that time, it had already been settled that WTO law does not have a direct effect in the EU.[79] However, the issue arose whether WTO obligations were relevant for determining a breach of the

[72] De Búrca and Scott, *supra* n. 48, pp. 12–16.

[73] Directive 2008/101/EC of the European Parliament and of the Council of 19 November 2008 amending Directive 2003/87/EC so as to include aviation activities in the scheme for greenhouse gas emission allowance trading within the Community, OJ [2009] L 8/3.

[74] Art. 2(2) of Regulation 925/1999 defines "recertificated civil subsonic jet aeroplane", and Art. 3 of Regulation 925/1999 prescribes that such planes cannot be registered in EU Member States.

[75] Art. 2(2) of Regulation 925/1999.

[76] Joined Cases C-27/00 and C-122/00, *The Queen* v *Secretary of State for the Environment, Transport and the Regions, ex parte Omega Air Ltd* and *Omega Air Ltd, Aero Engines Ireland Ltd and Omega Aviation Services Ltd* v *Irish Aviation Authority*, [2002] ECR I-2569.

[77] Ibid., par. 39–45, 54–61.

[78] Ibid., par. 40, 41.

[79] Within the WTO, the idea that WTO law should have a direct effect was rejected during the Uruguay round, and this was also held by the Panel in *United States – Sections 301–310 of the Trade Act of 1974* WT/DS152/R par. 7.72. Before the *Omega Air* case, many cases on the effect of WTO law in the EU had already been decided, e.g. Joined Cases 21 to 24/72, *International Fruit Company* v *Produktschap voor Groenten and Fruit*, [1972] ECR 1219; Case 70/87, *Fediol* v *Commission*, [1989] ECR 1781; Case C-69/89, *Nakajima* v *Council*, [1991] ECR I-2069; Case C-280/93, *Germany* v *Commission*, [1994] ECR 4873; Case C-149/96, *Portugal* v *Council*, [1999] ECR I-8395.

duty to provide reasons and the principle of proportionality. The ECJ, however, restated that WTO rules cannot be used to assess the legality of EU legislation, except in cases where the challenged piece of legislation is "intended to implement a particular obligation assumed in the context of the WTO, or where the Community measure refers expressly to precise provisions of the WTO agreements".[80] What is relevant in this case is that WTO compliance was invoked before the ECJ.

A more recent dispute concerning air transport's environmental effects deals with the Aviation Emissions Directive. This Directive sets up a system according to which airlines are required to purchase allowances for all their emissions on flights into or from the EU (including emissions caused above open seas, another country, or at an airport in another country). Unlike the mentioned Regulation on civil subsonic jet planes, this Directive does not directly regulate planes. However, it does affect the provision of air transport services and indirectly affects the type of planes which companies will use (trying to adjust engines, plane weight, etc., in order to lower their fuel consumption and emissions). The Directive was challenged before the ECJ by a number of US airlines on the grounds of being contrary to customary international law and certain international agreements, but the Court found the Directive to be valid.[81] What is interesting for our purposes is that WTO law is not mentioned anywhere in the case – either by the parties, the AG,[82] or the Court itself. It is true that the GATS explicitly excludes air transport services from its scope,[83] but there might be parts of WTO law which would still be applicable to the case. For example, studies by Bartels and Howse show that there might be parts of the GATT which would apply because the Directive limits trade in goods, and that the GATS could apply to the extent that the Directive restricts services other than air transport, e.g. tourism.[84] In

[80] *Omega Air*, *supra* n. 76, par. 93–94.

[81] Case C-366/10, *Air Transport Association of America and Others* v *Secretary of State for Energy and Climate Change*, judgment of 21 December 2011, n.y.r.

[82] Opinion of Advocate General Kokott in Case C-366/10, *Air Transport Association of America and Others* v *Secretary of State for Energy and Climate Change*, delivered on 6 October 2011. AG Kokott mentions WTO law incidentally when explaining the effects of international law in the EU legal order (par. 70–71, par. 100).

[83] GATS Annex on Air Transport Services.

[84] Lorand Bartels, 'The Inclusion of Aviation in the EU ETS: WTO Law Considerations; Trade and Sustainable Energy Series, with a Commentary by Professor Robert Howse', NYU School of Law, Issue Paper No. 6, International Centre for Trade and Sustainable Development, Geneva, 2012. See also Markus Gehring, 'Air Transport Association of America v. Energy Secretary before the European Court of Justice: Clarifying Direct Effect and Guid-

addition, some WTO officials have mentioned that it would be difficult, but not impossible, to bring a successful case before the WTO on this measure.[85] However, this point was not even mentioned in the EU's judicial procedure.

A conclusion which one might draw from a comparison of these two cases is that once the ECJ ignores any WTO law arguments in previous disputes, it is reasonable behavior of the parties not to invoke such arguments in a later case. However, one wonders whether the ECJ's indifference to the compliance of measures with WTO rules is prudent. Parties having lost a dispute in the EU could now turn to other available forums. Obtainable information suggests that interested companies are persuading their governments to initiate disputes within the WTO.[86] Regardless of whether it ever comes to a WTO dispute and whether the EU would be successful in that case, the question remains whether the ECJ should in some way take WTO compliance into account so as not to force parties to seek remedy in other forums.

3.3 *EU Measures under Challenge in the WTO*

The previous sections demonstrated that EU measures can present significant obstacles to external trade. It was also shown that interested parties or third countries are not always able to resolve an issue with the EU prior to the adoption of a measure, nor are interested parties afterwards able to successfully invoke WTO law before the ECJ. These reasons would appear to underlie WTO disputes in which the EU is a respondent.

Out of the 436 WTO disputes registered on the official WTO website, the EU participated in 274 disputes, which equals 63% of the total

---

ance for Future Instrument Design for a Green Economy in the EU', (2012) 12 *University of Cambridge Faculty of Law Legal Studies Research Paper Series*, available at: <http://ssrn.com/abstract=2063254>. For an analysis of the EU aviation emissions scheme and the principle of common but differentiated responsibilities and respective capabilities, see Joanne Scott and Lavanya Rajamani, 'EU Climate Change Unilateralism International Aviation in the European Emissions Trading Scheme', <http://www.indiaenvironmentportal.org.in/files/file/EU%20Climate%20Change%20Unilateralism.pdf>.

85 Reuters, 'EU Aviation Carbon Spat Seen Unlikely to Reach WTO', <http://www.reuters.com/article/2012/06/01/us-wto-aviation-carbon-idUSBRE8500WQ20120601>.

86 Brian Beary, 'Climate Change – Aviation Emissions Spat May End Up at WTO, Says Expert', Europolitics, 25 May 2012, <http://www.europolitics.info/external-policies/aviation-emissions-spat-may-end-up-at-wto-says-expert-art335116-46.html>; 'EU Aviation Emissions Levy Ruled Lawful by European Court as Measure Enters into Force', Bridges Weekly Trade News Digest, vol. 16, no. 1, 11 January 2012, <http://ictsd.org/i/news/bridgesweekly/123063>.

number.[87] It has been a respondent in 70 cases, which amounts to 16% of all WTO disputes.[88] This number is high, but it is in relative correlation with the Union's size and economic importance. However, the fact that the EU has frequently been a respondent is important not only in itself, but also because of certain incidental effects.

An important incidental effect is that the EU has frequently advocated regulator-friendly interpretations of WTO rules and has been motivated to employ such litigation strategies, sometimes successfully and sometimes not.

As an illustration, in connection with the GATT, the EC argued for regulator-friendly solutions in *EC – Asbestos*. In this case, the EC had to defend the French asbestos ban which was challenged by Canada. Canada argued that asbestos products were 'like' products in relation to products containing harmless PCG fibers so that they have to be treated alike. The Panel accepted that these were 'like' products, but it held that treating them differently was justified on grounds of public health. However, despite the fact that the Panel's decision was favorable towards the EC (because France was not required to change its measure), this decision was not regulator friendly enough for the Community. The EC appealed against the Panel's decision by arguing that two products cannot be 'like' in the meaning of Article III GATT if they can be distinguished on the basis of carcinogenicity. The EC claimed that determining 'likeness' exclusively on the basis of commercial factors would present "a serious curtailment of national regulatory autonomy".[89] In its view, non-commercial policy purposes listed as possible justifications in Article XX were not sufficient, due to their (arguably) exhaustive nature.[90] This is why the EC considered that some other legitimate policy purposes needed to be taken into account already in the analysis of national treatment under Article III GATT.[91] In other words, the Community argued that distinguishing between a carcinogenic and a non-carcinogenic product is not even prima facie contrary to the national treatment principle and thus needs no justification. The AB accepted the EC's reasoning. Thus, the AB's interpretation, pushed by

---

[87] Data taken from <http://www.wto.org/english/tratop_e/dispu_e/find_dispu_cases_e.htm#results> on 24/05/2012.

[88] Ibid.

[89] *EC – Asbestos*, AB Report, *supra* n. 17, par. 34.

[90] Ibid.

[91] Ibid.

the EC, gave more leeway to national regulators than the Panel's interpretation, against which the EC appealed.

Similar examples of regulatory-friendly interpretations and litigation strategies can be found in connection with the other agreements. In *EC – Hormones*, the EC partly succeeded in advocating a regulator-friendly interpretation of the SPS provision requiring national measures departing from an international standard to be based on a risk assessment by persuading the AB not to apply the procedural review.[92] In *EC – Sardines*, the EC convinced the AB that, under the TBT, a state which departs from an international standard should not be immediately required to justify its decision.[93] And in *EC – Biotech*, the EC even took a kind of litigation risk when it argued that one national rule which has two purposes can be subject both to the SPS and the TBT agreement; in this way, somewhat counter-intuitively, it increased the chances of the rule being saved.[94]

The aforementioned cases show how the EU, due to the high standards it has adopted internally, has an interest in developing a regulator-friendly WTO. The Union's litigation strategy testifies that it is engaged in developing mechanisms for guarding values within the WTO.[95] The EU also frequently intervenes as a third party in disputes between other

92 *European Communities – Measures Concerning Meat and Meat Products (Hormones)*, Complaint by the United States, Report of the Panel, WT/DS26/R/USA, 18 August 1997; *European Communities – Measures Concerning Meat and Meat Products (Hormones)*, Complaint by Canada, Report of the Panel, WT/DS48/R/CAN, 18 August 1997; *European Communities – Measures Concerning Meat and Meat Products (Hormones)*, Report of the Appellate Body, WT/DS26/AB/R, WT/DS48/AB/R, 16 January 1998. See also an analogous case on the EC ban of beef hormones decided by the ECJ, Case C-331/88, *The Queen* v *Minister of Agriculture, Fisheries and Food and Secretary of State for Health, ex parte: Fedesa and others*, [1990] ECR I-04023.

93 *European Communities – Trade Description of Sardines*, Report of the Panel, WT/DS231/R, 29 May 2002; *European Communities – Trade Description of Sardines*, Report of the Appellate Body, WT/DS231/AB/R, 26 September 2002.

94 *EC – Biotech*, Panel Report, *supra* n. 27.

95 Although the EU is frequently in favour of regulator-friendly interpretations, this is not always the case. For example, in *Tuna/Dolphin II*, the EC argued against considering measures on PPMs as covered by Art III GATT (*United States – Restrictions on Imports of Tuna*, unadopted Report of the Panel, DS29/R, 16 June 1994, par. 3.1, 3.3–3.5, 3.92–3.93, 5.6–5.10); in *United States – Taxes on Automobiles* it argued against the "aim and effects" test (*United States – Taxes on Automobiles*, unadopted Report of the Panel, DS31/R, 11 October 1994, the *CAFE* case) and it blocked the adoption of the Panel report. See Robert E. Hudec, 'GATT/WTO Constraints on National Regulation: Requiem for an "Aim and Effects" Test', (1998) 32 *International Lawyer*, pp. 619–649, p. 629.

WTO members, as it has an interest "to bring to Geneva (...) [its] legal interpretation".[96]

4. Conclusion

The EU's international identity, as perceived from the perspective of the WTO, is complex, multifaceted, and not merely a proxy of Member States' identities. This identity is created through the interaction of different levels of government (EU and Member States) as well as the interaction of the branches of government (legislative, executive and judicial).

One can already observe this complex international trade identity from the institutional perspective, since the EU represents both itself as well as each of its Member States before the WTO. This is relevant not only in rounds of WTO negotiations, or in regular meetings of WTO institutions, but also in dispute settlement where the EU acts as a complainant or as a respondent (or even as a third party) on behalf of itself and all its Members. On the one hand, the Union can raise a complaint against another WTO member even if only one of the EU Member States has an interest in the challenge. Whether the Union will undertake this challenge depends on its internal decision-making process. On the other hand, it is certain that the EU will find itself in the role of the respondent not only when its own measures are challenged, but also in situations where it has no influence over a challenged measure adopted by a single EU Member State. Thus, all the actions and identities of Member States influence how the Union is perceived in the WTO.

When one looks a bit deeper into the substance of EU identity in the WTO, one notices that the Union's international trade identity is under the dominant influence of its internal market activities. Some internal market rules (such as mutual recognition and partial harmonization) stimulate external trade, while others (primarily, strict harmonization) impede external trade.

EU decision-making presupposes taking account of the external effects of EU rules, and of their WTO compliance. This certainly happens within the Commission, as DG Trade can provide input on any measure. Public documents, including inter-institutional communication, also occasionally

---

96 Frank Hoffmeister, 'The Contribution of EU Practice to International Law', in: Marise Cremona (ed.), *Developments in EU External Relations Law*, Oxford: Oxford University Press 2008, p. 120.

refer to WTO law. However, this is not always the case. The two case studies presented here sought to shed some light on whether the approach of decision-makers in the EU towards WTO compliance is changing. While these case studies cannot lead to general conclusions, they both show that decision-makers in the EU (legislative institutions, national courts and the ECJ) took less account of WTO law in the recent examples than in the older ones. Not taking WTO law into account certainly affects the image of the EU within the WTO, and increases the chances of a WTO dispute.

The EU's participation in dispute settlement also affects its international identity, especially when it acts as a respondent, as it is then that its internal identity (reflected in its measures) gets questioned. As a respondent, the EU has frequently been in a position to argue for regulator-friendly interpretations of WTO rules, and in several cases, the Panels and the AB accepted some of its reasoning. The EU can thus appear in the WTO as a member that cares about non-trade values and is committed to an international trading regime sensitive to those values. However, in cases where the EU does not manage to persuade the Panel or the AB of its position, its identity is also affected, but in a different way. In these situations, the Union's view on a matter does not become the WTO's view. The EU then has to comply with a decision that it does not agree with, otherwise it will be perceived as acting unilaterally, and thus its official documents always stress its commitment to multilateralism. However, the Union occasionally does act unilaterally when there is another value which it does not want to put in jeopardy. A good example of such unilateral action is the hormones saga, where it lost the case, but did not change its measure, and instead offered alternative concessions to its trading partners. Thus, the EU principally bases its international trade identity on multilateralism, but makes it clear that non-trade values endorsed internally take precedence over external trade relations.

CHAPTER FIVE

FRATERNAL TWINS: THE EUROPEAN UNION AND THE COUNCIL OF EUROPE

Thomas Streinz

1. Introduction: Fraternal Twins

The European Union (EU) and the Council of Europe (CoE) are offspring of one common idea, that of European integration. For historic reasons, both organizations were born at the same time, in the aftermath of the Second World War.[1] As one would expect of twins, both organizations resemble each other to some extent. They overlap geographically,[2] are built on the same fundamental values,[3] share the flag of Europe[4] and the European anthem.[5] Their similarities contribute to the fact that both organizations are – just like twins – frequently confused with one another.[6] However,

---

1 The CoE was founded on 5 May 1949 by the Treaty of London (CETS No. 1), while the European Coal and Steel Community (ESCS), forerunner of what is now the EU, was proposed by French foreign minister Robert Schuman on 9 May 1950. The respective Treaty of Paris was signed on 18 April 1951 and came into force on 23 July 1952.

2 Twenty-seven of the forty-seven CoE member states also happen to be EU member states.

3 Among them are most notably democracy, the rule of law and human rights; see the preambles of the founding treaties of both organizations and recital 1 of the MoU between the CoE and the EU (the MoU is described in more detail *infra*, par. 4).

4 The flag was approved by the Consultative Assembly of the CoE on 25 October 1955, and adopted by its Committee of Ministers on 8 December 1955. The CoE encouraged the other European organizations to make use of the flag to promote the European idea. Its lobbying was successful: on 28 April 1983 the European Parliament (EP) decided to adopt the flag. The European Council in Milan of May 1985 followed suit, and adopted the flag for the European Communities (EC, now succeeded by the EU). Overtaken by its own success of promoting the flag, the CoE later created a distinctive logo by adding a green 'e'.

5 The idea to use Beethoven's instrumental version of 'Ode to Joy' as European anthem can be attributed to Count Richard Nikolaus von Coudenhove-Kalergi, founder of the International Paneuropean Union. He proposed this piece to the information's director of the CoE Paul M.G. Levy in 1955, but the decision was postponed. Encouraged by the Consultative Assembly, the CoM adopted it as the European anthem on 19 January 1972. Again, the European Council in Milan of May 1985 agreed to use it for the EC as well, a decision which was welcomed by the CoE.

6 The CoE even devotes a webpage to this issue under the title "do not get confused": <http://www.coe.int/aboutcoe/index.asp?page=nePasConfondre>. See also the written

their approach towards European integration differs significantly, which makes them easily distinguishable for the legal observer. The CoE, on the one hand, is still an example of a classic international organization,[7] following the intergovernmental approach based on consensus between its Member States. The EU, on the other hand, is the paradigm for a supranational organization, and has deepened integration among its Member States to an unprecedented extent. They are thus 'fraternal', and not identical twins. As is common in family relationships, the two have developed "very intensive and complex" relations over the past decades.[8]

The purpose of this chapter is to scrutinize this relationship. First, the formal status of the EU within the CoE shall be examined, including the legal fundamentals in both the CoE Statute and the EU Treaties (paragraph 2). Next, the evolution of their relationship will be described (paragraph 3), leading to an assessment of the status quo (paragraph 4). The subsequent part is devoted to the relationship between EU law and CoE law (paragraph 5). This relationship is set to change with the accession of the EU to the CoE's most prominent, most important, and most successful convention, the "Convention for the Protection of Human Rights and Fundamental Freedoms" (European Convention of Human Rights, ECHR).[9] The analysis will focus on the implications of this accession on the relationship between both organizations (paragraph 6). Finally, an attempt shall be made to sketch the 'international identity' of the EU within the CoE (paragraph 7).

2. The Legal Framework

The EU is neither a member of the CoE nor does it enjoy the status of observer. Neither the Statute of the CoE nor the EU Treaties allow for full

question by MEP Carlo Fidanza to the Council requesting measures for preventing confusion between EU and CoE institutions following the controversial ECHR judgment on crucifixes in Italian classrooms, P-5950/09.

[7] See already Jean Bruyas, 'Le Conseil de l'Europe', (1951) 55 *Revue Générale de Droit International Public*, p. 600: "Le Conseil de l'Europe apparaît, au premier regard, comme une simple association conventionnelle, fruit d'une coopération librement consentie entre les Etats."

[8] Frank Hoffmeister, 'Outsider or Frontrunner? Recent Developments under International and European Law on the Status of the European Union in International Organizations and Treaty Bodies', (2007) 44 *Common Market Law Review*, p. 50.

[9] Signed in Rome on 4 November 1950, ETS No. 5. For the history of the ECHR, see Ed Bates, *The Evolution of the European Convention on Human Rights*, Oxford: Oxford University Press 2010.

membership of the EU within the CoE. What they do allow for is mutual assistance and cooperation.

2.1 *The Statute of the CoE*

The Statute[10] of the CoE currently prevents the EU from acceding to the CoE. Article 4 clearly states that only a "European state" may become a member, which excludes a non-state entity such as the EU. This problem also stretches out to treaties adopted within the CoE framework.[11] There are no specific provisions in the Statute which address cooperation with the EU or other international organizations.[12] The sole exception is Article 23(b), which calls on the Parliamentary Assembly of the Council of Europe (PACE) to "have regard to the work of other European intergovernmental organizations to which some or all of the members of the Council are parties" when drawing up its agenda. In fact, the PACE has played an important role in connecting the two organizations by reaching out to its sister institution, the European Parliament.[13]

The Statute of the CoE as its 'constitution'[14] has never been changed by an amending protocol as foreseen in its Article 41(c). Rather, and not uncharacteristically, the CoE chose a flexible instrument. On its 8th session in May 1951, the Committee of Ministers (CoM) adopted a resolution with a view to its ultimate inclusion in a revised Statute (a so-called 'text of a statutory character'). This resolution addresses inter alia the relations with international organizations. The relevant passage reads:

> The [CoM] may, on behalf of the [CoE], conclude with any intergovernmental organization agreements on matters which are within the competence of the [CoE]. These agreements shall, in particular, define the terms on which such an organization shall be brought into relationship with the [CoE].

There is no doubt that the adoption of this resolution by the CoM in May 1951 was a reaction to the signing of the Treaty establishing the European Coal and Steel Community (ECSC), the preceding month. This Treaty was accompanied by a Protocol on relations with the CoE which stated that there was a "need to establish ties as close as possible between the

---

10 Signed by ten founding member states on 5 May 1949 in London, ETS No. 1.

11 See *infra*, par. 5.1.

12 Unlike the EU Treaties vice versa; see *infra*, par. 2.2.

13 See *infra*, par. 4.1.3.

14 Michaela Wittinger, *Der Europarat: Die Entwicklung seines Rechts und der Europäischen Verfassungswerte*, Baden-Baden: Nomos 2005, p. 27.

[ECSC] and the [CoE]", and contained a clause that allowed for agreements between the two organizations to provide for mutual assistance and cooperation.[15]

2.2 *The EU Treaties*

Nowadays, the CoE is mentioned three times in the EU Treaties. In Article 165(3) TFEU and Article 167(3) TFEU, where it is highlighted as an example for international cooperation in the areas of education, sport, and culture respectively. Both provisions concretize the more general principle laid down in Article 220(1) TFEU, which calls for cooperation of the EU with international organizations in general, naming the CoE among others.

2.2.1 *Article 165(3) TFEU*

Article 165(3) TFEU reads:

> The Union and the Member States shall foster cooperation with third countries and the competent international organizations in the field of education and sport, *in particular the Council of Europe*.[16]

The reference to the CoE is not merely symbolic. Rather, the TFEU recognizes the leading role of the CoE in this field.[17] With regard to education, there are abundant examples for this assessment: in cooperation with the United Nations Educational, Scientific and Cultural Organization (UNESCO), the CoE created the Convention on the Recognition of Qualifications concerning Higher Education in the European Region ('Lisbon Convention').[18] The CoE also plays an active role in the so-called Bologna Process aiming to create the 'European Higher Education Area'.[19] Furthermore, it promotes the study of foreign languages as a necessary prerequisite for European integration, and developed the well-known Common

[15] On the further development of their relations see *infra*, par. 3.
[16] Emphasis added.
[17] Notably, the parallel article 166(3) TFEU which calls for cooperation with third countries and the competent international organizations in the sphere of vocational training, does *not* mention the CoE.
[18] Signed in Lisbon on 11 April 1997, ETS No. 165.
[19] This aim was proposed by the Sorbonne Declaration of 1998 by the education ministers of France, Germany, Italy and the UK, and confirmed in 1999 through the namesake Bologna Declaration by thirty countries. Both declarations are non-binding.

European Framework of Reference for Languages (CEFR).[20] In the field of sports, two CoE conventions have been adopted: the European Convention on Spectator Violence and Misbehaviour at Sports Events, in particular at Football Matches,[21] and the Anti-Doping Convention[22] with an additional Protocol.[23] Besides, the CoE has recognized the importance of sport in the (revised) European Sport Charter, which is a non-binding recommendation of the CoM.[24] In contrast, the EU is limited internally by the non-harmonization clause in Article 165(4) TFEU, restricting it to encourage cooperation between Member States and, if necessary, support and supplement the actions of the latter. Due to the lack of an exclusive EU competence in the field, international agreements have to be concluded in the form of mixed agreements.[25]

2.2.2 *Article 167(3) TFEU*

Article 167(3) TFEU is drafted along the lines of Article 165(3) TFEU. Again, the reference to the CoE is not an act of symbolism but an acknowledgment of the achievements of the CoE in the relevant field. Among them is the European Cultural Convention,[26] the (revised) European Convention on the Protection of the Archaeological Heritage,[27] and the CoE Framework Convention on the Value of Cultural Heritage for Society.[28] According to the European Commission, 'culture' is a key element of cooperation with the CoE. The Commission refers to the joint implementation of the European Heritage Days and "some actions in the Western Balkans" as – rather unimpressive – examples.[29] However, one has to take into account that the EU competences with regard to culture are limited (Article 167(5) TFEU).

---

20 Its use is recommended by both the EU and the CoE. See CM/Rec(2008)7 of 10 July 2008 and the respective resolution by the Council of the EU of 10 January 2002.

21 Signed in Strasbourg on 19 August 1985, ETS No. 120.

22 Signed in Strasbourg on 16 November 1989, ETS No. 135.

23 Signed in Warsaw on 12 September 2002, ETS No. 188.

24 Recommendation No. R(92) 13 REV.

25 On 'mixity' in theory and practise, see e.g. Christophe Hillion and Panos Koutrakos (eds.), *Mixed Agreements Revisited*, Oxford: Hart Publishing 2010.

26 Signed in Paris on 19 December 1954, ETS No. 18.

27 Signed in Valleta on 16 January 19982, ETS No. 143.

28 Signed in Faro on 27 October 2005, ETS No. 199.

29 Communication from the Commission on a European agenda for culture in a globalizing world, COM/2007/242 final.

2.2.3 *Article 220(1) TFEU*

Article 220(1) TFEU mentions the CoE alongside other international organizations. It reads:

> The Union shall establish all appropriate forms of cooperation with the organs of the United Nations and its specialized agencies, the *Council of Europe*, the Organization for Security and Cooperation in Europe and the Organization for Economic Cooperation and Development.[30]

This newly drafted provision combines the former Articles 302–304 TEC, which dealt with each international organization separately and adds the Organization for Security and Cooperation in Europe (OSCE). Thereby prior nuances were lost: while Article 302 TEC called on the *Commission* "to ensure the maintenance of *all appropriate relations* with the organs of the United Nations and of its specialized agencies"; Article 303 TEC conferred the task to "establish *all appropriate forms of cooperation* with the Council of Europe" on the *Community* as a whole.[31] Without legal effect as regards the allocation of internal competences,[32] a symbolic implication was intended: the Community as a whole – and not just the Commission as one of its institutions – should engage with the CoE. Similarly, 'cooperation' was meant as a plus compared to 'relations'. The new Article 220 TFEU has eliminated these nuances, and raised the other international organizations to the same terminological level as the CoE. This should not be understood as setting back the CoE, for there exists no hierarchy but complementarity between the different international organizations with which the EU cooperates.

3. The Development of Relations between the EU and the CoE

There is no treaty governing the relations between both organizations. Other instruments from the international relations toolbox have been used instead. Originally CoE–EU relations were built on repeated exchanges of letters. In 2001, the common intention for cooperation and partnership was reaffirmed in a joint declaration. Four years later, Jean-Claude Juncker provided a new stimulus with a report entitled "A sole ambition

---

30 Emphasis added.
31 Emphasis added.
32 Article 302(2) TEC awarded this competence to the Commission.

for the European continent". Finally, in 2007, the EU and the CoE signed a Memorandum of Understanding (MoU).

3.1 *The Exchanges of Letters of 1959, 1987, and 1996*

Early on, the CoM of the CoE expressed its wish to establish close relations with the newly founded European Economic Community (EEC) and European Atomic Energy Community (EAEC).[33] The Secretary General (SG) of the CoE, Lodovico Benvenuti, and the President of the Commission of the EEC, Walter Hallstein, agreed on a number of 'arrangements', confirmed in an exchange of letters dated 18 August 1959, "without prejudice to the subsequent conclusion of a general agreement with the Community". Such a general agreement has never been entered into. Instead, the initial exchange of letters remained the basis for CoE–EU relations for almost thirty years. It provided for a sharing of reports, and allowed for regular contacts between the CoM and the Commission.

The initial arrangements of 1959 were only replaced in 1987. The new understanding provided for closer contact between the CoM and the Commission, as well as the SG and the Commission respectively. Amongst others, a senior official of each organization was named as a point of contact. Yet another exchange of letters of 5 November 1996 confirmed and updated the exchange of letters of 1987. This 'supplementing agreement' opened up the respective decision making bodies of the CoE for participation (without voting rights) by the Commission, at the invitation of the competent CoE authorities. Conversely, the Commission would 'consider' requests for participation by the CoE in Commission departmental meetings.

3.2 *The Joint Declaration on Cooperation and Partnership of 2001*

After the fall of the Iron Curtain, many Eastern European states applied for CoE membership. The EC encouraged this development by engaging in a number of joint programmes with the CoE to support the transition process.[34] Building on the exchange of letters of 1987 and 1996, the CoE and the EU signed a Joint Declaration on Cooperation and Partnership on 3 April 2001.[35] They hailed the success of their joint programmes, and

---

33 Resolution (57) 27, adopted on 13 December 1957, followed by Resolution (58) 11, adopted on 28 April 1958.

34 See *infra*, par. 4.2.

35 Available at <www.jp.coe.int/Upload/110_Joint_Declaration_EF.pdf>.

confirmed the determination of both organizations "to deepen our partnership and enhance our cooperation". An Appendix to the Declaration set out how the Joint Programmes should be planned, managed, implemented, and evaluated in the future.

3.3 *The Juncker Report of 2005*

In May 2005, the Heads of State and Government of the CoE Member States gathered in Warsaw for a summit to deliberate on the future course of the CoE. The year before, ten CoE Member States had acceded to the EU, giving the EU countries a majority in the CoE. Consequently, the summit decided to create a new framework for enhanced cooperation and interaction between the CoE and the EU in areas of common concern. To identify those areas, the Heads of State and Government entrusted their colleague from Luxemburg, Jean-Claude Juncker, with the task to prepare "in his personal capacity" a report on the relationship between the CoE and the EU. Juncker sent his report to the CoE Heads of State and Government on 10 April 2006, and presented it to the PACE on 11 April 2006.[36] He did not mince words and stated:

> Although each has enriched the other, the two organizations remain at best a shaky team. Although each has borrowed from the other, they have never been able to make themselves permanently complementary.[37]

To lift the relationship to a new level, he proposed reinforced cooperation in the areas of human rights, democracy, and the rule of law, and suggested inter-institutional reforms. Finally, he called for accession of the EU to the CoE by 2010. With this proposal Juncker went even further than the former CoE Secretary General Walter Schwimmer, who suggested setting up an associate partnership in 2003.[38] As we now know, both ideas have not materialized.[39]

---

[36] Jean-Claude Juncker, 'Council of Europe - European Union: "A sole ambition for the European continent" ', available at <www.coe.int/t/der/docs/RapJuncker_E.pdf>.

[37] Jean-Claude Juncker, *supra* n. 36, p. 2.

[38] See his Memorandum 'A Europe of Partners. Towards an Associate Partnership between the Council of Europe and the European Union', SG/Inf(2003)35 of 25 September 2003.

[39] For a legal analysis of EU accession to the CoE, see e.g. Oliver Mader, 'Beitritt der EU zum Europarat?', (2011) 49 *Archiv des Völkerrechts*, pp. 435–468.

3.4 *The MoU of 2007*

Instead, the CoE and the EU signed a MoU in May 2007, which sets out the current framework for cooperation between the two organizations. As intended by the Warsaw summit, the MoU serves a widespread purpose, namely to develop the relationship "in all areas of common interest".[40] Still a political agreement and not a legally binding treaty, the MoU makes several rhetorical statements. Among them is the oft-quoted and frequently repeated[41] mantra that "[t]he Council of Europe will remain the benchmark for human rights, the rule of law and democracy in Europe".[42] The MoU also contains a variety of operational arrangements with regard to consultation, coordination and cooperation.[43]

4. Contacts, Cooperation and Conflicts between the EU and the CoE

Regular contact has been established and reinforced between representatives of both organizations, and both organizations engage in a variety of forms of cooperation. However, it should not be overlooked that there have also been conflicts between the two organizations, especially with regard to the establishment of the EU Agency for Fundamental Rights (FRA).

4.1 *Contacts*

The CoE and the EU engage in regular and close consultations, both at political and technical levels.[44] In addition, an inter-parliamentary dialogue has developed between the PACE and the EP. With regard to institutional presence, the CoE and EU maintain offices in Brussels and Strasbourg respectively.

---

40 MoU, par. 9.

41 See for example the EU statement on cooperation between the CoE and the EU at the occasion of the 121st Ministerial meeting of 11 May 2011.

42 MoU, par. 10.

43 See for a detailed account Tony Joris and Jan Vandenberghe, 'The Council of Europe and the European Union: Natural Partners or Uneasy Bedfellows?', (2008–2009) 15 *Columbia Journal of European Law*, pp. 1–41.

44 MoU, par. 41.

4.1.1 *High Level Political Consultations*

According to the MoU, so called "quadripartite" meetings are devoted to the most important aspects of cooperation between the two organizations.[45] The four parties assembled at these meetings were the Chair of the CoM and the SG representing the CoE, and the President of the Council and the President of the Commission on behalf of the EU. The meetings were supposed to be held biannually. Since October 2009, there have been no quadripartite meetings. It does not seem to be a coincidence that the Treaty of Lisbon came into force shortly thereafter, substantially changing the Union's institutional structure. Consequently, it is now rather a "Tripartite"[46] meeting, in which the EU is represented by the High Representative for Foreign Affairs and Security Policy (HR). On occasions of common interest, the HR issues joint declarations together with the SG of the CoE.[47]

4.1.2 *Senior Officials' Meetings*

At the technical level, the Joint Declaration on Cooperation and Partnership of 2001[48] set up the Senior Official's Meetings (SOM) as annual gatherings for officials of the European Commission and the CoE "to draw up objectives, plan activities, monitor joint programmes and evaluate their implementation". They take place in turn in Strasbourg and Brussels, and are chaired either by the senior official of the European Commission or the senior official of the CoE, as foreseen under the 1987 exchange of letters.

4.1.3 *Inter-Parliamentary Dialogue*

The Parliamentary Assembly of the Council of Europe (PACE) and the European Parliament (EP) share their struggle for recognition, which is symbolized by their changing name.[49] In the beginning of the relationship between the two organizations, they regularly provided valuable input

[45] MoU, par. 44.

[46] This name, however, is already used by the CoE for meetings with the UN and the OSCE.

[47] See the recent declaration on the European and World Day against the Death Penalty, 10 October 2012.

[48] See *supra*, par. 3.2.

[49] The original Statute of the CoE of 1949 provided for a "Consultative Assembly", while the Treaty establishing the European Coal and Steel Community (ECSC) foresaw a "Common Assembly".

and worked closely together. They even established the practice of joint sessions of both assemblies.

However, in his report of 2005, Juncker noted that only two joint sessions had been held since 1995, to which he added "that these cannot be termed a success".[50] The PACE and the EP took this critique to heart. On the basis of Rule 63 of the Rules of Procedure of the PACE and Rule 189 of the Rules of Procedure of the EP, both institutions signed an agreement on the strengthening of cooperation between the PACE and the EP. It is likely that the accession of the EU to the CoE will link both institutions even more closely. EP members will even become PACE members for the purpose of electing ECtHR judges.[51]

4.1.4 *Institutional Presence*

The MoU stressed the importance of institutional presence.[52] The CoE had established a Liaison Office in Brussels already in 1974.[53] This office was upgraded in 2008 with the appointment of a Special Representative of the SG. Until recently, the EU lacked a permanent representation in Strasbourg. This changed in January 2011, when EU High Representative Catherine Ashton launched the official delegation of the EU to the CoE.[54]

4.2 *Cooperation*

The EU and the CoE cooperate in a variety of areas.[55] The MoU mentions amongst other the areas of human rights and fundamental freedoms, the rule of law, democracy and good governance, democratic stability, cultural diversity, education, youth, and social cohesion.[56] Next to the contacts described above, the EU may send representatives (without a right to vote) to the meetings of several CoE Intergovernmental Committees. In addition, the EU takes part in four CoE bodies which were set up as

---

50 Jean-Claude Juncker, *supra* n. 36, p. 26.

51 See *infra*, par. 6.6.1.

52 MoU, par. 51.

53 CoM Resolution (74) 13, adopted on 6 May 1974.

54 See 'Catherine Ashton EU High Representative for Foreign Affairs and Security Policy and Vice President of the European Commission, Remarks at the Official Opening of the EU Delegation to the Council of Europe', SPEECH/11/31, 19 January 2011, available at <http://europa.eu/rapid/press-release_SPEECH-11-31_en.htm?locale=en>.

55 For an overview, see Directorate of External Relations of the CoE, 'Co-operation between the Council of Europe and the European Union', DER(2009)1 of 30 September 2009.

56 MoU, par. 14.

(enlarged) partial agreements: the European Audiovisual Observatory,[57] the European Pharmacopoeia,[58] the Pompidou Group,[59] and – with a special status – the European Commission for Democracy through Law (Venice Commission).[60]

Among the various forms of cooperation, the joint programmes are worth highlighting.[61] These were initially intended as a tool to facilitate cooperation with new CoE members after 1989. After the accession of most Central and Eastern European states to the EU, the joint programmes now focus especially on the Western Balkans and the South Caucasus region. At the moment, 38 joint programmes are active to support the participation in the EU's Stabilization and Association Process and the European Neighbourhood Policy, respectively.

4.3 *Conflicts*

The CoE has been dubbed the "antechamber of the EU",[62] because it helped to prepare the Central and Eastern European states for accession. This nickname does not do justice to the CoE's achievements, but illustrates the differences between both organizations. The EU's financial and political power, as well as its publicity among citizens, by far outweighs

---

[57] The European Audiovisual Observatory seeks to create transparency in the European audiovisual sector and to provide information services for audiovisual experts. It is a partial agreement within the legal framework of the CoE, which counts 37 member states as well as the EU, represented by the European Commission. For more information, see <www.obs.coe.int>.

[58] The European Pharmacopoeia is a reference work for the quality control of medicines and a very good example of EU-CoE cooperation: it is based on a CoE convention (ETS No. 54, signed in Strasbourg on 22 November 1964) which was amended by a Protocol (ETS No. 134, signed in Strasbourg on 16 November 1989) to allow for accession of the EU (then the EC) – see also *infra*, par. 5.1. The EU Directives 2001/82/EC ([2001] OJ L 311/1), 2001/83/EC ([2001] OJ L 311/67), and 2003/63/EC ([2003] OJ L 159/46), as amended, on medicines for human and veterinary use make European Pharmacopoeia monographs mandatory when requesting marketing authorization.

[59] The Pompidou Group is an intergovernmental co-operation group to combat drug abuse and illicit trafficking in drugs. For more information, see <www.coe.int/T/DG3/Pompidou>.

[60] The Venice Commission is the CoE's advisory body on constitutional matters. It was established in 1990 to assist with the adoption of new constitutions in Eastern Europe. Today it acts as a legal think-tank. For more information, see <www.venice.coe.int>.

[61] A detailed website is devoted to these programmes: <www.jp.coe.int>.

[62] See Fabio Liberti, 'Why we need the Council of Europe', *Le Monde Diplomatique*, September 2012, available at: <http://mondediplo.com/2012/09/18council>.

that of the CoE. Its SG Thorbjørn Jagland started a reform process to raise the relevance of the organization.[63]

The CoE is frequently reduced to its achievements with regard to human rights, a policy area which was long neglected by the EU.[64] This might explain why the CoE insists so strongly on staying the 'benchmark for human rights in Europe'. The leading role of the CoE in this field was challenged when the EU developed into a 'human rights organization'[65] itself and introduced its own benchmark, namely the Charter of Fundamental Rights of the EU.[66] Certain tensions are even visible in the MoU. While it recognizes the "unique contribution" of the ECHR, the ECtHR, and other CoE standards and instruments for the protection of the rights of individuals, it is considerably less enthusiastic when "taking into account the importance of the Charter of Fundamental Rights of the European Union".[67]

A veritable conflict arose out of these underlying tensions, when the EU Fundamental Rights Agency was set up. In December 2003, the European Council decided to replace the existing European Monitoring Centre on Racism and Xenophobia[68] in Vienna with this new agency, a decision that the CoE did not greet with enthusiasm.[69] The PACE adopted a resolution warning that "there is no point in reinventing the wheel by giving the agency a role which is already performed by existing human rights institutions and mechanisms in Europe".[70] This appeal did not fall on deaf ears. Article 9 of the Council Regulation establishing the Fundamental Rights Agency calls on the Agency to coordinate its activities with those of the CoE

---

[63] For details on the reform process, see the dedicated website <http://www.coe.int/t/reform/default_en.asp>.

[64] See J.H.H. Weiler and Philip Alston, 'An "Ever Closer Union" in Need of a Human Rights Policy: The European Union and Human Rights', in: Philip Alston (ed.), *The EU and Human Rights*, Oxford: Oxford University Press 1999, pp. 3–66.

[65] Sceptical on that development is Armin von Bogdandy, 'The European Union as a Human Rights Organization? Human Rights and the Core of the European Union', 37 (2000) *Common Market Law Review*, pp. 1307–1338.

[66] See Pierre Drzemczewski, 'The Council of Europe's Position with Respect to the EU Charter of Fundamental Rights', (2001) 22 *Human Rights Law Journal*, pp. 14–32; Hans Christian Krüger and Jörg Polakiewicz, 'Proposals for a Coherent Human Rights Protection System in Europe', (2001) 22 *Human Rights Law Journal*, pp. 1–13.

[67] MoU, recital 2.

[68] Established by Council Regulation (EC) No 1035/97 of 2 June 1997, OJ 1997 L 151/1.

[69] See for a detailed account Olivier de Schutter, 'The Two Europes of Human Rights: The Emerging Division of Tasks between the Council of Europe and the European Union in Promoting Human Rights in Europe', (2008) 14 *Columbia Journal of European Law*, p. 517 ff.

[70] Resolution 1427 of 18 March 2005.

"in order to avoid duplication and in order to ensure complementarity and added value".[71] Based on the same provision, the EC and the CoE signed an agreement on cooperation between the Agency and the CoE in 2008, reaffirming the aforementioned goals.[72] Recent reports describe their cooperation as "evolving" and "a valuable learning process".[73] However, certain concerns about duplication remain.[74] The underlying concern of possible replacement of CoE (ECHR) standards by the EU may be diminished once the EU has acceded to the ECHR.[75]

5. The Relationship between EU Law and CoE Law

The spheres of EU law and CoE law display an unmistakable overlap. Although not a CoE member, the EU has signed and ratified several CoE treaties. Thereby, CoE law becomes an integral part of EU law. At the same time, CoE treaties regularly contain so-called 'disconnection clauses' to ensure that the obligations of EU Member States under CoE law do not undermine their obligations under EU law.

5.1 *The EU as a Party to CoE Treaties*

The CoE is a very active treaty-making organization.[76] Since its foundation in 1949, the CoE has adopted more than 200 treaties, which are now collected in the "Council of Europe Treaty Series" (CETS).[77] From the point of view of public international law, all of these agreements, conventions, charters and (additional) protocols are treaties within the meaning of Article 2(1)(a) of the Vienna Convention on the Law of Treaties

---

[71] Council Regulation (EC) No 168/2007 establishing a European Union Agency for Fundamental Rights, OJ 2007 L 53/1.

[72] OJ 2008 L 186/7.

[73] Overview of the co-operation between the European Union Agency for Fundamental Rights and the Council of Europe, October 2011, available online: <http://www.coe.int/t/dghl/standardsetting/hrpolicy/external_relations/Docs/FRA_CoE_ReportCooperation_2010–2011_en.pdf>.

[74] See the report of the Committee on Legal Affairs and Human Rights of the PACE 'The need to avoid duplication of the work of the Council of Europe by the European Union Agency for Fundamental Rights', Doc. 12272 of 31 May 2010.

[75] See *infra*, par. 6.

[76] See Jörg Polakiewicz, *Treaty-making in the Council of Europe*, Strasbourg: Council of Europe Publishing 1999.

[77] Treaties opened for signature between 1949 and 2003 were published in a "European Treaty Series" (ETS). See for a complete list merging ETS and CETS:<http://conventions.coe.int/Treaty/Commun/ListeTraites.asp?CM=8&CL=ENG>.

(VCLT) of 1969. The VCLT defines "treaty" as an international agreement concluded between *states*.[78] Furthermore, CoE treaties were originally limited to CoE members. Consequently, there are two problems, as the EU is neither a state nor a member of the CoE. Both problems are solved, however, by the insertion of a clause which allows for the EU to sign the treaty concerned.

A recent example[79] for such an 'opening clause', allowing the EU to accede to a CoE treaty, can be found in Article 75(1) of the CoE Convention on preventing and combating violence against women and domestic violence:[80]

> This Convention shall be open for signature by the member States of the Council of Europe, the non-member States which have participated in its elaboration *and the European Union*.[81]

Earlier examples such as Article 33(1) of the Convention on Human Rights and Biomedicine created the same opportunity for the EC.[82] Even older precedents referred to the EEC.[83] These clauses mirror the evolution of the EEC, to the EC, and finally the EU.[84] Today, there are fifty-one CoE treaties that allow for its signature.[85] The Union has signed 15 of them, four of which are pending for ratification.

There are however various CoE treaties that do not contain an 'opening clause'. A prominent example is the European Social Charter (ESC) of 1961.[86] When the ESC was revised in the mid-1990s, a draft version proposed in 1994 contained a clause allowing the CoM of the CoE to invite

---

78 The Vienna Convention on the Law of Treaties between States and International Organizations or between International Organizations of 1986 extends this definition to international organizations. This Convention has however not yet entered into force. It has been signed but not yet ratified by the CoE.

79 Another recent example is Article 28(1) of the CoE Convention on the counterfeiting of medical products and similar crimes involving threats to public health of 28 October 2011, CETS No. 201.

80 Signed on 11 May 2011 in Lanzarote, CETS No. 201.

81 Emphasis added.

82 Signed on 4 April 1997 in Oviedo, ETS No. 164.

83 Article 7(3) of the European Agreement on the Exchange of Therapeutic Substances of Human origin, signed on 15 December 1958 in Paris, ETS No. 26, as amended by as additional protocol signed in Strasbourg on 1 January 1983, ETS No. 109.

84 In accordance with Article 1(3) TEU, the Union has now replaced and succeeded the Community.

85 For a complete list, see <http://conventions.coe.int/treaty/Commun/ListeTraites.asp?CM=13&CL=ENG>.

86 ETS No. 35.

the EC to accede to the ESC.[87] This proposal was rejected by the CoM and was not part of the revised ESC of 1996.[88] Thus, the revised ESC also remains limited to the members of the CoE.[89] Even if such a provision existed, it remains doubtful whether the EU had the necessary external power to accede.[90] Concerning the ECHR though, both problems have been solved, as will be discussed below.[91]

5.2 *The Disconnection Clauses*

The so-called 'disconnection clauses'[92] are deemed necessary to protect the autonomy of the EU legal order. A standard example can be found in Article 23(3) of the CoE Convention on the Prevention of Terrorism:[93]

> Parties which are members of the European Union shall, in their mutual relations, apply Community and European Union rules in so far as there are Community or European Union rules governing the particular subject concerned and applicable to the specific case, without prejudice to the object and purpose of the present Convention and without prejudice to its full application with other Parties.

The insertion of such clauses into CoE conventions has been controversial.[94] To avoid misunderstandings, a declaration was adopted to clarify the purpose of the disconnection clauses. This declaration is part of the 'context' within the meaning of Article 31(2)(b) VCLT, and should govern the interpretation accordingly. Also it reflects the concerns that were raised by the non-EU high contracting parties. Therefore, it is worth quoting in full:

> The European Community/European Union and its member states reaffirm that their objective in requesting the inclusion of a 'disconnection clause'

---

87 Charter Rel. (84)23, Art. L.

88 ETS No. 163.

89 Article 35(1) ESC.

90 Strongly in favor of such accession is Olivier de Schutter, 'Anchoring the European Union to the European Social Charter: The Case for Accession', in: Gráinne de Búrca and Bruno de Witte (eds.), *Social Rights in Europe*, Oxford: Oxford University Press 2005, pp. 111–152.

91 See *infra*, par. 6.1.

92 For a detailed account, see Marise Cremona, 'Disconnection Clauses in EU Law and Practise', in: Christophe Hillion and Panos Koutrakos (eds.), *Mixed Agreements Revisited*, Oxford: Hart Publishing 2010, pp. 160–186.

93 Signed in Warsaw on 16 May 2005; CETS No. 196. Another recent example can be found in Article 43 (3) of the CoE Convention on the Protection of Children against Sexual Exploitation and Sexual Abuse, signed in Lanzarote on 25 October 2007, CETS No. 201.

94 For a detailed account of the debate, see e.g. Olivier de Schutter, *supra* n. 69, p. 536 ff.

> is to take account of the institutional structure of the Union when acceding to international conventions, in particular in case of transfer of sovereign powers from the Member states to the Community.
>
> This clause is not aimed at reducing the rights or increasing the obligations of a non-European Union party vis-à-vis the European Community/European Union and its Member states, inasmuch as the latter are also parties to this convention.
>
> The disconnection clause is necessary for those parts of the convention which fall within the competence of the Community/Union, in order to indicate that European Union Member states cannot invoke and apply the rights and obligations deriving from the Convention directly among themselves (or between themselves and the European Community/Union). This does not detract from the fact that the Convention applies fully between the European Community/European Union and its Member states on the one hand, and the other Parties to the convention, on the other; the Community and the European Union Member states will be bound by the convention and will apply it like any party to the convention, if necessary, through Community/Union legislation. They will thus guarantee the full respect of the convention's provisions vis-à-vis non-European Union parties.

The first paragraph points to the specific legal structure of the EU. Without a disconnection clause, a transfer of powers from the Member States to the Union level could be pointless, especially if they were already bound by CoE treaties in the field. The second paragraph seeks to dispel doubts with regard to the application of the relevant CoE treaty vis-à-vis *non*-EU countries. The Union and its Member States have to be looked at as one legal space governed by EU law. In relation to countries outside this space, the relevant CoE treaty applies. This is again reaffirmed by the third paragraph, which connects both lines of reasoning: defending the EU legal order on the one hand, while guaranteeing the application of the CoE treaty provisions vis-à-vis non EU parties, on the other. To avoid the notion of 'disconnecting' legal orders, Juncker suggested in his report to rename these clauses "EU clauses".[95] This would indeed make clearer what these clauses are really about: accommodating the specific structure of the EU.

6. The Accession of the EU to the ECHR

The pending accession of the EU to the ECHR will affect the relationship of the EU and the CoE in various ways. First, it will affect the EU legal order by incorporating the ECHR and two of its protocols. Second, it will

[95] Juncker, *supra* n. 36, p. 16.

affect the CoE legal order, since amendments to the ECHR are necessary to accommodate the EU. Third, it will affect the relationship between the Court of Justice of the European Union (CJEU) and the European Court of Human Rights (ECtHR). Fourth, after accession to the ECHR, the EU will be allowed to participate in CoE institutions whenever they exercise functions under the ECHR. Before these effects of accession are examined, let us first assess their legal fundamentals, as well as the (currently still on-going) accession process.

6.1 *The Legal Basis for Accession of the EU to the ECHR*

Article 6(2) TEU calls for accession of the Union to the ECHR, whereas the ECHR allows for such accession in its Article 59(2). Both provisions were only introduced recently, ending a long debate about whether accession of the EU to the ECHR was desirable and, if so, legally possible.[96]

Article 6(2) TEU entails a legal obligation of the EU to accede to the ECHR.[97] At the same time it confers upon the EU the necessary competence for accession, while making clear that the Union's competences in general shall remain unaffected. The provision was introduced by the Lisbon Treaty.[98] Protocol No. 8 annexed to this Treaty sets out several further requirements for the conclusion of the Accession Agreement, most notably the obligation to preserve the specific characteristics of the Union and Union law. The inclusion of a legal basis for accession was necessary after the controversial Opinion 2/94,[99] where the CJEU found that "[a]s Community law now stands, the Community has no competence to accede to the [ECHR]". At present, Union law stands differently.

The ECHR as the object of accession also required modifications, because Article 59(1) ECHR originally provided only for the accession of CoE Member States. The provision was changed by Article 17 of Protocol

---

96 For a "long story in a nutshell", see Jean-Paul Jacqué, 'The Accession of the European Union to the European Convention on Human Rights and Fundamental Freedoms', (2011) 48 *Common Market Law Review*, p. 998 ff.

97 This reading of Art. 6(2) TEU is less obvious in other but equally authentic (Art. 55 TEU) languages. The German ("tritt... bei") and the French ("adhère") version can easily be misinterpreted as both describe accession as if it were a unilateral act rather than a multilateral process.

98 The (failed) Treaty establishing a Constitution for Europe contained an identical provision in article I-9(2).

99 For a critical account, see e.g. Panos Koutrakos, *EU International Relations Law*, Oxford: Hart Publishing 2006, pp. 128–130, with further references in footnote 157.

No. 14,[100] inserting a new paragraph 2 which states that "[t]he European Union may accede to this Convention". Protocol No. 14 entered into force on 1 June 2010, after Russia finally ratified it on 18 February 2010.

6.2 *The Process of Accession of the EU to the ECHR*

Once these legal obstacles had been removed, the process of accession could finally get underway. On both sides, special proceedings were put into place.

On the EU side, the accession process is governed by Article 218 TFEU. On 4 June 2010, the Council authorized the opening of negotiations in accordance with Article 218(2) TFEU. The negotiation mandate was kept secret, and only a partially declassified version was made public.[101] The governing principles for the negotiations were revealed by a public document from the Presidency of the Council to the Committee of Permanent Representatives:[102] the principle of neutrality regarding Union powers, the principle of preservation of the ECHR system, the principle of neutrality regarding Member States' obligations, the principle of autonomous interpretation of Union law and the principle of equal footing.

On the CoE side, the Committee of Ministers entrusted its Steering Committee for Human Rights (Comité Directeur Droits de l'Homme, CDDH) to elaborate with the EU on the necessary legal instruments. To facilitate proceedings, CDDH set up an informal working group called CDDH–UE. It consisted of fourteen members, seven from EU Member States and seven from non-EU countries, so as to resemble the mixed composition of the CoE.

Between July 2010 and June 2011, CDDH–UE met eight times with representatives of the European Commission in order to elaborate on a possible accession agreement. The meeting reports of these negotiations have been made public.[103] The negotiations resulted in a draft legal instrument (DLI) accompanied by a draft explanatory report (DER).[104] The following

---

100 Signed in Strasbourg on 13.5.2004, ETS No. 194.

101 Harshly criticized by Theodor Schilling, 'Der Beitritt der EU zur EMRK – Verhandlungen und Modalitäten', (2011) *Humboldt Forum Recht*, p. 85.

102 Doc. Nr. 14842/11, 30 September 2011, par. 5, available at: <http://www.consilium.europa.eu/documents?lang=en>.

103 Available online: <www.coe.int/t/dghl/standardsetting/hrpolicy/Accession/Meeting_reports_en.asp>.

104 CDDH-UE(2011)16.

assessment is based on these documents. However, changes to both texts are not unlikely as the political decision-making process is still ongoing.[105]

6.3 *The ECHR as an Integral Part of EU Law*

The immediate impact of the accession of the EU to the ECHR is that the latter becomes an integral part of Union law (Article 216(2) TFEU). In this context it is worth noting that the EU will not only accede to the ECHR as such, but also to two of its protocols, namely Protocol No. 1[106] and Protocol No. 6[107] (Article 1(1) DLI). Both protocols have been ratified by all Member States of the EU.[108] Desirable as it may be,[109] Union accession to further ECHR Protocols seems unlikely, because this would – according to Article 216(2) TFEU – bind not only the EU, but also its Member States, including those who have deliberately decided not to accede to certain protocols.[110]

So far, the ECHR is not formally binding on the EU.[111] It serves 'only' as a source of inspiration for fundamental rights as general principles of Union law under Article 6(3) TEU.[112] This will change once the EU has acceded to the CoE. The ECHR (and the protocols the EU accedes to) will

---

105 Negotiations were restarted in July 2012 in a 47+1 setting, which means that all CoE member states discuss with the EU, represented by the Commission. Once an agreement has been reached, Art. 218(6) TFEU, in conjunction with the second sentence of Art. 218(8) TFEU, requires an unanimous decision by the Council and the consent of the EP to conclude the accession agreement. Furthermore, the accession agreement needs to be ratified by EU member states according to their national requirements. The accession agreement will only enter into force when all High Contracting Parties to the ECHR have expressed their consent to be bound by it (see Article 10 DLI for further details).

106 Signed in Paris on 20 March 1952; ETS No. 9. It contains most notably the protection of property (article 1 of the Protocol).

107 Signed in Strasbourg on 28 April 1983; ETS No. 114. It abolishes the death penalty.

108 The current status of ratifications is available from the Treaty Office of the CoE, <http://conventions.coe.int>.

109 For arguments in favor of accession of the EU to further ECHR protocols, see Martin Kuijer, 'The Accession of the European Union to the ECHR: A Gift for the ECHR's 60th Anniversary or an Unwelcome Intruder at the Party?', (2011) 3 *Amsterdam Law Forum*, p. 29.

110 Jacqué, *supra* n. 96, p. 1003 ff., advocates however that the Union should at least accede to all protocols that refer to rights guaranteed by the EU Charter of Fundamental Rights.

111 This is doubted by Bruno de Witte, 'The EU and the International Legal Order: The Case of Human Rights', in: Malcolm Evans and Panos Koutrakos (eds.), *Beyond the Established Legal Orders: Policy Interconnections between the EU and the Rest of the World*, Oxford: Hart Publishing 2011, p. 129.

112 See e.g. Joined Cases C-402/05 P and C-415/05 P, *Yassin Abdullah Kadi and Al Barakaat International Foundation* v *Council and Commission*, [2008] ECR I-6351, par. 283.

then be definitely binding on the EU institutions. This does not, however, answer the question where the ECHR will rank within the EU legal order.[113] Some authors suggest to confer on the ECHR a status equal to primary law (amending but not changing the existing primary law), because they interpret the unusual requirement of approval by Member States in accordance with their respective constitutional requirements in Article 218(8) TFEU as a specific treaty amending procedure.[114] The procedure may be unusual, but it is not unique (see Article 311(2) TFEU), and incapable of creating primary law as such. The desire to bring the ECHR on equal footing with the EU Charter of Fundamental Rights (which has primary law value according to Article 6(1) TEU) and fundamental rights as general principles of Union law (Article 6(3) TEU) is, however, understandable. The EU Charter of Fundamental Rights mitigates the problem (only) as far as correspondent ECHR rights are concerned by aligning meaning and scope of these rights (Article 52(3) of the Charter). A possible solution could be the powerful tool of interpretation in conformity with international law, which should also be applied with regard to EU primary law.[115] Yet, the ECJ has taken a differential attitude towards international agreements and their respective judicial institutions.[116] One would nevertheless expect that the ECJ will interpret EU law in conformity with the ECHR as far as methodologically possible, in order to avoid future judgments of the ECtHR condemning the Union in this regard.[117]

113 The rank of the ECHR within the EU Member States' legal orders differs significantly. For instance, it ranks above the constitution in the Netherlands, is on a par with the constitution in Austria, and subordinate to the constitution in Germany. For further details, see the contributions in Helen Keller and Alec Stone Sweet (eds.), *A Europe of Rights: The Impact of the ECHR on National Legal Systems*, Oxford: Oxford University Press 2008. These national differences will be levelled out by virtue of Article 216(2) TFEU, as far as the case at hand resides within the scope of Union law.

114 See e.g. Walter Obwexer, 'Der Beitritt der EU zur EMRK: Rechtsgrundlagen, Rechtsfragen und Rechtsfolgen', (2012) 2 *Europarecht*, p. 144.

115 See e.g. Case C-341/95, *Gianni Bettati* v *Safety Hi-Tech Srl*, [1998] ECR I-4355, par. 20. The possibility was rejected by the CFI in Case T-201/04, *Microsoft* v *Commission*, [2007] ECR II-3601, par. 798, but one could argue that Microsoft's argument was flawed anyway, because it tried to circumvent the settled case law which denies WTO agreements direct effect within the EU legal order.

116 For a thorough study, see Marco Bronckers, 'The Relationship of the EC Courts with Other International Tribunals: Non-Commital, Respectful or Submissive?', (2007) 44 *Common Market Law Review*, pp. 601–627.

117 On the future relationship between the Courts, see *infra*, par. 6.5.

6.4 *Changing a Running System: Further Amendments to the ECHR*

The insertion of Article 59(2) ECHR[118] removed the most obvious obstacle for EU accession. However, it was clear that more amendments would be necessary to accommodate the Union within the ECHR system.[119] The DLI clearly seeks to reduce the number of changes to the ECHR to a minimum. It refrains from changing provisions of the Convention simply because their terminology does not cover the EU.[120] The sole exception is the change of Article 33, where the term "inter-Party cases" shall replace the term "inter-State cases".[121] Two further amendments of the ECHR, namely of Article 59(5)[122] and Article 57(1)[123] are of a rather technical nature. The amendment of Article 36,[124] however, is substantial. It introduces a new and already controversial procedural tool into the ECHR system, the so-called "co-respondent mechanism".

The co-respondent mechanism is mainly designed to accommodate one distinct feature of the EU legal order,[125] namely the divergence between the creator and implementer of Union law. While secondary Union law is created by EU institutions, it is regularly implemented by the authorities of Member States.[126] Conversely, primary Union law is created by EU Member States as "Herren der Verträge", but (also) implemented by Union institutions. From the ECHR perspective, an application would normally only be admissible *ratione personae* against the implementer but not the creator of the act concerned and consequently only the respective implementer would be bound by an eventual judgment.

The co-respondent mechanism would bridge this gap.[127] An application both against the EU (as creator) and the respective Member State (as implementer) of the act concerned would no longer be inadmissible, if

118 See *supra*, par. 6.1.

119 See the explanatory report to Protocol No. 14, par. 101.

120 See Article 1(d) DLI, according to which the terms State and State Party (and their plural forms) shall be understood as referring also to the EU.

121 Article 4 DLI. The change also relates to Article 29(2) ECHR.

122 Article 1(3) DLI.

123 Article 2(2) DLI.

124 Article 3 DLI.

125 As required by Protocol No. 8 to the Treaty of Lisbon.

126 If Union law is implemented by EU institutions, the co-respondent mechanism does not apply. In these cases the EU will be treated just like any other High Contracting Party.

127 Cf. DER, par. 36 ff.

the implementing act by the Member State was determined by Union law.[128] Furthermore, it would allow the EU to become a party as co-respondent (and not only a third party intervener) in such cases, even if the original application was directed only against the Member State concerned. Conversely, it would allow EU Member States to become co-respondents to defend the compatibility of EU primary law with the ECHR, even if the original application was directed only against the EU, because only the EU Member States could remedy such a violation by changing EU primary law.

With regard to EU secondary law, this possibility will not exist. The Member State which implemented EU secondary law should be the respondent (and not 'co-respondent') anyway. Other EU Member States ought not be co-respondents in the proceedings, because it is the EU itself (and not its Member States) which is ultimately responsible for the underlying act; it is thus also the EU which should (together with the implementing Member State) be bound by a potential judgment by the ECtHR (Article 46 para 1 ECHR), and forced to take general measures to prevent further violations. Admittedly, the system is quite complicated, but nevertheless necessary "to avoid gaps in participation, accountability and enforceability in the Convention system".[129]

6.5 *The Future Relationship between the European Courts*

In the end, it will be the task of the two European Courts to reconcile the complex problems that arise from accession of a non-state entity to an instrument that was designed for external control of states. Their conduct to date suggests that both Courts will take a cautious approach towards each other. However, their relationship will change substantially after accession, and the new prior involvement procedure will introduce a procedural link between the two Courts.

6.5.1 *The Status Quo*

The relationship between the ECtHR and the ECJ has drawn much scholarly attention.[130] Both Courts have increasingly taken each others'

---

128 Notably if an alleged violation could not have been avoided otherwise than by disregarding Union law; cf. DER, par. 42.

129 See DER, par. 32.

130 For a recent pre-accession assessment, see Guy Harpaz, 'The European Court of Justice and its Relations with the European Court of Human Rights: The Quest for Enhanced Reliance, Coherence and Legitimacy', (2009) 46 *Common Market Law Review*, pp. 105–141, with further references.

judgments into account, and have generally avoided jurisprudential conflicts.[131] This can be illustrated by two striking examples. When, in the absence of Strasbourg case law, the ECJ ruled that Article 8(1) ECHR did not apply to business premises and the ECtHR later found the opposite,[132] the former acknowledged that the subsequent case law of the latter had to be taken into account.[133] The Strasbourg Court went even further: it recognized the protection of fundamental rights by Community law to be 'equivalent' to the ECHR, and created the so called *Bosphorus* presumption that an EU Member State "did not depart from the requirements of the [ECHR] when it implemented legal obligations flowing from its membership of the [EU]".[134]

6.5.2 *The End of Bosphorus*

Once the Union has acceded to the ECHR, a new hierarchy between the Courts will be established, with the ECtHR serving as a court of last resort for those who have not prevailed before the ECJ. For the latter, this means that its judgments will be reviewed in Strasbourg without the limitations established in *Bosphorus*. Once the EU is a high contracting party to the ECHR, there is no longer room for double standards.[135] This increase in coherence as regards fundamental rights protection may pose new challenges. The unrestricted application of the Strasbourg case law could even put the procedure before the ECJ itself into jeopardy, for the lack of a general possibility to reply to the reasoned submissions of the Advocate General could be deemed a violation of Article 6(1) ECHR by the ECtHR.[136]

---

[131] For a full account, see Sionaidh Douglas-Scott, 'A Tale of Two Courts: Luxembourg, Strasbourg and the Growing European Human Rights *Acquis*', (2006) 43 *Common Market Law Review*, p. 640 ff., with further references.

[132] Cf. ECJ, Joined Cases 46/87 and 227/88, *Hoechst* v *Commission*, [1991] ECR 2859 and ECtHR, *Niemietz* v *Germany*, Application No. 13710/88.

[133] ECJ, Case 94/00, *Roquette Frères* v *Directeur général de la concurrence, de la consommation et de la répression des fraudes*, [2002] ECR I-9011, par. 29.

[134] ECtHR, *Bosphorus* v *Ireland*, Application No. 45036/98.

[135] See also Tobias Lock, 'The ECJ and the ECtHR: The Future Relationship between the European Courts', (2009) 8 *The Law and Practise of International Courts and Tribunals*, p. 395.

[136] See ECtHR, *Kress* v *France*, Application No. 39594/98, where the role of the French *commissaire du gouvernement* at the *Conseil d'État* was at stake, which was the archetype for the creation of the Advocate General at the ECJ. The ECtHR found no violation with regard to the right to reply, because the parties were free to send a *note en délibéré*. Such a possibility does not exist before the ECJ. See Case 17/98, *Emesa Sugar* v *Aruba*, [1998] ECR I-665.

While it remains to be seen how this issue is resolved,[137] both Courts will need to find ways to cooperate within a new framework. While the European Court of Human Rights will apply (and if necessary adapt) its case law to the EU, it is to be expected that the ECJ will strengthen its own fundamental rights record further, to preemptively avoid negative verdicts by the ECtHR.[138]

6.5.3 *Prior Involvement of the ECJ*

It is also against this background that the ECJ has argued that "a mechanism must be available which is capable of ensuring that the question of the validity of a Union act can be brought effectively before the [ECJ] before the [ECtHR] rules on the compatibility of that act with the [ECHR]".[139] The problem arises because of the fact that there is no effective mechanism in place to ensure that national courts comply by their obligation enshrined in Article 267(3) TFEU. Therefore, the preliminary reference procedure cannot be considered a local remedy under Article 35(1) ECHR, because the applicant usually has no possibility to enforce it.[140] When delegations from the CJEU and the ECtHR met on 17 January 2011 in Luxembourg – as they regularly do – their Presidents Jean-Paul Costa (ECtHR) and Vassilios Skouris (CJEU) issued a joint communication, in which they addressed this issue.[141] They call for a procedure "which is flexible and would ensure that the [ECJ] may carry out an internal review before the EC[t]HR carries out external review". The DLI foresees such a procedure in Article 3(6),[142] giving the ECJ "sufficient time" to make its assessment, but also requesting that the EU ensures that such assessment is made "quickly". While the details of such a new procedure remain opaque at the moment, one can conclude that there will be a procedural

137 The *Bosphorus* backdoor used by the ECtHR in *Kokkelvisserij* v *Netherlands*, Application No. 13645/05, will be locked after accession.

138 Tendencies towards stronger fundamental rights protection are visible in recent case law, see e.g. ECJ, Joined Cases C-92/09 and C-93/09, *Volker und Markus Schecke GbR and Hartmut Eifert* v *Land Hessen*, [2010] ECR I-11063.

139 'Discussion document of the CJEU on certain aspects of the accession of the EU to the ECHR', available at <http://curia.europa.eu>.

140 There is an exception in Germany, where there is the possibility for a constitutional complaint based on Article 101(1), second sentence, of the Basic Law: "No one may be removed from the jurisdiction of his lawful judge." The prospects of success are slim, however, because the German Constitutional Court restricts its control to obvious cases, in which the obligation to refer the case to the ECJ was arbitrarily neglected.

141 Appendix III of CDDH-UE(2011)03, available at <http://curia.europa.eu>.

142 See also par. 57–61 DER.

link between the two European Courts. After all, the wish of the ECJ can hardly be ignored, given the fact that it will judge on the compatibility of the accession agreement with the EU Treaties (Article 218(11) TFEU).[143]

6.6 *New Forms of Participation for the EU within the CoE*

Next to judicial cooperation, new forms of participation in the competent CoE institutions will also be put in place. At first sight, this might come as a surprise, because the EU will not accede to the CoE but only to the ECHR (and two of its protocols). The CoE, however, is highly intertwined with its most important convention. Both the PACE and the CoM are entrusted with certain tasks under the ECHR. Therefore, accession of the EU to the ECHR without participation in these bodies is impractical.

6.6.1 *Participation by Members of the EP in the PACE*

According to Article 22 ECHR, the judges at the ECtHR shall be elected by the PACE. Once the Union has acceded to the ECHR, participation of the EU will be required whenever the PACE exercises this function. The PACE consists of members of the national parliaments. Since the European Parliament is the Union's equivalent to national parliaments, it seems logical to entrust an EP delegation with a representational task for this purpose. That solution is also envisaged in Article 6 DLI. The number of EP representatives shall be the same as the highest number of representatives to which any state is entitled under Article 26 of the Statute of the CoE. This number is eighteen at the moment.[144] After accession of the EU to the ECHR, the PACE will be increased by this number, leading to a new total of 336 representatives for the election of ECtHR judges.

6.6.2 *Participation by Representatives of the European Commission in the CoM*

The CoM exercises various functions within the ECHR system. It may, at the request of the plenary Court, reduce the number of judges of the Chambers to five (Article 26(2) ECHR). It may also request advisory opin-

---

[143] The Commission intends to ask the ECJ whether the envisaged agreement is compatible with the EU Treaties; see the Note from the Presidency to COREPER, *supra*, n. 102, par. 10.

[144] France, Germany, Italy, Russia and the United Kingdom currently have eighteen representatives in the PACE.

ions from the ECtHR (Article 47 ECHR). More important, however, is the supervision of the execution of friendly settlements (Article 39(4) ECHR) and judgments (Article 46(2–5) ECHR).

As a matter of principle, the EU shall be entitled to participate in the CoM with the right to vote in all these cases.[145] However, as far as the supervision of the execution of friendly settlements and judgments is concerned, special rules shall apply, as outlined in a draft rule to be added to the Rules of the CoM.[146] To understand the logic behind this, one has to take into account the extent to which Union law forces the EU and its Member States to act in a coordinated manner. It follows from the 'multifarious'[147] principle of cooperation, now enshrined in Article 4(3) TEU, that the Union and its Member States have to consult and to coordinate whenever their competence is shared. Consequently, when obligations of the EU (and/or one or more of its Member States) with regard to friendly settlements or judgments are at stake, the Union and its Member States are bound to express positions and to vote in a coordinated manner. To avoid a voting block of twenty-eight (EU Member States plus the EU itself), or as the DLI puts it "to ensure that the [CoM] effectively exercises its functions in those circumstances", the voting rights will be modified. Decisions by the CoM shall be regarded as adopted if a simple majority of the representatives of *non*-EU Member States is in favor. The same applies to referrals to the ECtHR for interpretation of a judgment and infringement proceedings,[148] where a majority of two thirds of the representatives of non-EU member states shall be sufficient. These modifications obviously favor the non-EU member states. Its effects in practice will likely be limited, as the CoM usually decides by consensus anyway. Rather, the adaption has a symbolic value by theoretically enabling non-EU countries to reach a decision against the EU and its member states.

Apart from the rights and duties of the CoM enshrined in the ECHR, the EU will participate in the CoM with a right to vote in two further cases: first, when the CoM adopts protocols to the ECHR, and second, when other texts or instruments are adopted or implemented that are either addressed to the ECtHR or all ECHR members, or relate to the functions

---

145 Article 7(1a) DLI.

146 Rule 18 – Judgments and friendly settlements in cases to which the European Union is a party, CDDH(2011)009, p. 14.

147 Cristophe Hillion, 'Tous pour un, un pour tous! Coherence in the External Relations of the European Union', in: Marise Cremona (ed.), *Developments in EU External Relations Law*, Oxford: Oxford University Press 2008, p. 27, with further references.

148 Rules 10 and 11 of the CoM.

exercised by virtue of the ECHR by the CoM or the PACE. Participation is insofar necessary, because the EU as the high contracting party to the ECHR shall not be excluded when the ECHR will be amended or when ECHR issues are discussed.

7. Conclusion: The Union's International Identity within the CoE

From the CoE's perspective, the 'international identity' of the EU is multifarious. The Union's forthcoming accession to the ECHR is a huge step, and one that is highly anticipated by the CoE. It marks the first time in history that a supranational organization submits its acts to external supervision by a court which belongs to another international organization. In this respect, the EU is treated on equal footing with the other parties to the ECHR, notwithstanding the specificity of the EU legal order, which requires adaptations to the ECHR system. The same holds true for other CoE conventions, where opening clauses and disconnection clauses accommodate the needs of the EU. The willingness of CoE Member States to grant those special rules mirrors the importance of the EU in the European arena, and confirms its exceptionality as a supranational organization.

At the same time, the Union is generally limited to mixed agreements within the CoE framework, because it lacks exclusive competence with regard to CoE affairs. Thus, the EU needs to coordinate with its Member States to reach a solidified position. Whenever such a position is reached, the twenty-seven EU Member States command a majority within the CoE. This poses a natural risk for the CoE to become divided between EU Member States on the one hand and non-EU member states on the other. However, it also offers an opportunity for the CoE, which could in the future serve as a platform for communication between both groups.

If the CoE's role is to "change from that of a standard-setter to that of standard-receiver",[149] there remains still the complementary function of acting as a 'standard-spreader' towards the rest of the world. This is especially important for an organization that keeps struggling to find a new place, alongside its ever more powerful twin. In recent years, after the successful efforts to integrate the Central and Eastern European states, both organizations have reached out to one another, in order to identify

149 De Schutter, *supra*, n. 69, p. 513.

new areas of cooperation. Moreover, it is a good sign that the largest sting has been taken out of the conflict with regard to the Union's Fundamental Rights Agency.

In the time to come, the promotion of further European integration will remain a common goal for both organizations. In this respect, it is highly symbolic that in 2012, the EU received the Nobel Peace Prize out of the hands of Thorbjørn Jagland, the Secretary General of the Council of Europe. Perhaps the fraternal twins are ever more closely growing together, once that all familial differences are sorted out?

CHAPTER SIX

THE EU-ILO PARTNERSHIP AND THE GLOBAL IDENTITY OF THE UNION'S SOCIAL MODEL

*Rudi Delarue**

1. Introduction

The International Labour Organization, established in 1919, is the only tripartite international organization. It brings together governments, employers and workers of 185 countries, and became the first specialized UN agency in 1946.[1] The ILO Office is the secretariat of the Organization, based in Geneva, which has offices in over 50 countries.[2] The ILO's mandate pertains to 'the world of work'. This mandate has been updated in 1944 and 2008, in order to better reflect new developments and needs, such as the social dimension of globalization and the pursuit of a better interplay between economic and social objectives. Since 2008, the promotion of decent work for all in the world constitutes its overarching strategic objective. The decent work agenda is backed up by a legal framework of eighty conventions and eighty recommendations classified by the ILO as up-to-date,[3] as well as a number of fundamental texts adopted by consensus by the ILO tripartite constituents of 185 ILO member countries.[4] All Member States of the EU have ratified the eight ILO fundamental

* The views expressed in this contribution do not necessarily reflect the official position of the ILO Office.

[1] In this contribution, 'ILO' denotes the International Labour Organization. The 'ILO Office' or 'Office' stands for the secretariat.

[2] In addition, the Office develops technical assistance operations and targeted technical advice initiatives in many other countries. It also provides technical advice to EU Member States, and this is expected to increase due to the financial and economic crisis, which affects employment, social dialogue and social inclusion in many Eurozone and EU countries, in particular countries on the periphery of the Eurozone.

[3] ILO conventions are adopted by the International Labour Conference and are legally binding after ratification. ILO recommendations are also adopted by the International Labour Conference, but do not require ratification. ILO conventions and recommendations can be found at the ILO website: <www.ilo.org>.

[4] The 2009 ILO Global Jobs Pact; the 2008 ILO Declaration on Social Justice for a Fair Globalisation; the 1998 ILO Declaration on Fundamental Rights and Principles at Work (nearly adopted by consensus, as some developing countries abstained in 1998).

rights conventions (including those on the freedom of association and collective bargaining), and Labour Inspection Convention No. 81. Almost all EU Member States have ratified priority and other up-to-date conventions, e.g. on employment policy, social security minimum standards, and minimum wage fixing machinery.

The ILO applies an integrated approach to the world of work, including in its governance and implementation tools: the adoption and supervision of international labor standards (conventions and recommendations); the adoption of policy frameworks and orientations; the complementary role of corporate social responsibility (CSR), research, knowledge basis, exchange of good practices and publications; capacity building of labor market actors and institutions and training.[5] It increasingly combines and diversifies its instruments, tools and methods of governance. Such a diversification of the policy and governance toolbox has also been taken up by the European Union, ever since the expansion of the latter's portfolio on employment and social policy, pursuant to the Treaty revisions at Maastricht, Amsterdam and Lisbon. EU legislation has been complemented by the Open Method of Coordination, with agreed objectives, indicators and peer reviews on employment, and at a later stage on social inclusion and social protection, social dialogue, CSR, strengthening capacity building through structural funds, analysis, the sharing of knowledge and good practices. This parallel expansion of the policy and governance toolbox both within ILO and EU resulted also in closer cooperation between the two institutions.

The Union's participation in the International Labour Organization, such as in ILO institutional meetings, as well as the EU–ILO cooperation more generally, has intensified significantly in recent years, covering a wide range of internal and external policies. The ILO and the EU share the same foundational values and principles such as social justice and solidarity. Moreover, they both pursue economic and social progress, as well as full employment, as attested by the ILO's constitution, mandate and standards, and successive EU Treaties, respectively.[6]

---

[5] The ILO has also a unique International Training Centre based in the EU (Turin, Italy), which operates both at its Turin Campus and in the field.

[6] These common foundational values are well illustrated by the address of the then ILO Director General, Juan Somavia, to the European Parliament on 14 September 2011, available at: <http://www.ilo.org/brussels/ilo-and-eu/european-parliament/lang--en/index.htm>.

The emergence of a tangible 'EU identity' within official ILO tripartite meetings has however been a long and complex process. Due to very strong divergence of views between the European Commission and EU Member States (often supported by their national social partners), in particular in the period 1983–2000, the Union's participation has had to overcome very considerable hurdles. These differences of opinion pertained to e.g. the right to represent the European Community, the coordination of EC Member States replies to questionnaires of the ILO Office on possible new ILO instruments, and the deposition of the instruments of ratification of ILO conventions. Nevertheless, a number of significant developments have contributed to the progressive intensification of ILO–EU interaction, among which, the emergence of an internal and external dimension of the Union's social model, the intensification of globalization, the expanding financial, economic and social crisis (since 2008), and the participation of both organizations in the G20.

The dynamics of this interaction, and the gradual expression of an EU identity within the ILO, cannot and should not be confined to a narrow legal and institutionally confined analysis, predicated on the formal observer status of the former, or the nature of the EU competences at stake. Unfortunately, many publications on EU–ILO cooperation display a tendency to narrow down their analysis to these formal institutional elements, highlighting the possible negative implications for e.g. presenting more progressive proposals by individual EU Member States, and the influence of national social partners. While such aspects certainly entail challenges for the expression of a true EU identity within the ILO, they can be addressed with relative ease. Yet, a complete absence of an EU identity within the ILO would represent a much bigger danger for the visibility of national social models of EU Member States at global forums, for their social partners, and for overall policy coherence and effectiveness. Such an absence would also risk resulting in the adoption of ILO standards that cannot be ratified by EU countries, for being contrary to Union standards.

Since many years, the ILO disposes of an Office for the EU and the Benelux countries. Its function and nature vis-à-vis the EU has progressively evolved from a 'liaison office' to a wider field of operation. This covers both internal and external Union policies, the facilitation of ILO–EU cooperation at all levels, the involvement of social partners, promotion of the ILO agenda within the Union's institutions and among stakeholders, as well as contributing to UN positions and actions towards the EU.

2. The Relevance of the ILO's Functioning and Mandate for the EU Identity

The ILO functions on the basis of its 1919 Constitution. This founding text was, and still is, a very progressive one. It includes many innovative features that are still highly relevant today, for instance on the role of organized civil society (employers and workers), the adoption and supervision of standards, and elements related to the direct effect of some constitutional obligations.[7] To some extent, some of these innovations have also influenced successive EU Treaties.[8]

The 1919 Constitution provides special rules for federal states, but not for regional integration organizations such as the EU. This has not prevented the latter to play an active and visible role in the ILO. Amendment of the ILO Constitution is possible, but requires a substantial number of ratifications before the changes can enter into force.[9] Fortunately the ILO Constitution and the ILO rules of procedure allow for a pragmatic approach that is responsive to new developments, in particular the establishment of regional integration organizations and their need to affirm their identity.

The highest authority within the ILO is the International Labour Conference (ILC), which meets once a year (in June), and is also convened in special sessions such as the Maritime Labour Conference. The ILO Governing Body (ILO GB) – composed of twenty-eight governments, fourteen workers and fourteen employers, as well as a number of associated and substitute members – meets three times a year.

[7] The principles and rights on freedom of association and collective bargaining are applicable to all ILO members, even without ratification of the corresponding Conventions N° 87 and 98. The practical consequence is that trade unions and employers' organizations of all 185 ILO member countries can lodge complaints with the ILO Tripartite Freedom of Association Committee for allegations concerning the violation, in law and practice, of freedom of association and collective bargaining. In addition, all ILO countries can be requested to present reports, even on non-ratified conventions (Art. 19 ILO Constitution). For more information on the ILO supervisory system, see *Rules of the Game – A Brief Introduction to International Labour Standards*, ILO 2009.

[8] Such as the direct applicability and direct effect of parts of Union law, and recognition of the role of EU social partners and social dialogue.

[9] Such amendments can enter into force when ratified or accepted by two-thirds (124/185) of the Members of the Organization, including five of the ten Members which are represented on the Governing Body as 'members of chief industrial importance'. At the time of writing (September 2012), the 1997 amendment enabling the ILO to abolish an obsolete convention had not yet passed that threshold (with four more ratifications being required).

The ILO's mandate touches not only upon the Union's employment and social policies, but also on economic, financial, entrepreneurial, and a wide range of sectoral policies, such as transport, home affairs, education, fishing and agriculture. The ILO and the domain of labor as such are also increasingly relevant for the Union's foreign, human rights, international trade, development, neighborhood and enlargement policies. This wide number of 'entry points' for EU–ILO cooperation presents both challenges and opportunities. Challenges, as action is required on many different fields, which strains the scarce human resources of both organizations. Opportunities, as it offers a phenomenal potential for developing their respective mandates and identities. The ILO's authority and its tripartite structure, reflected in operations at central, regional and national level, as well as its global membership, can greatly work to the benefit of the EU, both internally and in its operations in the wider world.

The ILO adopts international labor conventions and recommendations on all elements related to the world of work. Unlike the EU Treaties, ILO standard-setting is not restricted to (or more complicated in procedural terms for) parts of the labor and social protection domains. However, both the ILO and the EU face more resistance from the side of some constituents when launching new binding standards. Employers prefer to review existing conventions, and limit new conventions to those items where such a standard is absolutely required. Some EU Member States hold similar views in both organizations. A positive parallel development is that the Union increasingly relies on new ILO standards for its internal legislative and social dialogue agenda. This strengthens the interplay between the European and international standards, and their respective implementation.

The ILO supervises the compliance with ratified conventions and the respect for its constitutional principles, the freedom of association and collective bargaining, which are applicable to all its 185 members. Also, it promotes the ratification and effective application of conventions, recommendations and constitutional principles through technical cooperation, establishes policy frameworks, conducts research and policy in the field of labor, and provides training and information. In order to maximize its efforts and impact, the ILO collaborates with the UN and relevant specialized UN agencies, programmes and funds, international financial institutions (IFIs), the WTO, and regional organizations. Since the ILO's human and financial resources are rather limited compared to e.g. the IFIs, partnerships with inter alia the EU and others are both necessary and indispensable for ensuring decent work for all.

It is unsurprising that the ILO and the EU have developed intensive relations and cooperation for many years. The successive EU Treaties, the 1919 ILO Constitution, as well as the update of the ILO's mandate by the 2008 Declaration on Social Justice for Fair Globalization, reflect shared values and principles such as social justice, solidarity and rights at work. Both institutions combine economic efficiency with social justice, recognize the importance of social dialogue, establish and supervise standards, and are in a process of developing broader social economic governance frameworks and methods.

The ILO standards complement the secondary labor legislation of the EU, as the latter cannot enact legally binding standards on the level of wages, the detailed modalities of collective bargaining and the freedom of association, and can only adopt legislation on social security minimum standards or individual dismissal protection by unanimity in the Council.[10]

The increasing relevance of the ILO for the EU is also due to the enhanced role, visibility and authority of the ILO, in particular since 1998. This results from a number of internal and external factors. Internal factors were e.g. the adoption of the 1998 ILO declaration on Fundamental Principles and Rights at Work applicable also to those ILO members that have not yet ratified the eight corresponding conventions. The establishment of the World Commission on the Social Dimension of Globalization, which resulted in specific policy recommendations in February 2004, significantly increased the EU activity within the ILO.[11] External factors were e.g. the need for a stronger social dimension of globalization recognized by most emerging economies and developing countries, many industrialized countries, and the EU in particular; the evolution of the EU from an

[10] A serious challenge for the coherence of EU policy and the identity of the EU's social model are presented by the conditionalities imposed by the ECB, Commission and IMF Troika on financial assistance within the Eurozone, and the support for non-Eurozone countries as regards their balance of payments. This has already resulted in the imposition of reductions in minimum wages, pensions and health entitlements, as well as changes in employment protection and collective barraging structures without discussion or decision by the EPSCO Council or backing by the Parliament. On the other hand, the EU Treaties also require unanimity in the Council for the establishment of minimum standards on e.g. social security and individual dismissals.

[11] Communication on social dimension of globalisation, COM(2004) 383 final; Communication on promoting decent work in the world, COM(2006) 249 final; Renewed European Social Agenda, COM (2008) 412 final and SEC(2008) 2184; Council Conclusions on Core Labour Standards, 21 July 2003; Council Conclusions on the Social Dimension of Globalisation, 3 March 2005; Council Conclusions on Decent Work, 30 November–1 December 2006.

predominantly regional economic actor to a global player; the responses to the financial, economic and social crisis; and the inclusion of the international development agenda on the contribution of employment, decent work and social protection floors.[12]

The promotion of the Decent Work Agenda and of Social Protection Floors are not only ILO objectives, but also supported by the UN General Assembly, ECOSOC and the G20. It is also supported by the UN Chief Executive Board (CEB), the summits of all regions in the world, and last but not least, the EU.

The Director General of the ILO participates in both the G20's labor and employment ministerial meetings, and general G20 Summits. The EU is directly represented at the G20 labor and employment ministerial level by the European Commissioner for Employment and Social Affairs, and at the G20 Summit by the Presidents of the Commission and the European Council. This has also significantly increased the interaction between the EU and the ILO.

3. Formal Cooperation Agreements between the EU and the ILO

The origins of ILO–EU cooperation date back to the days of the European Coal and Steel Community (ECSC). The ECSC disposed of an integrated social and employment policy. Already in 1953, these two organizations signed a cooperation agreement.

In 1958, the ILO and the Commission signed a cooperation agreement, as the EEC Treaty included several social provisions and articles on gender equality. Over time, in correspondence with the amendment of the latter, this agreement has been repeatedly revised.

The exchange of letters (EoL) of 21 and 22 December 1989,[13] following the entry into force of the Single European Act, formed a decisive new step: the Community, represented by the Commission, obtained the official observer status in the International Labour Conference and in the ILO Governing Body. However, this did reflect an earlier practice. In turn, the Commission agreed to ensure that ILO representatives, where appropriate,

[12] Commission Proposal for the EU Employment Package, 18 April 2012, COM(2012) 173 final.

[13] Exchange of Letters between the EC and the ILO of 21 December 1989 and 22 December 1989, OJ [1990] C 24/8.

are invited to attend meetings of bodies which deal with social and employment issues that may be of interest to the ILO.

In May 1999, the Amsterdam Treaty entered into force, which entailed a strengthening of the social dialogue in the EU and new competences in the area of employment and social policy. It also strengthened the Union's role as a global player on ILO related issues.[14] Against this background, the Commission and the ILO Office renewed the EoL on 14 May 2001.[15]

Reconfirming the Community's observer status within ILO, the 2001 EoL also established the overall strategic framework for the cooperation, as it covers all relevant internal and external EC policies. Furthermore, it recognizes the ILO as a political organization that functions on the basis of a political mandate defined in its constitution, and as a regulator establishing international labor standards. It underlines the relevance of the ILO as an actor that is present at the global, regional as well as national level, through its services and in particular through its tripartite constituents dealing with technical, development and political cooperation aiming at promoting the effective implementation of its strategic objectives. The two organizations agreed to organize annual high level meetings (with already the tenth installment taking place at the end of 2012).

The 2001 EoL framework facilitated the pledge of adherence of the ILO to the EC–UN Financial and Administrative Framework Agreement (2003), and to the strategic partnership on development cooperation (2004).[16] However, contrary to a similar partnership with EU Member States, the strategic partnership with the Community did not come with allocated funding. It mainly establishes a framework for policy dialogue on development, which can result in financial support of the EU for ILO technical cooperation, based on specific thematic, regional or country-

---

[14] For instance, the EC negotiation mandate for the WTO Seattle Ministerial Conference in 1999 also contained a detailed reference to the need for strengthening the ILO and the cooperation between the ILO and the WTO. Another example forms the Cotonou Agreement concluded between the EU and the ACP countries, which contains provisions on the ILO's core labor standards.

[15] Renewed Exchange of Letters, 14 May 2001, OJ [2001] C 165/23.

[16] The strategic partnership in the field of development cooperation was based on a 2001 Commission Communication on establishing partnerships between the EC and UN Agencies, Programmes and Funds. However, it has to be stressed that the ILO's functioning, institutional framework and mandate are very different from that of UN programmes and other UN agencies. The ILO combines normative, political, technical and development-oriented activities, and through the tripartite delegations at the ILC, all its 185 members are involved on an equal basis.

specific funding. Practice has revealed that the programming of funding does not automatically follow new policy objectives.[17] This lack of consistency between development policies and financial programming has complicated more effective cooperation, in particular on issues where EU development cooperation has been very weak (e.g. on core labor standards, social dialogue and social security).[18] There now exists a significant potential for change, with the recognition of the Decent Work Agenda, social protection schemes and floors as important elements for inclusive growth and sustainable development in developing countries.[19] The Union's founding Treaties state explicitly nowadays that it shall seek to develop partnerships with global organizations which share its principles (Art. 21 TEU; Art. 212 TFEU).[20]

The EU is increasingly active within the ILC and ILO GB, both through coordination and agreed positions among the Member States. Just like the Community before it, the Union enjoys an observer status. This means that it can intervene at the ILC, ILO GB, or ILO tripartite sectoral or technical meetings. For many years, the ILO Office has pragmatically facilitated the EU's internal organization and external expression within the ILO. As a result, the EU is able to speak with one voice, and thereby affirm a common identity. This is closely circumscribed though by the Union's internal decision-making process, which is much more complex than that of federal states such as the US or Brazil.

The 2001 EoL has not yet been adapted to the new institutional and policy context that emerged from the entry into force of the Lisbon Treaty (2009). The EU has acquired official legal personality and taken over all the rights and obligations of the Community. Nonetheless, the EU is still experimenting with new arrangements within the ILO, such as the

---

17 European Consensus on Development, 20 December 2005, OJ [2006] C 46/1.

18 The EU's development cooperation policy has traditionally been marked by a reductionist approach on social and human development, i.e. essentially focusing on primary education and action against diseases and epidemia. The original Millennium Development Goals adopted in 2000 were not helpful in that regard, as they focused on fragmented outcomes, and underestimated the contribution to a country's development of decent employment, social protection, social dialogue, equity, taxation, and a greening of its economy.

19 Commission Communication, Increasing the impact of EU Development Policy: An Agenda for Change, 13 October 2011, COM(2011) 637 final.

20 In addition, the Union and the Member States are to comply with the commitments and take account of the objectives they have approved in the context of the UN and other competent organizations (see Art. 208(2) TFEU).

functioning of a team – consisting of the EU Delegation in Geneva, representatives of the country holding the rotating Presidency of the Council and the European Commission – for the daily coordination, representation of Union positions, and burden-sharing between Member States and the EU institutions.[21]

After the signing of the Lisbon Treaty and even before its entry into force, the ILO Office had already modified the seating arrangements of the EU within the ILO Governing Body. The Union's institutions (mainly the Commission/EU Delegation) are seated behind the EU nameplate, and represent positions coordinated or agreed among the Member States. Recent practice confirms also that the Commission intervenes in the debate, e.g. by informing the ILO GB and the ILC on Union actions and initiatives.

In 2005, the European Economic and Social Committee (EESC) also signed a Memorandum of Understanding with the ILO. This MoU illustrates the relevance of the role of organized civil society in EU–ILO relations. The EESC cannot represent the Union in external forums though, since it is a consultative committee that receives input from national representatives of employers, workers, organizations of consumers, farmers and other groups.[22] The ILO and EESC hold joint meetings on a biannual basis. The ILO Office contributes expertise to EESC preparatory work on opinions, and together, they encourage the involvement of social partners and social-economic councils in EU neighborhood policies, and consultations of civil society on the social and employment implications of free trade agreements.

The ILO has significantly increased its cooperation with the European Parliament. Delegations of the EP regularly visit the ILO, and consult on key issues such as on the EU response to the financial, economic and social crisis, greening the economy, EU legislation on migrant workers, and other labor standards. The EP has looked for ILO expertise on concrete EP legislative and policy work. The Parliament has significantly

---

[21] For the ILO GB, in practice this comes down to positions agreed in the EU that are or were not read out by the EU delegation or the Member State holding the rotating Presidency, but by another EU country that is an ILO GB member.

[22] The Amsterdam Treaty recognized the important role of bipartite European social dialogue, and the Lisbon Treaty recognized the Union's tripartite summit for employment and growth, bringing together the leaders of the EU social partners and the heads of the Union's institutions. Unlike the role played by the EESC, this social dialogue process is not only of a consultative nature, but can result in actual Europe-wide agreements.

strengthened its support for ILO actions, for instance on decent work, and standards for maritime labor, domestic work and social protection. This cooperation is not covered by a formal agreement, but forms part of the ILO outreach to parliaments.

The ILO has fostered cooperation with relevant EU agencies such as the EU Foundation for Improving Living and Working Conditions, the European Agency for Health and Safety at Work, the Agency for Vocational Training, and more recently the EU Fundamental Rights Agency. This cooperation is not covered by formal agreements either.

4. Participation of the EU within the ILC and ILO GB

The evolution of Union participation in ILO institutional meetings has been more complex than their general cooperation. The ILO is also a standard-setting and supervision organization, thereby touching on extremely sensitive issues for the relations between EU Member States and institutions, in particular questions of competence and representation.

In the 1980s and 1990s, the nature of the cooperation has raised significant tensions between the Commission and the Member States. This resulted in various legal disputes, whereby EU countries were often supported by the social partners at national level.[23] These disputes negatively affected the reputation and role of the EU (at that time still the Community) within the ILO and beyond. Unfortunately, they pushed to the side the debate on the substantive questions, such as the need for balanced, up-to-date and well-designed standards that can be ratified and applied by both industrialized and developing countries.

Many EU Member States even preferred coordination through the informal group of Industrialized Market Economies (IMEC), established in 1980, which knows a strong participation of and support by non–European countries such as the US, Australia and New Zealand.

The issue of Community competence with regard to ILO matters was raised for the first time during the preparation and adoption of the ILO

[23] For a detailed overview of the EU's participation within the ILC and ILO GB and the treatment of ILO conventions in areas of Union competence, see Rudi Delarue, 'ILO–EU Cooperation on Employment and Social Affairs', in: Jan Wouters, Frank Hoffmeister and Tom Ruys (eds.), *The UN and the EU: An Ever Stronger Partnership*, The Hague: T.M.C. Asser Press 2006, pp. 93–114.

Convention Nr. 153 on working hours and rest periods in road transport (1977–1979). At that time, this area was covered by Regulation 543/69 EC.[24] Similar problems arose with the preparation of other conventions, e.g. Convention Nr. 162 concerning health and safety in the use of asbestos (1983–1986), and in relation to Convention Nr. 170 concerning safety in use of chemicals at work (1988–1990).

In 1991, the Commission requested an ECJ opinion on the EC's competence to conclude ILO Convention No. 170. The ECJ delivered its Opinion 2/91 on 19 March 1993. The Court declared that the conclusion of ILO Convention Nr. 170 was a matter which fell within the joint competence of the EC and its Member States. All in all, it took a pragmatic approach and underlined the duty of cooperation between the Community institutions and the countries concerned. But, as under the ILO Constitution, the EC itself could not accede to its conventions, it had to act through its Member States. The ECJ did however not provide operational guidance on how this cooperation should or could be organized, which resulted in a protracted deadlock.[25]

An unfortunate coincidence for the image and position of the EC was that workers fiercely criticized it for requesting Member States, without proper consultation of social partners, to denounce ILO Convention Nr. 89 on prohibition of night work for women in industry. On 25 July 1991, the ECJ had ruled that this was contrary to EC Directive 1976/207 on equal treatment for men and women. In the meanwhile, the ILO approved Convention Nr. 171 on protecting both men and women during night work. On 23 November 1993, the EC adopted Directive 1993/104 on the organization of some elements of working time including some provisions on night work.

Since 2006, the Council and the Commission have endorsed the position that EU Member States should put more effort in ratifying and applying up-to-date ILO conventions. The Commission's 2012 Work Programme features a proposal for a Council Decision authorizing EU Member States to ratify ILO Convention N° 170 (1990) for those aspects where Union

---

[24] Council Regulation 543/69/EC of 25 March 1969, OJ [1969] L 77/49.

[25] In 1994, the Commission presented a Communication and draft Council Decision on the exercise of the Community's external competences at the ILC, but the EC Member States could not reach an agreement. Since then, a number of proposals originating in the 1994 package (such as the organization of effective coordination meetings, consultations with EU social partners, the presentation of positions and amendments by the EU Presidency) have been applied ever more frequently in practice.

competences are affected, as well as for ILO Convention N° 189 (2011) on domestic work.

From 2003 onwards, the EU's policy participation within the ILC and ILO GB improved dramatically, as did the relations between the Community, the Member States and social partners. The legalistic approach and hair-splitting debates with regard to competences shifted, with a stronger focus being placed on substance and joint results. The gradual emergence of a more coherent social and economic agenda, endorsed by all Union institutions, also buttressed the EU's positions at the ILC and the ILO GB. Before the entry into force of the Lisbon Treaty, the Presidency of the Council presented the Union's positions and amendments. Within the ILO as well, the practice of burden-sharing between the Presidency and the Member States was introduced, since smaller countries do not always have the resources to cover all items on the agenda of the ILC. In case the country holding the Presidency is not on the ILO GB, the Union's positions are presented by another Member State that is an ILO GB member. It was also agreed that the Commission could present Union positions in case exclusive competences were at stake (e.g. mobility of workers, trade related policies), but also when they pertained to shared competences on issues where the EU has a strongly integrated approach (e.g. the social dimension of transport policy, health and safety at work). From that time on, the Commission was also able to present EU initiatives or policies in for instance general debates at the ILC, the ILO GB Working Party on the Social Dimension of Globalization, and equally on concrete agenda items in other committees, in its capacity as observer and representative of the Community.

Unfortunately, the implementation of the complex external dimension of the Lisbon Treaty has introduced once again elements of uncertainty between the EU Member States on the one hand, and the Union institutions on the other.

5. Progressive Intensification of EU–ILO Interaction

As just noted, since 2003, EU participation within ILO has intensified considerably, both in terms of quality and quantity. The main driver behind this development has been the social dimension of globalization. As also mentioned earlier, Union participation within the ILO covers almost all relevant dimensions, including standard-setting and supervision, adoption and implementation of policy frameworks, research, training, and technical cooperation. The only important dimension where the EU is virtually absent is the ILO GB programme and finance committee. This remains very much a Member State (and IMEC) issue, which also has operational implications, e.g. on the presence or absence of ILO Offices in regions such as Europe and Central Asia, sub-regions such as the European Union, and available resources.

As indicated above, the ILO Office has facilitated in a pragmatic way the possibility for the EU to express its views within the ILO. It does not only do so because the EU is an important partner. Forms of regional integration are a reality in other regions as well, and becoming increasingly relevant in global governance, although the European integration process continues to be specific and quite unique. On all recent (major) ILC negotiations, regional and sub-regional groups have played a key role, at least at the level of governments.[26]

Therefore, EU–ILO interaction stretches far beyond the formal observer status of the EU within the ILO, and is not restricted by the mere fact that many ILO labor standards provisions do not touch upon exclusive Union competences but mainly deal with shared ones. All the same, the number of ILO conventions that contain one or more specific provisions touching upon exclusive or strongly integrated Union competences is increasing.[27] This means that ratification by an EU Member is only possible through an EU Council Decision, based on a proposal from the Commission. This Decision has to authorize the EU Member States to ratify the convention for those competences that touch upon Union competences.

Many of the authors that have previously sought to portray EU–ILO relations display a tendency to ignore the wider dynamics of the interaction between the two organizations. This particularly holds true for

---

[26] E.g. the 2008 ILO Declaration on Social Justice for a Fair Globalization, the 2009 Global Jobs Pact, Convention N° 189 on Domestic Work and recommendation N° 202 on Social Protection Floors.

[27] Almost all ILO Conventions adopted since 2005 contain one or more provisions affecting or touching upon exclusive Union competences. This is the case for the 2006 maritime labour Convention (Regulation 4.5.4, §4) and the Work in Fishing Convention N° 188 (2007) on social security coordination (art. 37), the Domestic Work Convention N° 189 (2011) on mobility of workers within EU (art. 8), the Seafarers' Identity Document Convention N° 185 (2003) on EU visa competences. For the older up to date conventions, reference can be made to the Chemical Substances Convention N° 170 (1990) and EU internal market requirements, the Maintenance of Social Security Rights in case of Migration Conventions N° 118 (1962) and 157 (1982), touching on EU coordination of social security within EU and the migrant workers; as well as Conventions N° 97 (1949) and 143 (1982), affecting mobility of workers within the EU and the special legal status of the EU non-discrimination directives.

those analyses focusing narrowly on the pertinent legal and institutional boundaries.[28] Yet, ILO–EU relations cannot be assessed in isolation from the (intensifying) process of globalization, with the emergence of various new players, the development of wider European and global governance frameworks and forums such as G20, and the progressive fleshing-out of a social and economic model of EU integration (e.g. encompassing social dialogue, integrated employment and economic guidelines for the Member States, and human rights that include social rights).

Other authors do take a broader view, but emphasize the dangers for the ILO of the EU acting as a block, and the possible bypassing of (national) social partners.[29] Yet, these challenges are not as such related to the emergence of the EU, and have to be addressed by the rules and practices adopted within the Union framework. This can be illustrated by two examples.

The first example is that, according to some views, the EU coordination within the ILO, based on the EU Directives on for instance health and safety at work,[30] might have resulted in too high ILO standards that cannot possibly be ratified by developing countries. However, the origin of the problem, if any, lies not so much with the EU acting as a block, but with the fact that the reference point for the coordination within the Union might have been the level of protection provided for in the relevant EU Directive. Similar problems can be resolved by ensuring that the parameters for EU coordination are, on the one hand, the need for adopting a global standard that can be ratified by all the ILO members; and on the other, that the standard takes into account the specific situation of regional integration entities (as was the case for e.g. the 2006 Maritime Labour Convention, the Work in the Fishing Sector Convention N° 188 (2007), Domestic Work Convention) N° 189 (2011). In addition, both the EU and the ILO's current standards on health and safety at work have the same origin, dating back to the emergence of the preventive approach to health and safety risks developed in Sweden. In fact, these

---

28 Gisbert Brinkman, 'EU Participation in ILO Standard-Setting', in: Julia Lieb, Nicolai von Ondarza and Daniela Schwarzer (eds,), *The EU in International Fora*, Baden-Baden: Nomos 2011, p. 190.

29 Alish Johnson, 'EU–ILO Relations, Between Regional and Global Governance', in: Jan Orbie and Lisa Tortell (eds.), *The EU and the Social Dimension of Globalisation – How the EU Influences the World*, London-New York: Routledge 2009, p. 81.

30 EC framework Directive on health and safety at work, EC/1989/391.

standards might even be considered as having become part of the EU and ILO's identity.[31]

A second example is that EU coordination might indeed result in a lower involvement of national social partners. However, the EU Treaties, in particular since the Amsterdam revisions, explicitly refer to the promotion of social dialogue by the EU.[32] The Union has developed a practice to organize e.g. preparatory meetings on all main items on the ILC agenda, which feature a consultation of social partners. This absolutely does not prevent Member State authorities to consult their national social partners on the position to be taken at the EU and at ILO meetings. Likewise, it does not prevent timely and proactive networking by national, European and international social partners towards Union Member States and institutions. Union positions are discussed at coordination meetings, but in practice, EU countries do intervene in the debate, highlighting the importance they adhere to specific issues. In many cases, these interventions build on the EU positions. In case there is no EU position, the Member States of course dominate the debates. Yet, they have to take care not to act against common EU policies or legislation. Of course, this is of particular relevance for exclusive competences and for those items where Union has already enacted standards. The active role and presence of the Commission is in that case of paramount importance in order to avoid inconsistencies, and ending up with standards that cannot be ratified by the Member States (because they run counter to, or diverge from, the European standards dealing with exclusive competences or firmly established rules and systems).

Of course, the Council's mandate for engaging in ILO negotiations can result in an authorization to accept international obligations in case the Union's rules are, for instance, outdated, or even obsolete. Otherwise, the EU would stand in the way of adopting new global standards, should the modified global rule be launched sooner than the European one. In that case, ratification of the ILO standard and the implementation of the necessary changes to EU law might require subsequent (internal) legislative initiatives and decisions.

[31] The preventive approach protected for instance men and women against risks of night work, instead of prohibiting night work for women only, as was the case in older, obsolete, conventions. This preventive approach also resulted in a shift from rewarding dangerous work by wage premiums, to the identification, reduction and elimination of risks.

[32] Art. 152, 154 and 155 TFEU.

6. Zooming in on the Role of EU Member States

The emergence of a common 'EU identity' certainly does not mean that there is no role left to play for its Member States. After all, they are members of the ILO, and only states and national social partners' delegates enjoy voting rights. Furthermore, only countries are able to ratify the conventions and, once ratified, assume the corresponding reporting obligations. In addition, the Member States pay the regular membership contributions to the ILO. All this follows from the rules and procedures of the ILO Constitution. As indicated earlier, not only is it very difficult to change the ILO Constitution, but at this stage, a number of EU Member States probably would not even endorse possible modifications of the ILO Constitution that were to result in full membership of the Union.

At present, in comparison to the EU, several Member States have developed a much more coherent partnership policy towards the ILO for voluntary contributions used for technical cooperation. The EU might remedy this by adopting a more coherent approach between support for multilateral commitments within the ILO, and the allocation of parts of EU external assistance programming and funding.

The ILO and the EU have already agreed on specific multi-annual partnership frameworks, such as on social dialogue within the Union and EU enlargement. This has yielded significant added value for both organizations, especially as regards promoting social dialogue and capacity-building of social partners in times of financial, economic and social crisis. Another example is the partnership set up between the ILO and the Flemish Community (part of Belgium, an ILO member country), on the funding of external assistance. Just like the EU, Flanders itself is not an ILO member, but it has recognized the added value of ILO operations through a multi-annual partnership that covers emerging economies and Southern Africa. This partnership complements the larger one concluded by Belgium's federal authorities.

The EU identity within the ILO benefits mostly from a constructive cooperation between its institutions, the Member States, social partners at all levels, and its outreach to and dialogue with other parts of the world.[33]

---

[33] This is well illustrated by the successful European coordination, representation, outreach to third countries, and to social partners and EU follow-up action on the consolidated Maritime Labour Convention (2006), the Convention N° 187 on the Promotional Framework for Health and Safety at Work (2006), the 2008 ILO Declaration on Social Justice for a fair Globalization expressing the Decent Work Agenda, the 2009 ILO Global

In contrast, isolated Member States will have, at least in most cases, much less impact in global negotiations involving 185 countries, including emerging economies that are much more assertive than in the past. Isolated EU Member States are also likely to be approached by other groups that do not always take care of EU policies and interests.

7. How Important and Effective is the ILO–EU Collaboration?

As remarked, the EU is engaged in outreach and dialogue with various other regions, emerging economies, and developing countries within the ILC and ILO GB. The ILO offers an excellent platform for the projection of Union values and explaining its approaches. For example, in the margin of the ILC and ILO GB, the ILO hosts or facilitates tripartite ministerial and technical meetings involving EU neighborhood countries, ASEM or G20 labor ministerial issues.

The Union's coordination and agreed positions within the ILO are presently no longer restricted to standard-setting activities, but also include wider policies and frameworks such as on the social dimension of globalization, on the ILO framework for labor migration and on decent work. The EU has gradually become a positive force within the ILC and ILO GB, capable of neutralizing or softening extreme negative positions taken by some other groups. For example, at the 2004 discussion on the ILO (non-binding) framework for a rights-based approach to labor migrants, some IMEC group members such as the US, Australia and Japan adopted tough positions. In contrast, the EU position was much more balanced, and more in line with the approach of employers and workers.[34]

Similarly, the EU has begun to participate in the ILO discussions on serious and systematic application of core labor standards problems in specific countries, as it had adopted EU policies and positions on some of the cases at stake (e.g. Myanmar, Belarus, Fiji, Bahrain and Zimbabwe).

Jobs Pact, the Convention N° 189 on Domestic Workers (2011), the 2012 ILO Recommendation on Social Protection Floors (Recommendation N°202), the 2012 ILO Action Plan on Fundamental Rights and Principles at Work, and the 2012 ILO Call for Action on Youth Employment. The detailed records of all proceedings and positions, including the EU, are registered in the provisional records of each ILC session. These can be consulted at the ILO website: http://www.ilo.org/ilc/ILCSessions/101stSession/reports/provisional-records/lang--en/index.htm. All EU statements in ILO are available here: <http://eeas.europa.eu/delegations/un_geneva/eu_statments/ilo/index_en.htm>.

[34] Provisional Record N° 22 of the 2004 ILC (92nd session).

The EU's GSP+ trading scheme makes the associated benefits conditional upon ratification and application of the eight ILO core labor standards conventions. In case a partner country violates those standards in a serious and systematic way, the general GSP scheme can be temporarily withdrawn. The EU's assessment takes into account the findings of the ILO supervisory system.

Since many years, the ILO (both the Office and the Organization) has recognized the reality of regional integration. Recent ILO conventions such as the Maritime Labour Convention (2006), the Work in the Fishing Sector Convention (2007) and the Domestic Workers Convention (2011) explicitly include provisions geared towards regional integration organizations on specified items, such as social security coordination and mobility of workers. The same goes for the 2008 ILO Social Justice Declaration and the 2009 Global Jobs Pact.

As indicated already, the EU is increasingly relying on new or other ILO standards for its internal legislative and the social dialogue agenda. This strengthens the interplay between EU and ILO standards and their respective implementation. Equally, it offers a solid approach for ensuring a level playing field, both within and outside the EU, and ensures a consistency of standards.

8. Some Illustrations

8.1 *The Maritime Labour and Work in Fishing Sector Conventions*

The preparations, adoption, ratification process and implementation of the consolidated ILO Maritime Labour Convention (MLC) constitutes one of the most remarkable and outstanding achievements in contemporary international standard-setting. Moreover, it represents one of the most comprehensive illustrations of the emergence of internal EU cohesion and a true 'EU identity' at the global level, which has worked to the benefit of social progress for all and the fostering of maritime safety. This convention formed a response to social dumping practices on board ships that were registered in countries with so-called 'flags of convenience', which resulted in mayor shipping disasters along the EU Atlantic coastline.[35]

[35] For a more detailed overview, see Lisa Tortell, Rudi Delarue and Jeffrey Kenner, 'The EU and the Maritime Labour Convention: "In Our Common Interest and in the Rest of the World"', in: Jan Orbie and Lisa Tortell (eds.), *The EU and the Social Dimension of*

The building up of this cohesion and common identity was accompanied by a number of remarkable paradoxes, such as the significant UK support for a synchronized European approach with regard to this dossier, the constructive cooperation between some Member State departments dealing with maritime transport on the one hand and employment and social policies on the other (e.g. in France), and the rather divergent views within other EU countries.[36]

The highly significant Union involvement in the consolidation of the sixty ILO conventions and recommendations on maritime labor started in 2004, with the High Level Tripartite Working Group on Maritime Standards (hosted by France, chaired by China). In April 2005, the EU's Council of Ministers adopted a negotiating mandate aiming at ensuring consistency with Union standards, cooperation between Member States and the supranational institutions, and the adoption of a global standard that could be ratified by both developed and developing countries. The EU actively participated in successive preparatory ILO meetings. Its positions were represented by the rotating Council Presidency or by other Member States, based on the aforementioned principle of burden-sharing. The Commission played not only an active role with regard to the coordination, but also in informal and formal outreach, in particular on issues that touched upon exclusive competences, such as the applicable social security standards based on the EU social security coordination Regulations. It co-funded the ILC conference of February 2006, which resulted in the adoption of the MLC, as well as a number of publications aiming at a better (worldwide) understanding of its content. In June 2006, the Commission swiftly presented a Communication on the strengthening of maritime labour standards.[37] In June 2007, the Council adopted Decision 2007/431/EC, authorizing the EU Member States to ratify, and requesting them to do so before (preferably) the end of 2010. The social partners in the shipping sector implemented important substantive parts of the MLC through an agreement, and jointly requested the Commission to table a proposal for a Council decision implementing their agreement on the

Globalisation – How the EU Influences the World, London-New York: Routledge 2009, pp. 113–130.

[36] This is all the more remarkable in light of the fact that the emergence of a common EU identity at the International Maritime Organization (IMO), based in London, was sometimes strongly resisted by some EU Member States, represented by the maritime transport authorities.

[37] COM (2006) 287 final.

basis of Article 155 TFEU.[38] In March 2012, the latter presented two proposals, implementing the MLC chapters on inspection and supervision.[39] Their objective is to ensure a level playing field with the internal market, as the quality and impact of inspection in ports and by flag-states on labor conditions onboard ships differ significantly. With the threshold of thirty ratifications being reached in August 2012, the MLC and the EU Directive implementing the social partners' agreement are to enter into force in summer 2013. Paradoxically, flags of convenience states and some emerging economies have ratified the MLC more quickly than most EU Member States. By March 2013, 17 EU countries have ratified the Maritime Labour Convention, while others are still in the process of completing the ratification process and putting the final touches to their internal legislation.[40]

In 2007, the ILO adopted a Convention (N° 188) and Recommendation on Work in the Fishing Sector, as the MLC excluded fishing from its scope of application. The new convention revised existing specific ILO standards on work in the fishing sector, and also covered other key issues such on health and safety at work. Yet again, the EU was very active and visible within the ILC. On 21 May 2012, EU social partners in the fishing sector concluded an agreement based on Convention N° 188, and once more lodged a joint request with the Commission to propose a decision implementing this agreement based on Article 155 TFEU.

8.2 *The Social Protection Floors Recommendation*

The June 2012 ILC adopted the landmark Recommendation Nr.202 on social protection floors, which was the result of a long process building on support for the extension of social protection to those that were hitherto excluded. The global financial and economic crisis provided evidence that social protection not only provided protection to people, but also

---

38 Directive 2009/13/EC, OJ (20 May 2009), L 124/30. According to Article 155 TFEU, an EU social partners agreement can be implemented by a decision of the Council on a proposal from the Commission. The term 'decision' in Article 155 TFEU can also refer to a directive.

39 COM(2012) 129 final and COM(2012) 134 final on inspection by respectively the port state and the flag state.

40 Including Member States with significant shipping and/or port operations, such as Belgium, Italy, Ireland, Germany, Portugal and the UK. EU Member states have an interest in speedy ratification as most of them have significant shipping and/or port operations. The lack of ratification could very much backfire against their flags, as only ILO member countries that have ratified can issue maritime labour certificates. This constitutes a prima facie indication for port state inspectors all over the world that the ship is respecting the MLC.

rendered economic development more resilient. Thus, social protection functions as an almost automatic stabilizing force. In the EU, even in the middle of the sovereign debt crisis, this has been recognized through the Commission's 2012 Annual Growth Strategy.[41]

Increasing global support was expressed, as from 2005, in the G8 labor ministerial meetings, the G20 labor ministerial and G20 Summit of 2011, the 2005 review of the Millennium Development Goals (MDGs) by the UN General Assembly, the 2009 Global Jobs pact, the 2011 report of the UN advisory group on the Social Protection Floor, and the 2011 ILC conclusions on the ILO strategy on extending social protection coverage.

The EU played an important role in this global agenda-setting process. For one thing, it actively took part in the ILC discussions. The 2011 ILC discussions also coincided with the implementation of the Lisbon Treaty with regard to the Union's role and activities in international organizations. The latter gave rise to some confusion for external partners, in light of the multiple interventions by different Member States in representing the Union's position, pursuant to the principle of burden-sharing. Nonetheless, the agreed positions firmly supported the ILO's actions and standard-setting that resulted in Recommendation Nr. 202.

In the last decade, the EU developed a number of other relevant initiatives such as the EU social protection and social inclusion strategy. The 2010 European Development Report dealt with social protection, and also contributed to the global process. On 20 August 2012, the Commission issued a Communication on social protection in development cooperation which referred directly to Recommendation Nr. 202.

9. New Challenges and Opportunities

In all likelihood, the implementation of the Lisbon Treaty, the new orientations for Union external action, the preparations for a new global development framework (post-MDG 2015 and sustainable development goals), and the European and international responses to the financial, economic and social crisis provide the currently most significant challenges and opportunities for the interplay between the ILO and the EU.

The 2001 Exchange of Letters between the ILO and the Commission, which builds further on the 1989 Exchange of Letters, has not yet been

---

[41] COM (2011) 815 final.

adapted to the functioning of the Union post-Lisbon. However, just as in 1989, actual practice often precedes the legal formalization of arrangements. Nevertheless, it is up to the EU to ensure that its external representation is organized in accordance with the EU Treaties, and in line with what is possible under the current constitutional rules of the ILO.

During the November 2012 and March 2013 ILO GB, the EU coordination meetings were chaired by the tandem consisting of the EU Delegation social affairs counselor in Geneva, and the representatives of the rotating Council Presidency. The Union positions at the 2012 ILC were presented by the rotating Council Presidency and the EU Delegation in Geneva, respectively. At the March and November 2012 and March 2013 sessions of the ILO GB, some of the Union's positions were presented by the EU Delegation in Geneva, and others by the rotating Presidency, or an EU country that was member of the ILO GB. When more information or clarification on Union initiatives was needed, the Commission intervened. 'The EU actively and constructively intervened at the 9th ILO European and Central Asia Regional Meeting, organized in Oslo, 8–11 April 2013. EU positions were presented by the Council Presidency, but the Commission and also the Parliament actively participated in panel discussions. ILO Regional meetings do not have standard-setting and supervisory capacity. However they determine ILO means of action and ILO policy objectives for the region.

For third countries, social partners and the ILO, it is important that the EU continues to express and pursue coherent positions that correspond with international commitments, as well as with the policies and instruments endorsed by its institutions and Member States. Yet, the representatives of the latter, intervening on the basis of burden-sharing, or even when acting on behalf of the Council Presidency, are not always informed or aware of the relevant EU policies and instruments and their interplay with global standards or positions agreed in other relevant forums such as the G20, the UN, and regional meetings such as ASEM. Moreover, some Member States might pursue policies that are not necessarily consistent with the EU Treaties, secondary legislation or established policies. Unfortunately, in some old and new Member States, the European culture of social dialogue, which forms an intrinsic part of the Union's treaties and practices, is not applied in practice.

Preferably, EU positions and ILO outcomes are followed up by implementation action whenever that is required, for instance by facilitating the ratification of conventions and their implementation through national and or European standards and actions. The Commission, on some issues the EEAS, the Council (including its Secretariat and Working Groups), the Parliament, the Member States and social partners all have a role in this.

Recent EU policy documents reflect the relevance of decent work for EU development, trade and external assistance policies and actions. The EU, UNEP and ILO have convergent approaches for the RIO+20 outcomes and for the next steps on sustainable development and greening the economy, green jobs and social protection floors.[42] However the current EU programming practices still result in fragmented operational support for the ILO on technical cooperation, as implementing partners are often selected by a call for proposals, mixing up the ILO with NGOs or national development agencies as 'implementing service providers'. The current provisions of the strategic partnership between the ILO and the Commission in the field of development (2004), which stipulate that both may use a multi-annual direct funding arrangement for jointly agreed objectives and outcomes, are not yet applied in a consistent manner. Consequently, the EU is missing opportunities to benefit from the involvement of ILO tripartite constituents in the field, and equally, is not realizing its full potential as a global actor within the ILO that is capable of mobilizing its policies and actions in a coherent way, in line with the Lisbon Treaty reforms.[43]

The global financial, economic and social crisis has very much affected the Eurozone and the wider Union, due to the systemic failures in the global financial order, and the lop-sided EMU that did not, and still does not, dispose of an effective, EU-wide reaction capacity (although some progress has been made with the ESM). During the first phase of the crisis (Fall 2008–Spring 2010), the EU responded in line with the 2009 ILO Global Jobs Pact, insisting on support for the real economy, protecting people, and building on the employment potential of greening the economy and green jobs.[44] The Commission and the ILO Office cooperated in conducting analyses and evidence-based policy research on adequate responses to the crisis. Yet, the second phase changed the perception of the EU's agenda and confused partners with regard to the Union's identity. As from May 2010, with the rise of the sovereign debt crisis in Greece, Ireland and other periphery countries, the economic and financial authorities

[42] See e.g. Commission Communication on Social Protection in EU Development Cooperation, COM(2012) 446 final.

[43] Art. 21 EU; Art. 208; Art. 209 and Art. 212 TFEU.

[44] The EU was (and is) well-placed to set a good example, and provides much-appreciated guidance and leadership, bilaterally and at global forums, to emerging economies and other developing countries that are progressively building up their employment and social policies.

took over. This resulted in an almost total dominance of the preparatory work on the reform of EU economic governance by the ECOFIN Ministers and related authorities such as EC DG ECFIN.[45] International partners saw this as a message that the EU had changed its approach, and now merely considered employment and social policy as dimensions that were subordinate to the economic and financial priorities. Some argued that this approach de facto resulted in the suspension of several Treaty provisions, such as the horizontal social clause and the provision on the role of social dialogue.[46]

Since 2010, the discussions on reforming EMU governance, and the definition of the successive conditions for assisting Greece and other periphery countries, has almost totally been dominated by ECB, the ECOFIN Council and the IMF. In 2012, this inter alia resulted in the condition that Greece had to reduce the national collective agreement fixing the minimum wage in the private sector by 22%. Greek employers and workers jointly resisted this reduction, and jointly published a list of possible alternatives. Their views were ignored, which resulted in the total breakdown of social dialogue. Meanwhile, the ILO supervisory system has received observations from the Confederation of Greek Trade Unions on alleged violations of over ten ratified ILO conventions, including the fundamental rights convention N° 98 on collective bargaining. The ILO supervisory system concluded – taking into account the complexity of the problems – that an ILO high level mission should be sent to Greece and have exchanges with the EU and IMF.[47] This mission, which also visited the Commission and the IMF, took place in September 2011. It published a detailed report, which was incorporated in the 2012 Report of the ILO Committee of Experts on the Application of Conventions and Recommendations (CEACR). In two separate resolutions (2011 and 2012), the

---

[45] The legal basis for action restricted to Eurozone (Art. 127 TFEU) focuses on the Eurogroup finance ministers, with only a consultative role for the Parliament. However, the Eurogroup and IMF, ECB and Commission 'Troika' decisions extended to conditions on working time, wages, collective bargaining systems, labour protection or social security, without any role for the Parliament, social partners or labour ministers.

[46] The Union's Employment, Social Affairs and Social Inclusion Commissioner László Andor fiercely criticized some of the conditions imposed by the Troika. The strong ECOFIN dominance was somewhat adjusted through interventions by the European Council President, and through amendments made by the EP to the legislative 'six-pack on economic governance'. These amendments introduced a specific role for labour markets actors, social partners, and respect for fundamental rights at work in EU economic governance.

[47] CEACR, 2011, report; Provisional Record of the conclusions of the ILO tripartite committee on the application of standards, ILC, June 2011.

European Parliament had requested as well that ILO should be involved in the Troika, and that its role should not be restricted to dealing with the consequences of the Troika decisions.[48] At present, the ILO attends the consultation meetings of the Commission's task force for Greece. The mandate of this taskforce consists in assisting Greece to mobilize and implement EU structural funds for promoting growth, investment, employment and better governance.

The third phase in the Union's response to the crisis once again marked a turn towards a more job-oriented approach, as highlighted by the April 2012 employment package proposed by the Commission, and the European Council Compact for Jobs and Growth.[49] At the same time, the ILO issued the World of Work Report in May 2012, and the Eurozone Jobs Crisis Report of July 2012.[50] The renewed convergence was made clear at the EU High Level Employment Conference of 6 and 7 September 2012, drawing explicit support from the Presidents of the European Council, the Commission and the Parliament. The Director General of the ILO concluded the EU conference expressing the hope that the EU effectively embrace a job-oriented recovery, and engage in a balanced reform of labor markets with full involvement of social partners. Furthermore, he highlighted the willingness of the ILO to engage in a partnership with the EU, both internally and at global level, such as in the G20.[51]

10. Conclusions

The EU has achieved a strong identity within the ILO, and their interaction has intensified forcefully and visibly over the course of the past decades. This interaction goes far beyond the formal remit of the Union's observer status. Furthermore, it would seem to coincide with the emergence, between 2000 and 2010, of a more coherent and integrated European social model, combining economic, employment, social and environmental objectives, and the recognition of its external dimension

---

[48] European Parliament, Adoption of the final report of the committee on the financial, economic and social crisis, 6 July 2011, and Resolution on the 2012 Annual Growth Strategy, 15 February 2012.

[49] COM(2012) 173 final.

[50] Available at: <http://www.ilo.org/global/research/publications/WCMS_184965/lang--en/index.htm>.

[51] The Employment Policy Conference, 'Jobs for Europe', organized by the European Commission, 6 and 7 September 2012. For the text of the concluding intervention of the DG-elect, see the ILO Brussels website: <http://www.ilo.org/brussels>.

by both EU institutions and Member States. This specific dimension of the integration process was also perceived in positive terms by the Union's bilateral and multilateral partners. This model of development is also in line with the integrated approach to the world of work, as reflected in the final 2004 report of the World Commission on the Social Dimension of Globalization (established by the ILO) and the Decent Work Agenda.[52] All this contributed greatly to the uptake of labor and social protection in emerging economies.

At the same time, the EU and Eurozone governance of the global financial, economic and social crisis as from May 2010 (the 'second phase', which gave rise to the sovereign debt crisis), excessively dominated by economic and financial authorities, has not only affected social cohesion in the EU, but also the perceptions of the Union in the eyes of third countries. The latter observe a progressive erosion of employment, social policy and social dialogue. If no rebalancing takes place, this will strongly impact on the Union's global identity. Fortunately, the April 2012 employment package, the December 2012 youth employment package, and the social investment package of February 2013 would appear to provide the initial building blocks for such a rebalancing, at least with regard to a more coherent social and economic governance. This is supported by the December 2012 European Council orientations towards a more genuine Economic and Monetary Union, with the intention to take into account the social dimension, including social dialogue.

The cooperation between the EU and the ILO has been able to exploit the potential of the ILO's 1919 Constitution and the ILC and ILO GB Standing Orders and Rules of Procedures to the maximum. As noted, the ILO standards and initiatives are relevant for a wide variety of internal and external EU policies, mostly affecting non-CFSP, and in some cases also CFSP issues, such as parts of the ILO supervisory findings and activities on non-EU countries. Recent ILO instruments refer to REIOs in order to take into account the specific legal and operational framework of the EU and other such organizations. It cannot be excluded that in the future, the ILO Constitution will have to reflect the legal reality of multiple regional integration organizations, just as it did for federal states, already in 1919. To be sure, amending the ILO constitution is a lengthy and cumbersome process, but that provides no justification for not bringing it into line with this new reality.

---

52 Available at: <http://www.ilo.org/global/meetings-and-events/campaigns/voices-on-social-justice/WCMS_099766/lang--en/index.htm>.

On a daily basis, the EU coordinates actions on almost all substantive items discussed at the ILC, and is reaching out to third countries as well as social partners. This often results in joint positions expressed by the rotating Council Presidency, another Member State (as part of burden-sharing), the EU Delegation, and in some cases the Commission. As highlighted, the Commission also intervenes in policy debates and general discussions that are relevant for its initiatives, EU policies and standards, in particular when these debates and discussions have the purpose of explaining policies. The implementation of the Lisbon Treaty has resulted in some adjustments already, such as the functioning of the team (the EU Delegation in Geneva and rotating Council Presidency) for dealing with on-the-spot coordination in Geneva.

The preparatory and substantive follow-up work in Brussels is organized by the Commission and the rotating Presidency, involving the Member States and (for some aspects) also European and international social partners. The Union's preparatory and follow-up work on the ILO may be expected to expand, as for instance almost all recent ILO conventions and frameworks are relevant for several sectoral policies, and affect, in one way or the other, exclusive and other strongly integrated EU competences and actions. The role of the Commission is and remains key in ensuring effective preparatory work and follow-up.

The EU and the ILO Office increasingly meet and cooperate outside the ILO, in particular through the UN system, the G20, and regional or sub-regional meetings and events. The new generation of EU FTAs with third countries, and the GSP and GSP+ trade arrangements refer to ILO standards and frameworks, the supervisory system, and its technical involvement. The Union's new development cooperation policy orientations of 2011 strongly refer to the decent work agenda as well. The EU human rights strategy of 2012 equally refers to ILO cooperation and its core international labor standards. Evidently, the EU Member States must continue to play a constructive role within ILO as they ratify, apply and report on ILO conventions and they pay their financial contribution. In that respect, it is striking that many EU Member states apply a much more coherent development cooperation partnership approach to the ILO than the EU. At the end of the day though, the effective impact of the Union's Member States at the ILO can benefit greatly from a coherent and coordinated EU position within that organization, followed by effective implementation, mobilizing all relevant EU internal and external policies, instruments, tools and programmes.

CHAPTER SEVEN

THE EUROPEAN UNION AND THE HAGUE CONFERENCE ON PRIVATE INTERNATIONAL LAW – FORCED MARRIAGE OR FORTUNATE PARTNERSHIP?

Jan-Jaap Kuipers

1. Introduction

Passionate arguments have been made that, in contrast to regulatory law, private law is deeply rooted in national legal culture.[1] If rules of private law are truly the expression of cultural values, we could expect to see significant differences from one state to another. Within Europe, and even more strongly on the global level, states have indeed adopted remarkably divergent conceptions of marriage, divorce and parentage but also have developed fundamentally different views on politically less sensitive questions such as 'what is a fair and efficient body of contract law'. Material differences between the private laws of states are in itself not problematic. However, a growing number of transnational legal relationships have a connection with more than one legal system. In such a case, the question arises which courts have jurisdiction to hear a potential dispute and which law should be applicable. In order to co-ordinate the problems stemming from the existence of multiple sovereign legal orders, states have resorted to private international law (PIL).[2]

The problems stemming from the divergence of laws at the substantive level would not be adequately resolved if states would exclusively rely upon their own rules of PIL to do justice in international cases. International cooperation is therefore essential. Already in 1893, the first steps towards such cooperation were taken in the framework of what would later become the Hague Conference on Private International Law. The

---

[1] Pierre Legrand, 'European Legal Systems are not Converging', (1996) 45 *International and Comparative Law Quarterly*, pp. 52–81.

[2] Jean-Michel Jacquet, 'La Fonction Supranationale de la Règle de Conflit de Lois', (2001) 292 *Recueil des Cours*, pp. 155–248; Pierre Mayer, 'Le Phénomène de la Coordination des Ordres Juridiques Étatiques en Droit Privé', (2007) 327 *Recueil des Cours*, pp. 23–377.

objective of the Hague Conference is to reinforce legal security by striving for the progressive harmonization of the rules of PIL.[3] The Hague Conference became a permanent intergovernmental organization in 1955, and currently counts 72 members. An important distinction should be drawn between membership of the Conference and being bound by a Hague Convention. The Hague Conference offers a framework for the negotiation of Hague Conventions, but membership of the Hague Conference does not mean that a state is automatically party to a Hague Convention. The question which states and/or entities may accede to a Hague Convention is determined by the respective Convention itself. Should a member of the Conference decide to accede to a Convention, a separate act of ratification is required. On the other hand, it is also possible that a Hague Convention is ratified by a state that is not a member of the Hague Conference. At the time of writing, there are 39 Hague Conventions, and more than 130 different states that have ratified at least one Hague Convention.

Whereas for long, the Hague Conference occupied a monopoly position in the area of international co-operation relating to PIL, the European Union has over the past two decades emerged as an important institutional player. Since the Hague Conference has traditionally mainly been a European initiative, the development of civil cooperation as a policy area within the European Union threatened to undermine the pertinence of the Conference. The increasing activities of the Union in PIL thus necessitated the Hague Conference to come up with an institutional response. This chapter will explore that institutional response, by first describing the evolution of EU competences in PIL (paragraph 2), then sketching the simultaneously evolving institutional relations between the Union, its Member States and the Hague Conference (paragraph 3 and 4), discussing the accession of the Union to the Hague Conference (paragraph 5) and, finally, by analyzing the interplay between Union law and Hague Conventions (paragraph 6).

---

[3] On the role and function of the Hague Conference, see the bundle edited by the T.M.C. Asser Institute: 'The Influence of the Hague Conference on Private International Law', Leiden: Martinus Nijhoff 1993.

2. Judicial Cooperation in Civil Matters

The relationship between Union law and PIL has often been described as a tale of two uneasy bedfellows.[4] It is true that the original EEC Treaty merely made one reference to PIL. In Article 220 EEC (subsequently Article 293 EC, but now repealed by the Lisbon Treaty), it was stipulated that Member States would enter into negotiations with each other concerning the simplification of recognition and enforcement of judicial decisions. Strictly speaking, the EEC therefore enjoyed only a competence in PIL limited to the recognition and enforcement of foreign decisions, but not with regard to the jurisdiction of national courts in international disputes and the rules determining the applicable law. Despite the shaky legal basis, Art. 220 EEC did function as the legal basis for the Brussels Convention on jurisdiction and the enforcement of foreign judgments in civil and commercial matters (1968). The harmonization of the rules on jurisdiction was deemed necessary to generate a high level of mutual trust between the courts of the Member States, thereby creating the essential parameters allowing for the free movement of judgments. The Rome Convention on the Law applicable to Contractual Obligations (1980) was

[4] The literature on this topic is voluminous, see e.g.: Katharina Boele-Woelki, 'Unification and Harmonization of Private International Law in Europe', in: Jürgen Basedow et al. (eds.) *Private Law in the International Arena: Liber Amicorum Kurt Siehr*, The Hague: T.M.C. Asser Press 2000, pp. 61–78; Jürgen Basedow, 'The Communitarisation of the Conflict of Laws under the Treaty of Amsterdam', (2000) 37 *Common Market Law Review*, pp. 687–708; Jona Israël, 'Europees Internationaal Privaatrecht', (2001) 19 *Nederlands Internationaal Privaatrecht*, pp. 135–149; Hans Ulrich Jessurun d'Oliveira, 'The EU and a Metamorphosis of Private International Law', in: James Fawcett (ed.), *Reform and Development of Private International Law: Essays in Honours of Sir Peter North*, Oxford: Oxford University Press 2002, pp. 111–136; Pierre Lagarde, 'Développement futurs du droit international privé dans une Europe en voie d'unification: quelques conjectures', (2004) 68 *Rabels Zeitschrift für ausländisches und internationales Privatrecht*, pp. 225–243; Andrew Dickinson, 'European Private International Law: Embracing New Horizons or Mourning the Past', (2005) 1 *Journal of Private International Law*, pp. 197–236; Lajos Vékás, 'Der Weg zur Vergemeinschaftung des Internationalen Privat- und Verfahrensrechts – eine Skizze', in: Vesna Tomljenović, Johan A. Erauw and Paul Volken (eds.), *Liber Memorialis Petar Šarčević, Universalism, Tradition and the Individual*, München: Sellier European Law Publishers 2006, pp. 171–187; Michael Bogdan, *Concise Introduction to EU Private International Law*, Groningen: Europa Law Publishing 2006, pp. 6–14; Johan Meeusen, 'Who Is Afraid of European Private International Law', in: Gabriella Venturini and Stefania Bariatti (eds), *Liber Fausto Pocar: New Instruments of Private International Law*, Milano: Giuffrè 2009, pp. 685–700; Jan-Jaap Kuipers, 'Bridging the Gap: The Impact of the EU on the Law Applicable to Contractual Obligations', (2012) 76 *Rabels Zeitschrift für ausländisches und internationales Privatrecht*, pp. 562–596.

even more loosely connected to the EEC legal order. The Rome Convention lacked any explicit legal basis in the EEC Treaty but was based instead upon the desire to continue the unification of PIL as initiated by the Brussels I Convention.

After the adoption of the Brussels and Rome Convention, and in the light of continuing initiatives of the Member States within the framework of the Hague Conference, it seemed therefore safe to state that the influence of the European Union on PIL would be fairly limited and only gradual.[5] However, starting with the Maastricht Treaty (1991) the competences of the Union to act in the area of PIL were gradually enlarged. Most significant was the incorporation of Article 65 by the Amsterdam Treaty (1999) in Title IV of the TEC allowing for the adoption of measures relating to civil cooperation in cross-borders matters insofar as necessary for the functioning of the internal market. The Treaty of Lisbon continued the trend of broadening the EU competences in PIL. Article 81 TFEU allows the Union to act, *in particular* when necessary for the functioning of the internal market.[6] The adding of the words "in particular" demonstrate that the Union may also act in subjects of PIL having a more remote link with the functioning of the internal market, such as international family law and legal relationships having a connection with third states. Article 81 TFEU is part of Title V on an "Area of Freedom, Security and Justice". Denmark, Ireland and the United Kingdom enjoy a special position regarding measures adopted on the basis of this title. While the latter two Member States may decide ad hoc whether they participate in a specific measure, Denmark is not at all bound by measures adopted on the basis of Article 81 TFEU, but may conclude international conventions with the Union to reach the same substantial effects.[7]

---

[5] Peter North, 'Is European Harmonisation of Private International Law a Myth or Reality', in: Ted de Boer (ed.) *Forty Years On: The Evolution of Postwar Private International Law in Europe*, Kluwer: Deventer 1990, pp. 29–48.

[6] Gerard-René de Groot and Jan-Jaap Kuipers, 'The New Provisions on Private International Law in the Treaty of Lisbon', (2008) 15 *Maastricht Journal of European and Comparative Law*, pp. 109–114; Heinz-Peter Mansel, Karsten Thorn and Rolf Wagner, 'Europäisches Kollisionsrecht 2009: Hoffnungen durch den Vertrag von Lissabon' (2010) 30 *IPRax*, pp. 1–27; Isabelle Barrière Brousse, 'Le Traité de Lisbonne et le droit international privé', in: (2010) 137 *Journal du Droit International*, pp. 3–34.

[7] Damian Chalmers, Gareth Davies and Giorgio Monti, *European Union Law*, Cambridge: Cambridge University Press 2006, pp. 620–621. With regards to Brussels I: Agreement between the European Union and the Kingdom of Denmark on jurisdiction and the recognition and enforcement of judgments in civil and commercial matters OJ [1995] L 299/62.

In the past decade, the Union has developed an ever greater appetite for PIL.[8] The progressive harmonization of PIL was deemed necessary for the creation of a genuine European justice area.[9] The Brussels and Rome Convention were transformed into the Brussels I and Rome I Regulation. Moreover, the Union has adopted a range of instruments dealing with jurisdiction, applicable law and recognition and enforcement in both commercial and family-related PIL. In fact, it cannot be excluded that within the near future the national rules on PIL will have become completely replaced by measures adopted at the Union level.[10] However, civil cooperation on the internal market is necessarily limited to cooperation between the Member States of the European Union. An international harmony of decisions cannot be ascertained by the Union acting on its own. Even if national PIL would be completely replaced by rules adopted at the Union level, Member States will continue to have a keen interest in participating in the progressive harmonization of the rules of PIL in the framework of the Hague Conference to safeguard cooperation with third states.[11]

3. The European Union and the Hague Conference

3.1 *Potential Tension*

The Hague Conference has always been quite liberal in allowing international organizations, non-governmental organizations and non-member states to act as observers in the Conference, to participate in its meetings and to submit proposals. Despite the existence of only limited competences, what we presently know as the EU was, from its very inception in 1957, consistently invited to participate as an observer in the Hague Conference. In 1960, at the occasion of the first Diplomatic Session of the Conference after the establishment of the EEC, the Union was granted the

---

8 Eva Storskrubb, 'Civil Justice – A Newcomer and an Unstoppable Wave', in: Paul Craig and Gráinne de Búrca, (eds.), *The Evolution of EU Law*, Oxford: Oxford University Press 2011, pp. 299–322.

9 Presidency Conclusions, Tampere European Council 15 and 16 October 1999.

10 Pierre Lagarde, 'Développement futurs du droit international privé dans une Europe en voie d'unification: quelques conjectures', (2004) 68 *Rabels Zeitschrift für ausländisches und internationales Privatrecht*, pp. 225–233.

11 Fausto Pocar, "The 'Communitarization' of Private International Law and its Impact upon the External Relations of the European Union", in: Alberto Malatesta, Stefania Bariatti and Fausto Pocar (eds.), *The External Dimension of EC Private International Law in Family and Succession Matters*, Milan: CEDAM 2008, pp. 3–18.

status of formal observer. The involvement of the EEC in the workings of the Hague Conference initially raised no significant problems from the perspective of the Conference. The Hague Conference adheres to a rather informal method of preparing new Conventions. In The Hague, a preliminary draft Convention is negotiated in a specially established commission that meets several times over the course of a few years. The discussions in that commission are of a rather technical nature and tend not to be too much politicized. Participants function primarily as experts instead of national delegates. At the last meeting of the special commission, a preliminary draft Convention is adopted by vote. The final step is the adoption of the Convention in a Diplomatic Session.[12] It is at the Diplomatic Session where discussions become more formal and politicized. Prior to 2000, a new Convention was adopted at the Diplomatic Session by a simple majority.[13] The expanding activity of the Union in PIL could thus easily be resolved in the informal procedures of the Hague Conference. It has been said that the position of the Union corresponded factually more or less with that of a member.[14]

The growing activity of the Union in PIL was however followed with close interest in The Hague. In particular the autonomous lawmaking powers conferred upon the Union by the Amsterdam Treaty (1997) was a cause of concern. For long, the Hague Conference was the sole international organization dedicated to the promotion of international cooperation in PIL. Although the Hague Conference had the aim to strive for the global harmonization of PIL, its members were mainly European states. To give an impression: when the Amsterdam Treaty was signed in 1997, thirty-one out of the forty-five members of the Hague Conference were European countries. All EU Member States, fifteen at that time, were simultaneously members of the Hague Conference. Moreover, European states were much more active in the Hague Conference than non-European states. Whereas

[12] Hans van Loon and Andrea Schulz, 'The European Community and the Hague Conference on Private International Law', in: Bernd Martenczuk and Servaas van Thiel (eds.), *Justice, Liberty, Security: New Challenges for the External Relations of the European Union*, Brussels: VUBPress 2007, p. 260.

[13] Andrea Schulz, 'The Accession of the European Community to the Hague Conference on Private International Law', (2007) 56 *International Comparative Law Quarterly*, p. 942.

[14] Ibid., p. 944.

for example the United States had ratified by 1997 no more than four Hague Conventions, the count for the Netherlands stood at twenty-four.[15]

At one point, it was feared that the enhanced regional cooperation in civil matters would gradually come to overshadow the work of the Hague Conference, that EU Member States would direct their resources primarily at harmonizing PIL within the Union, and consequently, contribute less to the work of the Hague Conference. Closer regional convergence would then come at the expense of global cooperation.[16] In the most favorable scenario, even if the EU Member States would still be dedicated to the work of the Hague Conference, the risk would occur that EU Member States would become too dominant in the Conference. As a matter of Union law, the powers of the EU Member States to act on the international scene are restricted once the Union has exercised its competences. Moreover, even in the absence of harmonization, Member States could become too dominant by adopting common positions prior to the negotiations. The Hague Conference benefits immensely from the input of national experts. If the EU Member States were only to defend a common position, the richness of their own PIL traditions would not be reflected in the framework of the Conference. This would be a blow to the plurality of debate in The Hague. Moreover, the risk would grow that the content of future conventions would be wholly dictated by EU Member States. If new Hague Conventions were to place a too strong emphasis on the European PIL tradition, they simply would not get ratified outside of Europe.

3.2 *The Response of the Hague Conference*

The response of the Hague Conference was twofold. First, it sought to guarantee the commitment of the EU Member States, and second, to reduce its dependence on European states. In order to achieve the latter, the Hague Conference started a campaign encouraging non-European countries to become member of the Conference.[17] At the same time, the ratification

---

[15] The ratifications of the different members can be viewed at: http://www.hcch.net/index_en.php?act=states.listing, as of 5 October 2011.

[16] Gülüm Bayraktaroglu, 'Harmonization of Private International Law at Different Levels: Communitarization v. International Harmonization', (2003) 5 *European Journal of Law Reform*, pp. 127–172.

[17] Rolf Wagner, 'Die Haager Konferenz für Internationales Privatrecht zehn Jahre nach der Vergemeinschaftung der Gesetzgebungskompetenz in der justiziellen Zusammenarbeit in Zivilsachen', (2009) 73 *Rabels Zeitschrift für ausländisches und internationales Privatrecht*, p. 222.

of conventions by non-European states was promoted. This campaign has been rather successful. Between 1955 and 2000, on average two to four new members joined the Hague Conference every five years.[18] However, in the period after 2000, there has been a remarkable surge in the membership of the Conference. For example, in the 2000–2005 period, eighteen new members joined. Those new members included Brazil, India, the Russian Federation and South Africa. Compared to 1997, the year when the Amsterdam Treaty was signed, the total number of members of the Hague Conference has, at the time of writing, nearly been doubled. Many of the new members are emerging economies, and the global representativeness of the Hague Conference has improved dramatically. The campaign to enhance the ratification of Conventions has also borne fruit. For example, the 1980 Hague Convention on the Civil Aspects of International Child Abduction has been ratified by twenty-five states not being member of the Conference. Whereas only seven of such ratifications were made before 1997, the large majority, eighteen, only ratified the Convention in or after 1997.

Evidently, it remains difficult to determine precisely to what extent the increasing interest amongst non-European states in the work of the Hague Conference was caused, directly or indirectly, by the enlarging competences of the European Union in PIL. It is clear however that with the emergence of civil cooperation in cross-border cases as an EU policy area, the Hague Conference repositioned itself as a more representative international organization. The strategy of the Hague Conference to be less dependent on European states, and hence on internal developments in Europe, has ensured its continued pertinence on the international stage. The enlargement of the Hague Conference means that the Union and the Conference may act in the same policy area, but serve the needs of different markets. Within the Area of Freedom, Security and Justice, the uniform interpretation and application of European PIL is guaranteed by the European Court of Justice. The harmonization in the AFSJ may therefore go deeper than the harmonization envisaged by the Hague Conference, but the territorial reach of the Hague Conventions is potentially much larger. From the perspective of the European states, the particularities of European integration may call for closer cooperation in civil matters

[18] An exception was the period 1991–1995 when nine new members joined. The temporary increase of new members could be possibly be attributed to the fall of the iron curtain.

between the Member States, but due to the differentiation in international civil cooperation, deeper integration on the European level does not necessarily have to come at the price of reduced cooperation with third countries.

The greater involvement of emerging economies in the Hague Conference is a strong safeguard against the potential dominance of the EU Member States resulting from the participation in negotiations as a block. Nevertheless, a further safeguard was introduced. A change in the decision-making procedure ensured that non-EU Member States would not simply be outvoted by the EU block. Whereas new Hague Conventions were traditionally adopted by majority-voting, in 2000, the procedure was changed into the adoption of decisions by consensus.[19]

The gradual shift of the Hague Conference from a primarily European forum towards a truly international organization has undeniably contributed to the realization of its own statutory goal, the progressive unification of the rules of PIL. The strengthened global representativeness, and the subsequent enhanced plurality of debate, adds to the legitimacy of the Hague Conventions. More states, even if not a party to the Hague Conference, may therefore be expected to ratify Hague Conventions. The conferral upon the Union of the power to adopt measures in the area of PIL by the Amsterdam Treaty could from this point of view be seen as a stimulus to the strive of the Hague Conference for the progressive unification of the rules of PIL.

4. The Participation of the Member States in the Hague Conference

The increased participation of non-European states in the Hague Conference adequately buttressed the threat of reduced pertinence of the Conference following the enlarging powers of the Union in PIL. Yet, even if the Union were to succeed in completely unifying the rules of PIL applicable in the Member States, the common rules would evidently not bind third countries. From the perspective of the EU Member States, there would still be the necessity, and framework, to pursue broader international cooperation.[20] The broadening of the basis of the Hague Conference did

---

19 Wagner, *supra* n. 17, p. 224.

20 The Joint Council and Commission statements on Council Regulation 44/2001 on jurisdiction and the recognition and enforcement of judgments in civil and commercial

however not solve the ambiguity surrounding the representation of the EU Member States or the Union in the Hague Conference. As remarked, as a matter of Union law, Member States become severely restricted to act on the international scene once a policy area has been harmonized internally.[21] Even in the absence of harmonization, there may already be an obligation upon the Member States to speak with one voice.[22] After the entry into force of the Treaty of Amsterdam, it was unclear whether the mere attribution of competence upon the Union in some way affected the powers of the Member States to act individually in the framework of the Hague Conference.

Moreover, the exact scope of the powers of the Union to act on the international stage in matters related to PIL was not unequivocally clear. Article 65 EC only provided the legal basis to adopt measures insofar as necessary for the functioning of the internal market. A plausible argument could thus be made that the powers of the Union were limited to the harmonization of PIL between the Member States, but that the Member States had retained competence with regard to international relationships lacking a clear connection with the internal market, such as the recognition in a Member State of a judgment awarded by a court in a third country.[23]

By the mid-1990s, the Union's formal status of observer became increasingly unsatisfactory. It was evident that the informal recognition of the powers of the Union could only be sustained temporarily. Although the Union could participate in the meetings of the Hague Conference, its formal status as observer meant that its Member States had retained the power

---

matters recognize that The Council and the Commission hold that establishing this area within Europe should not rule out the possibility of concluding international agreements of broader geographical scope with third States or international organization which might allow the creation of a global or regional legal environment conducive to the circulation of judgments in civil and commercial matters. See: Note 13742/00 Justciv 131.

[21] Piet Eeckhout, *EU External Relations Law*, Oxford: Oxford University Press 2011, p. 70.

[22] See further: Marise Cremona, 'Defending the Community Interest: the Duties of Cooperation and Compliance', in: Marise Cremona and Bruno de Witte (eds), *EU Foreign Relations Law – Constitutional Fundamentals*, Hart Publishing 2008, pp. 125–170; Andrés Delgado Castelleiro and Joris Larik, 'The Duty to Remain Silent: Limitless Loyalty in EU External Relations?', (2011) 36 *European Law Review*, pp. 522–539.

[23] Bernard Hess, 'Les compétences externes de la Communauté européenne dans le cadre de l'article 65 CE', in: Angelika Fuchs, Horatia Muir Watt and Étienne Pattaut (eds.), *Les conflits de lois et le système juridique communautaire*, Paris: Dalloz 2004, pp. 81–100; Pascal de Vareilles-Sommières, 'La Compétence internationale de l'espace judicaire européen', in: Tristan Azzi et al. (eds.), *Vers de nouveaux équilibres entre ordres juridiques, Liber amicorum Hélène Gaudemet-Tallon*, Paris: Dalloz 2008, pp. 397–417.

to vote. Moreover, the Hague Conventions in force at that time did not foresee in the possibility of ratification by a non-state entity. Accession was thus not open to the Union, despite the fact that, after the entry into force of the Amsterdam Treaty, many of the issues covered by Hague Conventions fell within the competence of the Union. Although with regard to the latter problem, the Union could authorize the Member States to ratify a specific Convention in the interest of the EU,[24] the issue of the limited formal standing of the Union became an ever greater nuisance. The catalyst was the 'judgments project' initiated by the Hague Conference. On a proposal of the United States, it was decided at the 17th Session of the Hague Conference (1993) to place the question of jurisdiction, and recognition and enforcement of foreign judgments in civil and commercial matters on the agenda of the Hague Conference. Formal negotiations started in 1996, and by 1999, a preliminary draft Convention had been adopted. The draft Convention followed the approach of a mixed convention, meaning that it laid down both rules on jurisdiction as well as on recognition and enforcement of decisions in civil and commercial matters.[25]

The draft Convention thus significantly overlapped with the Brussels Convention on jurisdiction and the enforcement of foreign judgments in civil and commercial matters (1968). At the end of the 1990s, the Brussels Convention was also subject of legislative reforms and in the process of being transformed into the Brussels I Regulation. There was consensus that, at least with regard to the question of jurisdiction, the transformation of the Brussels Convention into a genuine instrument of Union law would result in the exclusive external competence of the Union.[26] The ongoing negotiations within the framework of the Hague Conference could not be interrupted pending the developments in Brussels. The immediate problem was resolved by the arrangement that the Union would be jointly

[24] See for example Council Decision 2003/93/EC of 19 December 2002 authorizing the Member States, in the interest of the Community, to sign the 1996 Hague Convention on jurisdiction, applicable law, recognition, enforcement and cooperation in respect of parental responsibility and measures for the protection of children, OJ [2003] L 48/1.

[25] Paul Beaumont, 'Hague Choice of Court Agreements Convention 2005: Background, Negotiations, Analysis and Current Status', (2009) 15 *Journal of Private International Law*, pp. 125–160.

[26] Charles Kotuby, 'External Competence of the European Community in the Hague Conference on Private International Law: Community Harmonization and Worldwide Unification', (2001) 48 *Netherlands International Law Review*, pp. 1–30, p. 21; Alegria Borrás, 'The Effect of the Adoption of Brussels I and Rome I on the External Competences of the EC and the Member States', in: Johan Meeusen, Marta Pertegas and Gert Straetmans (eds.), *Enforcement of International Contracts in the European Union*, Cambridge: Intersentia 2004, pp. 1107–1179.

represented in the negotiations by the European Commission, the European Parliament and the Council. The speaker's role was essentially fulfilled by the Commission and the national delegation of the Member State holding at that time the rotating Presidency of the Council.[27] Although the solution was pragmatic, the adoption of the Brussels I Regulation in 2000 made the absence of voting rights of the Union increasingly pressing. In December 2002, the European Union (at that time still: Community) formally applied for membership of the Hague Conference.[28]

5. The Negotiations in the Hague

5.1 *Regional Economic Integration Organization (REIO)*

The Statute of the Hague Conference were not modified since its foundation in 1955. As many international organizations shortly after the Second World War, this Statute followed the traditional state model and only endorsed the accession of states to the Conference. Consequently, accession was not possible for another international organization. However, drawing on the experience with the Judgments Project, there was significant political will on the side of the Hague Conference and its members to acknowledge the formal standing of the Union. At the occasion of its 20th session in 2005, a number of amendments to the Statute of the Hague Conference were approved. The most significant change was the insertion of a new article 3 which allowed for the accession of a Regional Economic Integration Organization to the Hague Conference.

The term 'Regional Economic Integration Organization' is defined in Article 3(9) as "an international organization that is constituted solely by sovereign States, and to which its Member States have transferred competence over a range of matters, including the authority to make decisions binding on its Member States in respect of those matters". The term was chosen to strive for consistency with other instruments of international law, such as the Constitution of the United Nations Food and Agricultural Organization, which had been likewise amended to enable the accession

[27] Wagner, *supra* n. 19, p. 221.

[28] Letter of Commissioner Vitorino requesting the admission of the European Communities to the Hague Conference of 19 December 2002.

of the Union.[29] The discussion on the notion 'REIO' preceding the 20th Session primarily related to larger geopolitical sensitivities that had little to do with PIL. Russia expressed concerns that the notion could exclude international organizations transcending national boundaries, such as the Eurasian Economic Community. On the other hand, China was afraid that an international organization of which Taiwan was a member could accede to the Hague Conference, and hence indirectly, provide Taiwan standing in the Hague Conference.[30]

In particular because the term 'REIO' is more widely used to enable the accession of the Union to international organizations, the amendment of the Statute of the Hague Conference was seized as an opportunity to make wider political statements to guarantee a solid negotiating position on the future accession of the Union to other international organizations. Be that as it may, for the purposes of Article 3(9), the term 'REIO' in Article 3(9) thus does not exclusively refer to the EU. However, since there is currently no other international organization to which members have transferred competence to adopt measures in the field of PIL, it is not to be expected that the example of the Union will soon be followed.[31]

5.2 *The Division of Competences between the Union and Its Member States in the Hague Conference*

The definition of 'REIO' was however not the most controversial object of debate. The members of the Hague Conference held varying opinions

---

29 The definitions are not completely the same. For example, contrary to the constitution of the FAO (Art. II (4), art. 3 (9) does not require that a majority of the members of the REIO are simultaneously members of the Conference.

30 Schulz, *supra* n. 13, p. 945. The definition of 'REIO' in the Statute of the Hague Conference is slightly different than in the FAO. Due to the Chinese objection, art. 3 (9) specifies that the international organization must be constituted solely by sovereign states. The meaning of 'constituted' immediately proved a source of ambiguity. Some delegations insisted that it referred to organizations being established by sovereign states, while other delegations supported the interpretation that an organization should consist out of sovereign states. In the former interpretation, an international organization would be eligible for Hague Conference membership if a non-state entity joined the international organization after its creation, while in the latter interpretation the date of accession to the Hague Conference is relevant. Hence, while in the first interpretation an international organization would be eligible for membership if Taiwan would join that international organization after its creation, in the second interpretation, Hague Conference membership would be barred if Taiwan would have become member at any point.

31 The Organization of American States (OAS) is also active in the area of PIL, but its members have not transferred any competence. The OAS merely coordinates, in the same way as the Hague Conference on a global level, cross-border cooperation in civil matters.

on the question how the internal division of competences between the Union and its Member States should be communicated towards non-EU Member States, and whether the Union should exercise its membership rights concurrently with the EU Member States or on an alternate basis. Although the exercise of membership rights and the communication of EU competences can be expected to constitute the more controversial issues in any accession of the Union to an international organization, the issues have to be seen through the specific perspective of the Hague Conference. Hague Conventions are prepared in a rather informal manner. It is only at the Diplomatic Session, when a draft Convention is finalized and official governmental positions are being expressed, where it would become important to ascertain whether the REIO or its Member States have the authority to make binding statements. With regard to the issue of voting, precisely in order to mitigate the dominance of EU Member States, since 2000, decisions were to the furthest extent possible taken on a basis of consensus.[32] The issue of whether the Union could express a single vote, or rather as many votes as there were EU Member States, thus seemed to have lost much of its relevance.

With regard to the issue of competence, some Hague Conference members found it necessary, however, to be able to ascertain whether the Union or the Member States were competent regarding a specific issue. As has been described above, there has been quite some ambivalence with regard to the external PIL competence of the Union.[33] The determination of whether the Union has competence on a specific issue can only be made on a case-by-case basis. Article 65 TEC merely provided the Union with the competence to act insofar as necessary for the internal market. At least a defensible argument could be made that the conclusion of international conventions in specific areas of PIL would not interfere with the measures adopted by the Union. The territorial scope of application of Brussels I Regulation was for example limited to defendants domiciled in a Member State.[34] The national rules of the Member States determined the international jurisdiction of their courts when the defendant was domiciled in a third country. Also the free movement of judgments only extends to judgments granted by a court in another Member

[32] Art. la Rules of Procedure of the Hague Conference.

[33] Hess, *supra* n. 23; Michael Wilderspin and Anne-Marie Rouchaud, 'La Compétence externe de la Communauté européenne en droit international privé', (2004) 93 *Revue Critique de Droit International Privé*, pp. 1–48.

[34] Art. 4 (1) Brussels I Regulation.

State. However a couple of months before the 20th Session of the Hague Conference, the European Court of Justice made clear in the *Owusu* case that the Brussels Convention was not intended to apply only to situations in which there would be a real and sufficient link with the working of the internal market, which would by definition involve a number of Member States. The common rules on jurisdiction were also applicable to a situation involving only one Member State and a third country.[35] The Brussels Convention could thus also affect the question of jurisdiction in disputes having a connection with a third country.

In fact, the external competences of the Union are to a large extent dependent on the exercise of its internal competences, and therefore not static. On the other hand, the scope of the projects in the Hague Conference is subject to continuous change as well. The Hague Conference Judgments Project for example started in 1996 with the aim of providing rules on jurisdiction and recognition and enforcement of judgments in civil and commercial matters, but was gradually narrowed down to choice of court agreements.[36] Therefore, requiring the Union to indicate its competences at the beginning of a new project would be highly impractical. The negotiations of new Conventions would, in the light of their evolution, have to be constantly interrupted with a view to verifying the Union's competence. A more flexible solution was therefore preferred. Article 3 provides:

(3) Each Regional Economic Integration Organisation applying for membership shall, at the time of such application, submit a declaration of competence specifying the matters in respect of which competence has been transferred to it by its Member States.
(4) Each Member Organisation and its Member States shall ensure that any change regarding the competence of the Member Organisation or in its membership shall be notified to the Secretary General, who shall circulate such information to the other Members of the Conference.
(5) Member States of the Member Organisation shall be presumed to retain competence over all matters in respect of which transfers of competence have not been specifically declared or notified.

---

35 ECJ, Case C-281/02, *Andrew Owusu* v *N. B. Jackson*, [2005], ECR I-1383. In more detail, see Thalia Kruger, *Civil Jurisdiction rules of the EU and their Impact on Third States*, Oxford: Oxford University Press 2008.

36 Beaumont, *supra* n. 25.

(6) Any Member of the Conference may request the Member Organisation and its Member States to provide information as to whether the Member Organisation has competence in respect of any specific question which is before the Conference. The Member Organisation and its Member States shall ensure that this information is provided on such request.

The basic rule is thus that upon accession, the REIO specifies in which areas its Member States have transferred competence onto it. When the EC finally acceded to the Hague Conference in 2007,[37] it however refrained from giving a detailed statement of its powers.[38] The declaration merely summarized the ECJ case-law relating to the doctrine of implied external powers, and indicated which internal legislative bases could potentially give rise to external powers in the area of PIL. Moreover, it provided for a list of Regulations and Directives that were adopted on the basis of Article 61(1)(c) in conjunction with Article 65 EC (currently art. 67 and 81 TFEU). The declaration concluded with the statement that "[t]he extent of competence which the Member States have transferred to the European Community pursuant to the EC Treaty is, by its nature, liable to continuous development", and the Community pledged that any change regarding its competences would be promptly notified to the Secretariat General of the Hague Conference.

At the time of accession, it would have been possible for the Union to provide a much more detailed indication of its competences. A year before the declaration was made, the ECJ delivered its *Lugano* Opinion.[39] The Lugano Convention sought to extend the regime established by the Brussels I Regulation to Iceland, Norway and Switzerland. According to the ECJ, the Lugano Convention could affect the internal rules of the Union or alter their scope. Because the system of jurisdictional rules in

---

[37] Council Decision of 5 October 2006 on the accession of the Community to the Hague Conference on Private International Law, OJ [2006] L 297/1.

[38] Declaration of competence of the European Community specifying the matters in respect of which competence has been transferred to it by its Member States, <http://www.hcch.net/index_en.php?act=status.comment&csid=992&disp=resdn>, as of 28 November 2009.

[39] ECJ, Opinion 1/03, *Competence of the Community to conclude the new Lugano Convention on jurisdiction and the recognition and enforcement of judgments in civil and commercial matters*, [2006] ECR I-1145. See also Marc Fallon, 'L'applicabilité du règlement ‹Bruxelles I› aux situations externes après l'avis 1/03', in: Tristan Azzi et al. (eds.), *Vers de nouveaux équilibres entre ordres juridiques, Liber Amicorum Hélène Gaudemet-Tallon*, Paris: Dalloz 2008, pp. 241–264.

civil and commercial matters was so closely intertwined with those relating to recognition and enforcement, the Union enjoyed an exclusive external competence in both areas. The *Lugano* Opinion therefore not only ended any remaining uncertainty about whether Article 65 EC provided the Union with the competence to act externally in the area PIL, but also decided that the Union could do so at the exclusion of the Member States.

The *Lugano* Opinion has consequences that bear well beyond Brussels I. By analogy, the Union would have equally, at least with regard to multilateral conventions, an exclusive external competence in the matters covered by Brussels II bis.[40] Yet, despite its pivotal importance, the declaration does not refer to the *Lugano* Opinion at all.

The Union has also refrained from providing a detailed account of the subsequent modifications of its powers. On 29 January 2010, a declaration was made that as from 1 December 2009, the date of entry into force of the Lisbon Treaty, the European Union replaced and succeeded the European Community, and would exercise all the Community's rights and assume its obligations, whilst continuing to exercise all existing rights and assume the obligations of the European Union. However, no mention was made of the fact that the Lisbon Treaty had also slightly broadened the Union's competences.[41] The consequence is that the declaration made by the Union upon its accession to the Hague Conference does not enable an innocent outsider to swiftly identify whether a particular issue falls within the sphere of competences of the EU or of the Member States.

---

[40] Pieter Jan Kuijper, 'The Opinion on the Lugano Convention and Implied External Relations Powers', in: Bernd Martenczuk and Servatius van Thiel (eds.), *Justice, Liberty and Security: New Challenges for EU External Relations*, Brussels: VUBPress 2008, pp. 187–210. Moreover, the fact that the Union considers the area covered by Brussels II bis as an exclusive external competence is evidenced by Regulation 664/2009 establishing a procedure for the negotiation and conclusion of agreements between Member States and third countries concerning jurisdiction, recognition and enforcement of judgments and decisions in matrimonial matters, matters of parental responsibility and matters relating to maintenance obligations, and the law applicable to matters relating to maintenance obligations. The Regulation first confirms the competence of the Union, but then, subject to prior authorization of the Commission, enables Member States to conclude under certain conditions bilateral agreements with third states. See Jan-Jaap Kuipers, 'The Exclusive Competence of the Union under art. 81 TFEU. Lugano re-opened?', in: Marise Cremona, Jörg Monar and Sara Poli (eds.), *The External Dimension of the Area of Freedom Security and Justice*, Brussels: Peter Lang Publishing 2011, pp. 287–322.

[41] Whereas art. 65 EC allowed the Community to act insofar as necessary for the functioning of the internal market, art. 81 TFEU allows the Union to act *in particular* when necessary for the internal market. The changed wording reflects that the measures adopted by the Union should not by definition be directed at regulating a situation between two Member States, as well as that the competence of the Union extends beyond commercial PIL.

The general indication of competences gives the Union a lot of room for maneuvering. Two mechanisms have been put in place to ensure legal certainty for the Hague Conference and its members.[42] The first is a presumption that EU Member States have retained competence over matters in which a transfer of competence has not been specifically declared or notified. The international partners are thus protected against any ambivalence surrounding the competences of the Union, by being able to fall back on a general rule. The second mechanism is the prerogative of any member of the Hague Conference to request the Union and its Member States to indicate who enjoys competence with regard to any specific question pending before the Conference. The request will be addressed to both the REIO and its member states, and it is a matter of their internal rules to decide who has to answer the request of the third country. Should it therefore become relevant to ascertain who may lawfully represent the Union, a member of the Hague Conference will be able to obtain legal certainty from the Union and its Member States.

The result is a workable compromise. A competence catalogue, or constitutional straightjacket, would have placed too much strain on the functioning of the Union in the Hague Conference. The declaration made by the Union upon accession to the Hague Conference is nothing more than a broad indication of its competences. It does not enable an outsider to identify with absolute certainty whether, with regard to a specific issue, the Union enjoys an exclusive or shared competence, or no competence at all. However, a more detailed account of Union competences is not necessary. As has already been mentioned several times before, the exact delimitation of competences between the Union and its Member States will not be such a contentious issue, since the participants in the preparatory meetings function in a somewhat intellectually independent way from the member they represent, and in the more politicized diplomatic session, decisions are adopted by consensus.

5.3 *Accession to Hague Conventions*

The precise division of competences becomes extremely important however once a Convention has been adopted by the Diplomatic Session. The question is whether the Union, the Member States, or both should

[42] The mechanism has been modeled after the United Nations Convention on the Law of the Sea (1982). Article 5 of Annex IX provides for a similar mechanism.

ratify the Convention. The Hague Conventions adopted after 2002, the date of the Union's official request to join the Conference, enable the accession of a REIO to that Convention. These Conventions all contain a clause requiring a REIO to notify at the latest at the time of signature, acceptance, approval or accession of the relevant Convention the precise delimitation of competences.[43] At that point in time, the REIO shall notify the depositary in writing of the matters governed by the Hague Convention in respect of which competence has been transferred to that REIO by its member states. A REIO may also declare that it exercises competence over all the matters governed by the Convention concerned, and that its member states will not be Parties to that Convention but shall be bound by virtue of the signature, acceptance, approval or accession of the organization.[44]

5.4 *Specific Issues on the Position of Denmark, Ireland and the United Kingdom*

Article 81 TFEU is part of Title V on the Area of Freedom, Security and Justice. Denmark, Ireland and the United Kingdom have a special position with regard to the measures adopted on the basis of that Title. While Ireland and the United Kingdom may decide ad hoc whether they participate in a specific measure, Denmark is not bound by such measures at all. The special position of these three Member States is referred to in the declaration of competence made by the Union upon its accession to the Hague Conference. Since measures adopted on the basis of Article 81 TFEU do not bind Denmark, that Member State can also not be bound by the signature or ratification of a Hague Convention by the Union if the subject matter of that Convention would have fallen within the scope of Article 81 TFEU. An example is the Brussels I Regulation. Since Denmark is not bound by this Regulation,[45] there can be no exclusive external competence of the Union. The Union therefore ratified the Hague Convention

[43] Art. 18(2) Hague Convention on the Law Applicable to Certain Rights in Respect of Securities held with an Intermediary (2006); Art. 29(2) Hague Convention on Choice of Court Agreements (2005); Art. 59 (2) Hague Convention on the International Recovery of Child Support and Other Forms of Family Maintenance (2007); Art. 24(2) Protocol on the Law Applicable to Maintenance Obligations (2007)

[44] The Securities Convention does not have a clause allowing such a declaration.

[45] It did conclude an international convention with the Union to reach the same substantial effects. Agreement between the European Community and the Kingdom of Denmark on jurisdiction and the recognition and enforcement of judgments in civil and

on Choice of Court Agreements, but stipulated that the term 'European Union', for the purposes of that Convention, does not include Denmark. With regard to Ireland and the United Kingdom, the Union will only ratify the Convention if the Member State has exercised its right to opt-in. The ratification of the Protocol on the Law Applicable to Maintenance Obligations (2007) by the Union thus did bind Ireland, but not the United Kingdom, since the latter Member State has not made use of its right to opt-in to Regulation 4/2009.[46]

5.5 *Exercise of Membership Rights*

Article 3(7) of the Statute of the Hague Conference stipulates that the REIO shall exercise "membership rights on an alternative basis with its Member States that are Members of the Conference, in the areas of their respective competences". Despite the wording of Article 3(7), it appears that EU Member States may still participate in the Hague Conference, in particular in the early preparatory stages of a new Convention, even if the Union enjoys exclusive external competence. The United States had initially proposed to add the words "including participation in meetings" after "membership rights", so as to exclude the simultaneous participation of the Union and its Member States in Hague Convention meetings.[47] The proposal was however not adopted in the final text of the Statute, because it was considered necessary to protect the open and informal style of preparing Hague Conventions. The preparatory meetings leading to a new Hague Convention involved many interrelated issues. If the Union and the Member States could only participate in the meetings on an alternative basis, the relevance of the contributions of both the Union and the Member States would risk being undermined. Since the issues are often closely interrelated, it would be very difficult for a delegate who is only allowed to participate in certain parts of the negotiations to make informed contributions in the sessions.[48] Despite the possibilities of sharing information on an informal basis between the Union and the Member States, there would probably still be a negative impact upon the quality

---

commercial matters, OJ 2005 299R/62; see Peter Arnt Nielsen, 'Brussels I and Denmark', (2007) 27 *IPRax*, pp. 506–509.

[46] 47th recital to the preamble of Regulation 4/2009.

[47] Schulz, *supra* n. 13, p. 947.

[48] Schulz, *supra* n. 13, p. 947.

of the debate. There was thus a consensus on the need to preserve some flexibility, and it was therefore preferred that the level of participation would be controlled by the Chair of the meetings.[49] Therefore, as Van Loon and Schulz put it, "the principle of non-additionality as expressed in paragraph 7 applies generally in the Conference, including to participation and eligibility for offices such as membership of drafting committees or other subsidiary bodies, but is to be applied with some flexibility in order to achieve the best results in negotiations."[50]

The right to vote in the meetings is addressed in Article 3(8). The general principle in the Hague Conference is that one delegation only has one vote. It has already been observed that the issue whether the Union could only cast one vote or the total number of votes of all EU Member States it represented may appear relatively unimportant, since decisions are to furthest extent possible taken by consensus. However, when it is not possible to obtain consensus, decisions of the Conference shall exceptionally be made by a majority of the votes cast by delegations present at the time of the vote.[51] Moreover, majority voting is preserved with regard to a few specific questions, such as the accession of new members.[52] Should a vote be necessary, it was proposed by some delegations to give the Union only a single vote, at the exclusion of the right to vote of the Member States, but that position was ultimately abandoned.[53] If it was accepted that the Union could only exercise one vote, it would also be reasonable to assume that the Union would only have to make a single financial contribution. That contribution would likely to be much lower than the sum of all contributions of the Member States. Whether it was for this (pragmatic) reason or not, a consensus emerged that the Union should exercise a number of votes equal to the number of Member States which have transferred competence to the Union in respect of the matter in question. The principle of non-additionality applies here as well. If the Union exercises its right to vote, the Member States shall not exercise theirs, and vice versa.[54] Although it is not necessary for the EU Member States to be actually present at the time of voting, they do need

---

49 Van Loon and Schulz, *supra* n. 12, p. 292.

50 Van Loon and Schulz, *supra* n. 12, p. 292.

51 Art. 8 (2) Statute of the Hague Conference; Art. 1a Rules of Procedure of the Hague Conference.

52 Art. 2 (2) of the Statute of the Hague Conference.

53 Schulz, *supra* n. 13, p. 948.

54 Art. 2 of the Rules of Procedure of the Hague Conference.

to register for the meeting, otherwise they forfeit the right of the Union to cast their vote.[55]

5.6 *Interim Conclusions*

The Union was already since the early 1960s informally recognized in the structure of the Hague Conference. As a consequence of the enlarging competences of the Union in the area of PIL, its formal status of observer became increasingly unsatisfactory. The catalyst was the Judgments Project in The Hague and the simultaneous revision of the Brussels I Regulation by the EU. The formal application of the EU for membership in 2002 was followed by an amendment of the Statute of the Hague Conference in 2005, and ultimately by the Union's accession in 2007. The amended Statute ensures due regard to the obligations of EU Member States under Union law, as well as safeguards the plurality of debate within the Hague Conference. The negotiations leading to the 2005 Statute of the Hague Conference thus allowed for a synergy between the Union and the Hague Conference, and could potentially serve as a model of best practice for future EU accessions to international organizations. In order to formulate an answer to the question whether the – perhaps – forced marriage has resulted in a good partnership, the next section will analyze in more detail the interplay between EU law and the Hague Conventions, after the Union's formal accession in 2007.

6. The Interplay between EU Law and the Hague Conventions

6.1 *Participation of the Union in the Hague Conference*

The Hague Conventions adopted after the formal application of the Union for membership all contain a clause enabling a REIO to accede to that Convention. Accession by the EU to Hague Conventions adopted before 2002 is impossible, unless they are modified. Three Hague Conventions and one Protocol allow for ratification by a REIO. The Union has in fact acceded to the Protocol on the Law Applicable to Maintenance Obligations, has signed the Convention on Choice of Court Agreements and the Convention on the International Recovery of Child Support and Other

[55] Schulz, *supra* n. 13, p. 948.

Forms of Family Maintenance. The Union has thus signed or acceded to three out of the four Hague instruments foreseeing the accession of a REIO. Compared to the other Conference members, the high number of ratifications and signatures by the Union is rather impressive. As evidenced by the Maintenance Regulation,[56] within the Union, there exists a great amount of respect for the work of the Hague Conference.[57] The Maintenance Regulation lays down common rules on jurisdiction and recognition and enforcement in matters relating to maintenance obligations within the Union, but for the determination of the applicable law, Article 15 refers directly to the Hague Protocol on the Law Applicable to Maintenance Obligations. Although the Hague Protocol has not yet received the minimum number of ratifications for it to enter into force,[58] the Union has made an unilateral declaration stipulating that the Member States will already apply the Hague Protocol in their mutual relations.[59] Although it is much too early to draw any general conclusions, it appears at least for the moment that the accession of the Union to the Hague Conference has not mitigated the commitment of European countries to the Hague Conference.

6.2 *Disconnection Clause*

Ensuring the continuing commitment of the Union and its Member States to the work of the Hague Conference was one the primary motives of the Hague Conference to accommodate the Union in the structure of the Hague Conference. From the perspective of the Union, however, the commitments undertaken within the framework of the Hague Conference

---

56 Regulation 4/2009 on jurisdiction, applicable law, recognition and enforcement of decisions and cooperation in matters relating to maintenance obligations. See Frédérique Ferrand, 'The Council Regulation (EC) no 4/2009 of 18 December 2008 on Jurisdiction, Applicable Law, Recognition and Enforcement of Decisions and Cooperation in Matters Relating to Maintenance Obligations', in: Beatriz Campuzano Díaz et al. (eds.), *Latest Developments in EU Private International Law*, Cambridge: Intersentia 2011, pp. 83–111.

57 Michael Traest, 'Over de Haagse Conferentie en het Europese IPR', (2010) *SEW – Tijdschrift voor Europees en Economisch Recht*, pp. 94–102.

58 Art. 25(1) requires a number of at least two ratifications. On April 18, 2012 Serbia has signed the Protocol, but has not yet deposited an instrument of ratification.

59 The reason can be found in art. 76 of the Maintenance Regulation: "Except for the provisions referred to in the second paragraph, this Regulation shall apply from 18 June 2011, subject to the 2007 Hague Protocol being applicable in the Community by that date. Failing that, this Regulation shall apply from the date of application of that Protocol in the Community." The entry into force of the Maintenance Regulation was thus made dependent upon the applicability of the Protocol. The Declaration can be accessed at <http://www.hcch.net/index_en.php?act=status.comment&csid=1065&disp=resdn>.

should not undermine the effectiveness and coherence of the EU instruments of PIL. It is important to underline that the Hague Conventions to which the Union has acceded will coexist alongside the EU PIL. Therefore, firm criteria are required to coordinate the scope of application of both sets of rules. For that purpose, the Hague Convention on Choice of Courts and the Hague Convention on the International Recovery of Child Support contain a disconnection clause distributing the application of these Conventions with the relevant rules of Union law.[60] The rationale behind a disconnection clause is that an international agreement should not replace the rules of Union law that apply between EU Member States. Disconnection clauses are thus used more widely in international agreements to ensure that the Member States will apply Union law in their mutual relations instead of the rules of the relevant international agreement.[61] However, as the ECJ recognized in the *Lugano* Opinion,[62] disconnection clauses do have a special dimension in PIL.[63]

The Hague Convention on Choice of Court Agreements provides an excellent illustration of this special disconnection clause in PIL.[64] As has already been mentioned, there the Convention may overlap with the rules of the Brussels I Regulation. For example, the Convention does not merely require Contracting Parties to recognize an exclusive choice of court clause as grounds for jurisdiction; it also contains rules concerning

[60] Art. 26 (6) of the Hague Convention of 30 June 2005 on Choice of Court Agreements; Art. 47 of the Hague Convention of 23 November 2007 on the International Recovery of Child Support and Other Forms of Family Maintenance. A disconnection clause is however for example not required in the Hague Protocol on the Law Applicable to Maintenance (2007) because Regulation 4/2009 on jurisdiction, applicable law, recognition and enforcement of decisions and cooperation in matters relating to maintenance obligations refers, in art. 15, the question of applicable law to the Hague Protocol.

[61] Constantin Economides and Alexandros Kolliopoulos, 'La clause de déconnexion en faveur du droit communautaire : un pratique critiquable', (2006) 110 *Revue générale de droit international public*, pp. 273–302 ; Marise Cremona, 'Disconnection Clauses in EC Law and Practice', in: Christophe Hillion and Panos Koutrakos (eds.), *Mixed Agreements Revisited – The EU and its Member States in the World*, Oxford: Hart Publishing 2010, pp. 160–186.

[62] *Lugano* Opinion, *supra* n. 39, par. 155.

[63] Alegria Borrás, 'Les clauses de déconnexion et le droit international privé communautaire', in: Heinz-Peter Mansel et al. (eds.), *Festschrift für Erik Jayme*, München: Sellier European Law Publishers 2004, pp. 57–72.

[64] Catherine Kessedjian, 'La Convention de La Haye du 30 juin 2005 sur l'élection de for', (2006) 133 *Journal du Droit International*, pp. 813–850; Rolf von Wagner, 'Das Haager Übereinkommen vom 30. 6. 2005 über Gerichtsstandsvereinbarungen', (2009) 73 *Rabels Zeitschrift für ausländisches und internationales Privatrecht*, pp. 100–149; Peter Arnt Nielsen, 'The Hague Judgements Conventions', (2011) 80 *Nordic Journal of International Law*, pp. 95–119.

the recognition and enforcement of judgments. After the Convention has entered into force, it will thus become necessary to determine whether a court in an EU Member State should seize jurisdiction either on the basis of Brussels I or on the basis of the Convention. Article 26 (6) provides that:

> This Convention shall not affect the application of the rules of a Regional Economic Integration Organisation that is a Party to this Convention, whether adopted before or after this Convention
>
> *a)* where none of the parties is resident in a Contracting State that is not a Member State of the Regional Economic Integration Organisation; *b)* as concerns the recognition or enforcement of judgments as between Member States of the Regional Economic Integration Organisation.

Contrary to the standard disconnection clause in EU external relations, the disconnection clause in the Choice of Court Convention does not have the effect of ensuring the applicability of Union law in every instance where it is applicable. For example, a party established in Austria and a party established in Italy may agree to litigate any dispute between them before the courts of London. In breach of the exclusive choice of court agreement, the Italian party brings an action for non-liability in Italian courts. Under Brussels I, the London court has to stay any subsequent proceeding brought concerning the same subject matter until the Italian court has ruled on its jurisdiction (lis pendens). The bringing of a claim before a manifestly incompetent court, referred to as an 'Italian Torpedo', is often used as a litigation tactic with the aim of delaying the actual proceedings.[65] The Italian Torpedo will however be less effective if the choice of court agreement was made between an Italian and a Californian company. After the Italian company has launched proceedings in Italy, the Californian company may respond by initiating proceedings in London in accordance with the choice of court agreement. The dispute would fall within the scope of application of Brussels I, and Article 23 would again require the London court to stay the proceedings. However, since both parties are established in a state that has acceded to the Hague Convention, the disconnection

[65] ECJ, Case C-116/02, *Erich Gasser GmbH* v *MISAT Srl*, [2003] ECR I-14693. See Mario Franzosi, 'Worldwide Patent Litigation and the Italian Torpedo', (1997) 19 *European Intellectual Property Law Review*, pp. 382–385; Isabella Betti, 'The Italian Torpedo is Dead: Long Live the Italian Torpedo', (2008) 3 *Journal of Intellectual Property Law & Practice*, pp. 6–7. The issue of the Italian Torpedo is taken up in the revision of Brussels I. The Heidelberg Report proposes to modify Brussels I to the effect that courts other than the chosen court have no jurisdiction unless the chosen court has determined its jurisdiction Burkhard Hess, Thomas Pfeiffer and Peter Schlosser, 'General Report of the Study on the Application of Regulation Brussels I' (Heidelberg Report), Study JLS/C4/2005/03 (2007).

clause would apply and require the applicability of the Convention.[66] As main rule, the Convention does not oblige the chosen court to stay proceedings but instead obliges the court not chosen to dismiss proceedings.[67] Whereas the London court cannot hear the case in the former situation, it can in the latter. The rules of the Convention will thus take precedence over Brussels I, despite the fact that the relation between an English and Italian court is at stake.[68]

The disconnection clause in the Choice of Court Convention is not meant to guarantee the application of Brussels I every time it is applicable. The Choice of Court Convention will prevail if one of the parties is domiciled in a non-EU Member State, provided that the respective state has ratified the Convention. The disconnection clause thus differs from general disconnection clauses seeking to regulate the concurrent application of an international agreement and Union law. The justification lies in the particularity of PIL and the objectives pursued by the Hague Conference. The development and implementation of common rules of PIL, in order to co-ordinate the relationships between different private law systems in international situations, means that individual members of the Hague Conference cannot always insist upon the mandatory application of their own laws. There would be little point for non-EU Member States to accede to the Choice of Court Convention if the EU Member States would continue to apply Brussels I to situations where a party is domiciled in a third country. Greater convergence in civil procedure can only come about when the members are prepared to make concessions when a foreign party is involved. However, precisely because of the fact that the international convention may alter the scope of the applicable instruments of Union law, the EU will possess an exclusive external competence.

7. Conclusion

The recognition of the European Union in the framework of the Hague Conference could very well function as a best practice. Despite the initially rather limited competences in private international law, already in

---

[66] Trevor Hartley and Masato Dogauchi, *Explanatory Report Convention of 30 June 2005 on Choice of Court Agreements*, para. 309 and 310. Available at: <http://www.hcch.net/upload/expl37e.pdf>, as of 30 April 2012.

[67] Art. 5 and 6 of the Hague Convention on Choice of Courts.

[68] The consequence is thus that in the same situation, an American company would enjoy a better protection against an Italian torpedo than a European company.

1960, the precursor of the EU was awarded the status of formal observer. This swift recognition can be explained by the fact that it were traditionally the European states that were active in the Hague Conference, which could thus exercise significant influence on the recognition of the Union, and by the fact that the initial phases of preparing a Hague Convention are rather informal. In the informal stages, participants in drafting committees enjoy a large amount of intellectual autonomy, and primarily participate as experts, rather than national delegates. More importantly perhaps, the Hague Conference had a clear interest to accommodate the EU in its structure, for the Union's gradually enlarging competences and expanding activity in the field of PIL constituted a direct threat to the pertinence of the Hague Conference. The reaction of the Conference was twofold. Firstly, the Conference sought to reduce its dependence on European states, by stimulating non-European states to join the Conference and promoting the ratification of Hague Conventions across the globe. Secondly, the Hague Conference responded by amending its Statute, in order to allow for the Union's formal accession. Overall, the response of the Hague Conference has been rather successful. The publicity campaign has made the Hague Conference much less dependent on the internal developments within the Union, while the latter's formal accession has ensured the continuing commitment of EU Member States to the Conference.

The eventual formalization of the Union's position in the Hague Conference strikes a delicate balance between the special needs of the Union legal order on the one hand, and the traditional functioning of the Hague Conference on the other. In the informal stages, depending upon the degree of flexibility required, the Union and its Member States may cumulatively participate in the deliberations. This arrangement safeguards the plurality of debate in the Conference, which is essential for the preparation of a new Convention. The principle of non-additionality will apply more formally once the stage of official drafting committees has been reached, and with regard to the exercise of formal membership rights (such as the right to vote). Moreover, the arrangement allows the EU Member States to comply with their obligations under EU law, while at the same time, it leaves sufficient flexibility to do justice to the spirit of the Hague Conference. The reconciliation of objectives also becomes apparent in the Hague Choice of Court Convention. Its disconnection clause allows the Member States to apply, in most instances, the Brussels I Regulation in their mutual relations, but does not guarantee the application of that instrument in every scenario where it is applicable. Thus, the mandatory application of Brussels I has been sacrificed by the Union on the altar of civil cooperation at the global level, which serves the primary objective of the Hague Conference.

Whereas initially, the gradually increasing activity of the EU in the field of PIL constituted a threat to the pertinence of the Hague Conference, the latter has managed to change the tide in a manner that is fully consistent with its own statutory goals. All in all, the Union's recognition in the framework of the Hague Conference constitutes an excellent example of a fruitful cooperation between two international organizations.

CHAPTER EIGHT

THE EU'S INTERNATIONAL IDENTITY: THE CURIOUS CASE OF THE OECD

*Joren Verschaeve and Tamara Takács**

1. Introduction

Ever since the promotion of effective multilateralism became a key objective of the European Union's foreign policy, scholars have been increasingly studying the relationship between the EU and other international organizations (IOs).[1] Up until now, however, the relationship with the Organization for Economic Co-operation and Development (OECD) has barely gained academic attention. This is extremely remarkable as the OECD covers a wide range of policy areas in which the EU upholds strong competences or has clear international leadership ambitions, e.g. trade, climate or development cooperation. Therefore, in order to fill this gap in literature, this chapter provides a first systematic overview of the EU's identity in the OECD. In so doing, we build upon empirical data retrieved from interviews with EU and OECD officials, document analysis (OECD archives), and participatory observations.

This chapter begins with a brief description of the origins of the OECD (2.1), its mandate, structure and functioning (2.2) and membership (2.3). Then, we take a closer look at the EU's identity in the OECD and demonstrate that it is better to refer to a multiplicity of Union identities rather than a single one. In order to explain this unusual situation, we develop a general framework (3.1) in which we unravel the EU's identity into four dimensions. Next, we take a closer look at the Union's day-to-day position in two important OECD Committees (3.2) – the Economic Development and Review Committee (EDRC) and the Development Assistance

* The authors are grateful to officials at the European Commission and the European External Action Service in Brussels, the EU Delegation to the OECD and DAC delegates in Paris, who all provided invaluable insight through interviews (referenced below), and wish to remain anonymous.

[1] Knud Erik Jørgensen, *The European Union and International Organizations*, London: Routledge 2009, p. 188.

Committee (DAC) – in order to put our framework to the test. Finally, we conclude with some general reflections on the EU's international identities in the OECD and show that, despite this multiplicity, the EU holds a much stronger position in this Organization than in many other IOs.

2. The OECD in a Nutshell

2.1 *History*

The OECD is an intergovernmental organization that promotes global economic and social well-being. It was established in Paris in 1961, but its origins go back to 1948, as the OECD succeeded the earlier established Organization for European Economic Co-operation (OEEC). This European organization administered the Marshall Plan for the reconstruction of Europe, but by the end of the 1950s, its very existence was heavily criticized for two major reasons. On the one hand, the Marshall Plan had already evaporated by 1952, and by the end of that decade, all Western economies had recovered from the Second World War. On the other hand, the OEEC was also contested by two newly established organizations, the European Economic Community (EEC) and the European Free Trade Association (EFTA), which quickly became the new driving forces behind further European integration. As a result, the OEEC increasingly became an irrelevant player, counting its last days.[2]

The OEEC was nevertheless not truly abolished, as the organization was replaced by the OECD in 1961, after the signing of the Convention on 14 December 1960. The rationale behind this transformation was twofold. On the one hand, transatlantic relations in the late fifties were more problematic than ever before. Especially the relationship between the French president, Charles de Gaulle, and the US became increasingly tense on a number of NATO issues. Moreover, Western countries were divided on whether to follow a supranationalist (EEC) or intergovernmentalist (EFTA) path towards European integration. Therefore, the US wanted to establish a permanent forum for transatlantic cooperation, the OECD, in order to streamline Western relations.[3] On the other hand the US, UK and other EFTA members were also frightened by the creation of the

---

[2] See, generally, Richard Woodward, *The Organization for Economic Co-operation and Development*, London: Routledge 2009.

[3] Peter Carroll and Aynsley Kellow, *The OECD: A Study of Organisational Adaptation*, Cheltenham: Edward Elgar Publishing 2011, pp. 45–65.

EEC Common Market, as Article 1 of the Rome Treaty foresaw an economic liberalization that went far beyond traditional free trade areas. Therefore, in order to counter a possible discriminatory impact of this project, both the US and UK wanted to create a legal basis to weigh upon the EEC's economic policies. Moreover, the EEC members themselves also wanted to create a Western forum for economic cooperation in order to institutionalize their relations with all major non-EEC economies.[4]

2.2 *Mandate, Functioning and Structure*

The OECD's overarching objective is to promote "(...) the economic and social well-being of people around the world".[5] In so doing, the OECD holds a very broad and flexible mandate. Article 1 of the OECD Convention stipulates more specifically that the Organization shall promote policies designed to:

> a. (...) achieve the highest sustainable economic growth and employment and a rising standard of living in Member countries, while maintaining financial stability, and thus to contribute to the development of the world economy;
>
> b. (...) contribute to sound economic expansion in Member as well as non-member countries in the process of economic development; and
>
> c. (...) contribute to the expansion of world trade on a multilateral, non-discriminatory basis in accordance with international obligations.

Given this broadly defined mandate, the OECD covers virtually all (socio-) economic policy areas, varying from e.g. macro-economy policy, environment, corruption, employment, agriculture to taxation, education, development, trade or science.[6] Only in the fields of defense, culture and sports does it lack competences.[7] As a result, the OECD holds a rather unique

---

[4] Robert Wolfe, 'From Reconstructing Europe to Constructing Globalization: The OECD in Historical Perspective', in: Rianne Mahon and Stephen McBride (eds.), *The OECD and Transnational Governance*, Vancouver: University of British Columbia Press 2008, pp. 25–43; Richard T. Griffiths, 'An Act of Creative Leadership: The End of the OEEC and the Birth of the OECD', in: Richard T. Griffiths (ed.), *Explorations in OEEC History*, Paris: OECD Press 1997, pp. 235–250.

[5] OECD website, < http://www.oecd.org/about>.

[6] Carroll and Kellow, *supra* n. 3, pp. 8–11.

[7] Nicola Bonnuci and Gita Kothari, *Organization for Economic Cooperation and Development*, Max Planck Encyclopedia of Public International Law, available at http://www.mpeil.com.

position in the constellation of IOs, as most of its counterparts have a much more narrow and well-defined mandate.

When taking a closer look at the OECD's functioning, it also becomes clear that the Organization operates in a very distinctive way given its unique mix of soft-law working methods. As described by Martin Marcussen, the OECD is "the archetypical example of an international organization that governs through deliberation, persuasion, surveillance and self-regulation", and is "designed to be a meeting place, primarily for national civil servants with a focus on dialogue among equals".[8] It thus serves as a forum in which its members can share any kind of information, discuss best practices and seek solutions to common problems. These discussions are largely informal and deliberative with the member states in the driving seat, as opposed to the 'staff-driven' nature of other IOs.[9] As a result, the OECD functions as a forum for permanent consultation and international consensus building on almost all topics, varying from highly politicized issues[10] to technical discussions.[11] Therefore, it can be said to function as the "quintessential host of transgovernmental regulatory networks, as well as the catalyst for their creation".[12]

The OECD is also renowned for its statistical data, as its Secretariat collects and analyzes data, monitors trends and forecasts developments in all of the Organization's policy areas. This results in a wide range of policy options that member states (and others) can take into consideration.[13] The OECD, finally, also develops shared policies or standards in the form of binding decisions[14] or non-binding recommendations. In order to assess the implementation of the latter, periodic 'peer reviews' are conducted, a process in which one member's practices are evaluated by the rest of the

---

[8] Martin Marcussen, 'OECD Governance through Soft Law', in: Ulrika Mörth, *Soft Law in Governance and Regulation*, Cheltenham: Edward Elgar 2004, p. 103.

[9] Nicholas Bayne, 'Plurilateralism and Multilateralism: Comparing Institutions', in: Stephen Woolcock and Nicholas Bayne (eds.), *The New Economic Diplomacy: Decision-Making and Negotiation in International Economic Relations*, Farnham: Ashgate 2011, p. 212.

[10] On trade or climate, for example, the OECD has frequently served as a platform for reviving stalled international negotiations at the GATT/WTO or UN level.

[11] Bob Reinalda, *Routledge History of International Organizations: From 1815 to the Present Day*, London: Routledge 2009, p. 424.

[12] Anne-Marie Slaughter, *A New World Order*, Princeton: Princeton University Press 2004, p. 46.

[13] Woodward, *supra* n. 2, pp. 43–62.

[14] This, however, only happens on very rare occasions (e.g. the 1998 Convention on combating bribery of foreign public officials in international business transactions).

OECD members and the Secretariat.[15] Given this unique mixture of working methods, it has been noted that the OECD serves as an example for "the next generation of international organizations".[16] It enjoys three particular strengths: its capacity for cross-issue analysis (i.e., its 'horizontal' work) that covers a remarkable range of issues; the linkage between the analytical work of the Secretariat and policy-making in member capitals; and the coherence that comes from non-universal membership.[17]

Finally, it is also important to elaborate on the OECD's structure, as it is a strongly decentralized entity. Its center of gravity lies within its more than 250 committees, working parties or subgroups, even though the OECD Council[18] holds de facto the decision-making powers.[19] This can be explained by the fact that most of the work and interactions between the member states and OECD staff takes place within these bodies. Moreover, the OECD Convention itself also provides all first-level committees, which are the most important ones, a great deal of autonomy, as they determine their own agenda, working pace and the level of involvement of non-OECD members, NGOs and other IOs.[20] First-level committees can even establish new subcommittees and/or working parties with specific responsibilities.[21] This renders the OECD an amalgam of committees, each pursuing their own agendas in varying ways. As a result, one may conclude that the OECD is probably one of the most complex IOs, with a structure that proves extremely difficult to fathom.

---

[15] Anja Jakobi and Kerstin Martens, 'Conclusion: Findings, Implications, and Outlook of OECD Governance', in: Anja Jakobi and Kerstin Martens (eds.), *Mechanisms of OECD Governance*, Oxford: Oxford University Press 2010, pp. 260–279; Martin Marcussen, 'Multilateral surveillance and the OECD: Playing the Idea Game', in: Klaus Armingeon and Michelle Beleyer (eds.), *The OECD and European Welfare States*, Cheltenham: Edward Elgar Publishing 2004, pp. 13–32.

[16] James Salzman, 'The Organization for Economic Cooperation and Development's Role in International Law', (2011) 43 *George Washington International Law Review*, p. 256.

[17] Ken Heydon, 'The OECD: Lessons from Investment and Services', in: Stephen Woolcock and Nicholas Bayne (eds.), *The New Economic Diplomacy: Decision-making and Negotiation in International Economic Relations*, Farnham: Ashgate 2011, p. 232.

[18] The OECD Council is a permanent intergovernmental conference that brings together the members at the ministerial or permanent representative level (including the European Union) and meets twice a year.

[19] Convention on the OECD, Art. 7 and Art. 10(2).

[20] Woodward, *supra* n. 2, pp. 43–62.

[21] Carroll and Kellow, *supra* n. 3, pp. 31–45.

2.3 *Membership*

The membership of the OECD is in essence global, thus not limited to a particular region or group of countries. However, Western countries and especially EU (members) are overrepresented, given the Organization's 'European history', as detailed above.[22] Currently, twenty-one out of the thirty-four OECD members[23] are EU countries, and only seven member states are non-European (though equally wealthy). Because of this composition, the OECD is frequently referred to as a "rich man's club".[24] In more recent years however, it is strongly attempting to abandon this exclusive image, by pursuing good relations with a large number of third countries (especially the BRICS), civil society actors, the G20,[25] and a large number of other IOs such as the UN, FAO or ILO.[26]

Up until now, this 'outreach strategy' has only been partly successful. Apart from some reluctance from the side of the BRICS,[27] one of the major causes concerns the involvement of the 'recent' EU member states in the OECD. In particular, all non-EU members of the OECD, usually referred to as the APEC Group, expressed a notable resentment against including additional EU members, as they felt that the European Union was already more than sufficiently represented in the OECD. Eventually a compromise was reached on this issue, and both the EU and APEC agreed to grant membership to these countries as long as it would not disturb the 'balance of power', i.e. as long as non-EU countries were to join simultaneously.[28] As a result, Slovenia and Estonia were able to join the OECD in 2010 together with Israel and Chile. This means that countries of all

---

[22] Richard Woodward, *supra* n. 2, pp. 2–8.

[23] The OECD members are: Australia, Austria, Belgium, Canada, Chile, Czech Republic, Denmark, Estonia, Finland, France, Germany, Greece, Hungary, Iceland, Ireland, Israel, Italy, Japan, Korea, Luxembourg, Mexico, The Netherlands, New Zealand, Norway, Poland, Portugal, Spain, Sweden, Switzerland, Slovak Republic, Slovenia, Turkey, United Kingdom and United States.

[24] Rianne Mahon and Stephen McBride, 'Introduction', in: Rianne Mahon and Stephen McBride (eds.), *The OECD and Transnational Governance*, Vancouver: UBC Press 2008, p. 3.

[25] See Jan Wouters and Sven Van Kerckhoven, 'The OECD and the G20: An Ever Closer Relationship?', (2011) 43 *George Washington International Law Review*, pp. 345–374.

[26] OECD/C(2006)78/REV1/Final, *Revised resolution of the council on a new governance structure for the organisation*, 10/02/2011.

[27] Currently only Russia shows ambition for becoming a member of the OECD in the nearby future.

[28] Andrew Beatty, 'EU Gives Ground in OECD Membership Battle', *European Voice*, 4 April 2007.

continents are represented in the OECD, with the sole exception of Africa. Nonetheless, OECD membership still remains much more restrictive than for example, the UN or WTO, as developing countries are not represented in the Organization.[29]

3. The EU–OECD Relationship

As remarked above, the OECD is a highly decentralized organization, structured around more than 250 committees, sub-committees and working groups. Therefore, when studying the EU–OECD relationship, one is in fact confronted with a large and varying set of relations, as the bulk of interactions between both organizations take place within this heterogeneous committee structure.[30] Moreover, the EU–OECD relationship also displays great variations in tenor and significance, as the latter's mandate covers the whole spectrum of EU powers, varying from exclusive and shared competences (e.g. trade, development cooperation) to policy areas in which the Union has no competences (e.g. taxation). Therefore, it has been argued that it is "probably fruitless to talk about the relationship between the EU and the OECD", since much depends on the particular committee or issue one is looking at.[31]

Indeed, the multiplicity of relations between both organizations makes it nearly impossible to put forward general statements on the EU's international identity in the OECD. Nonetheless, in this chapter, we seek to capture EU–OECD relationship(s) by putting forward a general framework of analysis in which we distinguish five dimensions of the EU's identity in the OECD (paragraph 3.1 below). Moreover, we argue that one can only arrive at sound conclusions with regard to the Union's identity in a respective OECD body by making an in-depth analysis of the interplay of these dimensions. This claim is supported by the two case studies incorporated in this chapter (paragraph 3.2), as they exemplify that the EU's day-to-day identity in the OECD varies considerably.

---

[29] Ludo Cuyvers and Bart Kerremans, *Internationale Economische Organisaties*, Leuven: Garant 1999, pp. 87–105; Woodward, *supra* n. 2, p. 2 and p. 55.

[30] Carroll and Kellow, *supra* n. 3.

[31] Peter Carroll and Aynsley Kellow, 'The EU in International Organizations: The Case of the OECD', in: *Proceedings of the Fifth ECPR General Conference 2009*, p. 10.

3.1 *Dimensions of the EU Identity in the OECD*

3.1.1 *Legal Status*

A first dimension of the EU's identity in the OECD concerns its legal status in the organization, as this determines to what extent the Union is able to participate in the organization's work. Back in 1961, the EEC's legal status in the OECD triggered a highly politicized and contentious debate. As already emerged from our earlier discussion, the EEC fatally undermined the OEEC's *raison d'être*, and the conflicts between EEC and EFTA countries on the European Common Market sparked the formation of the OECD.[32] In this highly politicized context, the European Commission itself made a strong plea for full membership of the OECD. On one occasion Walter Hallstein[33] even went to Washington to garner support for this idea.[34] He had little success though, as most countries perceived membership of the EEC, a supranational IO, as contradicting the OECD's intergovernmental nature. Some countries also feared that this could set a precedent for other IOs, or generally rejected the idea of surrendering national sovereignty to an international organization, while others opposed EEC membership, as this would further strengthen the European overrepresentation within the OECD.[35]

As a result, the EEC missed out on OECD membership in 1961. However, the European Commission – in representation of the EEC – did obtain a particular status short of full membership. In a Supplementary Protocol to Article 13 of the Convention on the OECD, the signatory countries agreed that the European Commission "shall take part in the work of the Organization".[36] In so doing, Commission representatives were allowed to work alongside members in the preparation of texts, participate in discussions on the OECD's work program and strategies, and are involved in the work of the entire Organization and its different bodies.[37] Moreover, they can even (co-)chair OECD committees, or be elected to their respective

[32] Robert Wolfe, 'From Reconstructing Europe to Constructing Globalization: The OECD in Historical Perspective', in: Rianne Mahon and Stephen McBride (eds.), *The OECD and Transnational Governance*, Vancouver: University of British Columbia Press 2008, pp. 25–43.

[33] The first President of the European Commission (1958–1969).

[34] US Department of State, Office of the Historian, *Foreign Relations of the US (Vol. VII)*, 1959, documents 34–56.

[35] Carroll and Kellow, *supra* n. 3, p. 202.

[36] Convention on the OECD, *Supplementary protocol No. 1 of the Convention on the OECD*, 1960.

[37] OECD, Rules of Procedure of the Organisation (2011), pp. 7–9.

bureaus.[38] In 2012, the EU participates in 204 committees or subsidiary organs, chairs four, and vice-chairs twelve of them.[39] Only when decisions and recommendations are presented before the Council, the EU has no voting rights. In reality, however, this seldom happens, and if the OECD Council adopts a binding decision this is generally done by consensus.[40]

Therefore, if all the aforementioned elements are taken together, one can conclude that the EU's legal status in the OECD goes beyond that of a mere observer. This is why the EEAS, diplomats and scholars refer to it as a 'quasi-membership' of the OECD.[41] It should be noted though that the EU exceeds this 'quasi-membership' status in a small number of OECD bodies where it enjoys full membership. This can be explained by the large autonomy which some OECD committees enjoy in determining their own composition, as already described above. A first clear example relates to the Steel Committee that, ever since its creation in 1978, counts the EU among its full members.[42] This also holds for the Development and Assistance Committee, one of the most important OECD bodies, where the EU enjoys a full membership.[43]

3.1.2 *Coordination*

A second dimension of the EU's identity in the OECD relates to the coordination between the Union and its Member States, as this determines whether the EU can be seen as a single-voiced actor rather than an amalgam of different voices within the OECD. This focus on coordination is relevant for three important reasons. First, the OECD covers a large number of policy areas in which the necessity of coordination is self-evident (e.g. shared competences). Second, EU coordination is also needed in order to involve the non-OECD members of the Union in the work of the Organization. Third, there is a strong belief among a number of EU actors that

38 Carroll and Kellow, *supra* n. 31, pp. 1–7.

39 <http://webnet.oecd.org/oecdgroups/bodies/listbyroleview.aspx>

40 Woodward, *supra* n. 2, pp. 43–62.

41 Michele Comelli and Raffaello Matarazzo, 'Rehashed Commission Delegations or Real Embassies? EU Delegations Post Lisbon', 2011 1123 *IAI Working Papers*, p. 10; Sieglinde Gstöhl, 'Patchwork Power Europe? The EU's Representation in International Institutions', (2008) 2 *Bruges Regional Integration & Global Governance Papers*, pp. 15–16.

42 Decision of the Council establishing a Steel Committee, 26 October 1978, C(78)171(Final).

43 Carroll and Kellow, *supra* n. 3, pp. 207–209.

a 'single-voiced Europe' strengthens the Union's international position.[44] This is especially relevant in the case of the OECD, given the EU's numerical strength within the Organization.

Nonetheless, one should also be careful not to exaggerate the EU's coordination efforts. Because the OECD covers the entire gamut of EU competences, there are also a number of policy areas in which the Union is de jure forbidden to coordinate because it lacks competences, or is de facto unable to do so because of the sensitive nature of the issues discussed. On a number of topics there is also little need to coordinate, due to the nature of the OECD being a deliberative forum aiming at information sharing instead of position-taking. Bearing these nuances in mind, we choose to center our inquiry on those OECD issues where the EU engages intensively in coordination with its Member States (e.g. trade issues).[45] Hereby, we distinguish between the efforts that are undertaken within the EU institutions in Brussels and the coordination activities within the EU Delegation in Paris.

3.1.2.1 *Coordination in Brussels*

The European Commission is – and has always been – in charge of the overall coordination with regard to issues lying in the purview of the OECD. When we focus on the intra-Commission coordination, all Directorates-general (DGs) follow up on the issues falling within their respective competences and decide to what extent EU coordination is desirable with the Member States. In so doing, a number of DGs strongly favor a 'single-voiced Europe', while other take in a more pragmatic stand depending on the issue at hand or their available resources.[46] Within this system of intra-Commission coordination, DG Trade functions as a central clog, conducting the overall coordination via daily contacts with the respective desk officers in the other DGs. Moreover, DG Trade also steers an inter-service group (with participation of desk officers from the various DGs as well as the EEAS) to discuss pertinent horizontal OECD issues and

---

[44] Knud Erik Jørgensen and Ramses Wessel, 'The Position of the European Union in (Other) International Organizations: Confronting Legal and Political Approaches', in: Panos Koutrakos (ed.), *European Foreign Policy: Legal and Political Perspectives*, Cheltenham: Edward Elgar Publishing 2011, pp. 261–287.

[45] What follows draws largely on interviews conducted with officials in the Commission DG Trade in June 2012.

[46] Interview with a Commission official at DG Trade, Brussels, 15 June 2012.

questions related to the OECD's general functioning, such as accession or relations with third parties.[47]

Coordination between the Commission and the Member States takes place within the Council of the EU. In so doing, most DGs have adopted a pattern of coordination similar to the one encouraged by DG Trade. This means that the respective Committee and Working Parties of the Council – in casu the Trade Policy Committee (TPC) – serve as the forum in which the dialogue between the Commission and the Members States takes place. This can be both via written note or via discussions. Horizontal issues or questions related to the OECD's general functioning are dealt with in the TPC, even though they are not always in line with the scope of this Committee.[48]

Finally, it is also important to take a closer look at the European External Action Service (EEAS). With the entry into force of the Lisbon Treaty, all parties felt that DG Trade should continue to uphold its central coordinating role, as it was a flexible, well-functioning mechanism. However, since the EEAS is preoccupied with the EU's external representation, and because the OECD also deals with a number of multilateral issues, DG Trade now has to cooperate quite closely with this new Service, more specifically the EEAS's OECD coordinator from Managing Directorate VI, *Multilateral Relations and Global Issues*. The EEAS is consulted regularly on the rather 'political' OECD issues such as accession, relations with non-members, relations with the G20 or discussions that involve 'specific issues, themes related to countries or regions'.[49] So far, it is still unclear how this will influence the EU coordination in Brussels as the current situation remains a bit blurry, but one can conclude that it is very likely that the EEAS will have an increasing impact on the EU coordination and the role of DG Trade within this process.

3.1.2.2 *Coordination in Paris*

Also in Paris, the entry into force of the Lisbon Treaty spelled a number of important changes for EU coordination. Traditionally, the European Commission's Representation to the OECD (now EU Delegation), was in charge of the coordination on all issues falling under Community competences. In

47 Interview with an official at the EU Delegation to the OECD, Paris 5 September 2012.

48 Interviews with officials at DG Trade, and at the EU Delegation to the OECD, September 2012.

49 Interview with EEAS official, Brussels, 20 September 2012.

so doing, coordination meetings were organized by the Commission Representation and chaired by the representative of the country holding the Presidency. This changed significantly after 2009 as these coordination meetings are now organized and led by diplomats of the EU Delegation, or the European Commission when the former lacks capacities in the respective policy area.

An arrangement by the Belgian Council Presidency in 2010 aimed to ensure a more effective transition towards post-Lisbon cooperation and coordination[50] with the "withdrawal of the rotating Presidency from representing the EU".[51] If we take a closer look at this 'Belgian arrangement' (which was never formally adopted, yet seems to be the modus vivendi in Paris), it becomes clear that the role of the Presidency has evolved to assisting the EU Delegation in e.g. preparing common positions or organizing coordination meetings. These meetings are organized at the initiative of the EU Delegation – or on request of the Commission or one of the Member States – and take place at the level of the ambassadors, deputies and committees. Next to these coordination meetings, there are also monthly lunch meetings at ambassadors' and deputy level in which information is exchanged and possible common positions are identified.[52]

Finally, it is also important to note that the EU Delegation in Paris is not only concerned with coordination efforts among the EU Members represented in the OECD, but also tries, as much as possible, to involve those Member States that are not represented in the Organization. In so doing, a number of meetings are organized with a special emphasis on their respective interests.[53] In sum, one may conclude that the EU and its Member States have established a well-functioning coordination system in Paris. Especially when comparing it with the coordination in Brussels, the Lisbon Treaty has been fully operationalized here and poses no real unclarities.

3.1.3 *Representation*

A third dimension of the EU's international identity in the OECD relates to the Union's representation in Paris. This is extremely relevant as it not

50 Comelli and Matarazzo, *supra* n. 41, p. 10.

51 Rosa Balfour et al., *Upgrading the EU's Role as Global Actor*, Brussels: CEPS 2011, p. 97.

52 Interview with officials at the EU Delegation to the OECD in September 2012.

53 Implementation of the Lisbon Treaty; EU coordination and representation in OECD including IEA and NEA; Working arrangements between the EU Delegation and the Belgian Permanent Representation to the OECD.

only determines who speaks on behalf of the EU, but also to what extent the respective actor is able to do so (e.g. staff skills). If we now take a closer look at the EU representation in the OECD one must depart from the Treaty of Rome, as Article 231 TEEC mandated the European Commission to establish a 'close cooperation' with the OECD. This resulted inter alia in the opening of the Commission's Representation in Paris in 1964, composed of an ambassador and diplomats representing the EU institutions in (former) first pillar policy areas. Statements and declarations of the entire Union (and Community) were issued by the rotating Presidency, which intervened during the meetings in its individual capacity as an OECD member.

This changed significantly with the entry into force of the Lisbon Treaty, as the EU was finally granted international legal personality. Consequently, the Commission Delegation in Paris has been replaced by a 'Delegation of the European Union', operating as a part of the EEAS, and nameplates at the OECD now also display 'European Union'.[54] Statements and declarations are now issued by this EU Delegation, and in so doing, EEAS diplomats not only represent the EU institutions, but have also the right to speak in behalf of the entire Union every time a common position is reached on issues falling within areas of exclusive or shared competences.[55] However, reality proves to be different, as both the EU Delegation and the Member States continue to take the floor, even when dealing with exclusive competences. By way of pragmatic solution, the EU Delegation has been granted the right to speak first.[56] Furthermore, once there is a commonly agreed position in the OECD, Member States are expected not to go against the EU position and are bound by the principle of sincere cooperation whilst complementing statements made on behalf of the EU, as is prescribed by the General Arrangements for EU statements in multilateral organizations, a document adopted by the Council in October 2011.[57]

Remarkably, the EU Delegation can also represent the entire Union on issues falling under national competence, although this is only the case when Member States request it and assign a clear mandate to the EU

54 <http://eeas.europa.eu/delegations/oecd_unesco/oecd_eu/political_relations/legal_framework/index_en.htm>

55 Comelli and Matarazzo, *supra* n. 41, p. 10.

56 Interview with a Commission official at DG Trade in Brussels, 15 June 2012.

57 EU Statements in Multilateral Organisations – General Agreements, 15901/11, 24 October 2011.

Delegation. Moreover, special attention is given to coordination between the Member States and the EU Delegation, especially "when international agreed instruments and recommendations are elaborated".[58] Nevertheless, in reality this type of representation remains rare, as some Member States remain reluctant to grant the EU Delegation additional powers.[59]

Therefore, piecing all the aforementioned elements together, we see how the OECD proves to be a unique case when it comes to EU external representation. In a varying setting of exclusive, shared and even a number of non-EU competences, EU representation has been operationalized in a way that ensures both EU visibility as well as the right of Member States to engage directly in the discussions within the OECD.

3.1.4 *Competences*

A final dimension of the EU's identity in the OECD relates to Union's internal competences attached to the issues discussed within the Organization. More specifically, the EU upholds a much stronger identity in those OECD bodies dealing with exclusive competences such as trade or competition, than in those on e.g. taxation or welfare state reform. This can easily be explained by the fact that e.g. the EU possess expertise in these respective policy areas, or is not (or to a lesser extent) contested by its own Member States within the OECD.[60]

In a number of cases, however, the nature of competences is not always clear-cut, as emerges from the following case law. A first case, Opinion 1/75, concerned the existence of Community power to conclude the OECD understanding in a Local Cost Standard, an instrument that involved the standard to grant export credits within Member States as credits for the financing of local costs linked to export operations.[61] In this Opinion, the Court stressed that the export policy was an integral part of commercial policies, thus falling within the ambit of Article 133 TEEC. Then, the Court took into account both the objective of the OECD instrument and the manner in which Common Commercial Policy was conceived in the Treaty, and opined that regarding export policy and CCP, Member States should not exercise a power concurrent to that of

---

[58] 'Working Arrangements between the EU Delegation and the Belgian Permanent Representation to the OECD', working document of 1 September 2010, cited by Rosa Balfour et al., *Upgrading the EU's Role as Global Actor*, Brussels: CEPS 2011, p. 97.

[59] Comelli and Matarazzo, *supra* n. 41, p. 10.

[60] Carroll and Kellow, *supra* n. 31.

[61] ECJ, Opinion 1/75, *Understanding on a Local Cost Standard*, [1975] ECR I-1362.

the Community in both the EEC sphere of competence and the international sphere. Moreover, it was argued that an opposite interpretation would go against the very purpose of the CCP, and thus the Community's common interest. Therefore, based on the subject matter of this OECD instrument and its consequences for the CCP, the Court granted the Community – in casu the Commission – the exclusive power to participate in the OECD Understanding on Local Cost Standard.[62]

In another Opinion, the Court examined the issue of conclusion of the Third Revised Decision on National Treatment adopted by the OECD Council. The Commission envisaged the EC's participation in this instrument based on the free movement of capital (then Article 57 TEC) and the CCP (then Article 113 TEC).[63] In this Opinion, the Court found that the national treatment rule of the Decision applies as much to the conditions for foreign controlled undertakings in their participation in trade between Member States and non-EC countries (covered by CCP), as it related to their participation in intra-Community trade (governed by internal market rules). Therefore, it was argued that the competences to participate in this OECD instrument were shared.[64]

If we now once again take all the previous elements together, it becomes clear that the nature of EU competences attached to an OECD issue has a clear impact on the Union's identity in the Organization. Especially when dealing with exclusive competences, the EU upholds a strong and often leading role in the OECD, sometimes supported by the ECJ, as reflects from the first strand of case law.[65] When dealing with shared or unclear EU competences, our conclusions on the Union's identity must be less straightforward. On a number of these issues, the EU tries to assume a much stronger role *vis-à-vis* its Member States – especially when there are some linkages with exclusive competences as reflects e.g. from the second strand of case law – but at the same time, it also risks a backlash of its Member States who are not willing to give up their participatory rights. Therefore, the EU's identity on these issues is strongly determined by the respective EU and Member States interests and the possible view of the Court on this matter.

---

[62] Ibid., I-1365.

[63] ECJ, Opinion 2/92, *Competence of the Community or one of its institutions to participate in the Third Revised Decision of the OECD on national treatment*, [1995] ECR I-552.

[64] Ibid., I-558.

[65] Carroll and Kellow, *supra* n. 3, pp. 207–209.

3.2 *The EU Identity in Day-to-day Practice*

Having established a general framework for analyzing the EU's identity in the OECD, we shall now demonstrate that these four dimensions vary considerably within the different bodies of the organization, which results in a multiplicity of EU identities. This claim is supported by two case studies, in which we elaborate on the EU's day-to-day identity in the Economic Development Review Committee and the Development Assistance Committee.

3.2.1 *The Economic Development Review Committee*

The Economic Development and Review Committee (EDRC) is one of the oldest and most important Committees of the OECD, and is often seen as the cornerstone of the Organization's system of peer reviewing and economic surveillance. It was established in 1961, with its role being to "examine economic trends and policies in individual OECD countries, assess the broad performance of each economy and make policy recommendations".[66] These country reports are prepared by the OECD Secretariat – albeit in close consultation with the country under review – and adopted by all thirty-four members of the EDRC and the European Commission. As with most of the OECD's work, these country reports are legally non-binding. Nonetheless, a system of peer pressure is used to ensure their effectiveness.

Of particular interest for the EU's identity in the EDRC are the yearly reviews of the Euro area – conducted since 2001 – and the reviews of the entire EU economy (hereafter called 'EU-wide reviews'). The latter review was introduced in 2007 on demand of the APEC countries who wanted to bundle "all EC policies and EU wide policies"[67] into one review, instead of dealing with them in a "repetitive and fragmented manner in all individual Member States' EDRC reviews".[68] It was expected that this would provide a parity of treatment between the European Community and the other OECD members, as in the latter case all economic policies were open for examination. The European Commission and the Member

---

[66] <http://www.oecd.org/site/peerreview/peerreviewineconomicsurveystheroleoftheedrc.htm>

[67] Communication from the Commission to the Council on the Establishment of an OECD EDRC Examination of EC Economic Policies alongside to the Euro Area Survey, COM(2005) 150 final, p. 2.

[68] Ibid., p. 3.

States responded positively to this request, and after the Council had given its approval as well, the first 'EU-wide' review was conducted in September 2007.[69] In more recent times, reviews were carried out in 2009[70] and 2012.[71]

If we now take a closer look at the EU's identity in the EDRC, it is important to bear in mind that much depends of the respective issue one is looking at, in casu the Euro Area Review or the 'EU-wide' review. Only when focusing on the first dimension of the EU's identity – its legal status in the EDRC – one should not make this distinction, as the Union takes part in all aspects of the Committee's work as a 'quasi-member'. Moreover, with the introduction of the 'EU-wide' review, the difference between being a quasi-member and full member of the EDRC is less prominent as in other parts of the OECD. If we take a closer look at the EU coordination in the EDRC, it is important to make a distinction between the Euro Area and the 'EU-wide' reviews. More specifically, while the former review covers only seventeen EU Member States, the 'EU-wide' review focuses on policies that have been formulated and apply to all EU countries. This makes coordination on the 'EU-wide' reviews much more comprehensive, especially since six EU Member States are not represented in the OECD.

Also when focusing on the EU representation in the EDRC, it is important to make a clear distinction between the reviews on the Euro Area and those on the entire EU economy. More specifically, while the Commission, the European Central Bank and the (Eurogroup) Presidency jointly represent the Eurozone in the former case, the Commission is the lead representative of the entire EU economy in the latter case, making clear that the position it presents is coordinated with the Member States. With regard to the final dimension of the EU's identity, the intra-EU competences attached to the issues discussed in the EDRC, one should note that in preparation of the report to be represented by the Commission, Member States tend to be vigilant about the division of competences in the EDRC.[72] This comes as no surprise as the EDRC's works – especially the 'EU-wide' reviews – covers both EU (exclusive and shared) and national competences. Consequently,

---

69 Available at <http://www.oecd.org/economy/economicsurveysandcountrysurveillance/39311348.pdf

70 Available at <http://www.urv.cat/media/upload//arxius/Catedra_Innovacio/economic_survey_ue_ocde.pdf>

71 Available at <http://www.oecd.org/eco/49950244.pdf>

72 The most congested areas include e.g. taxation and financial supervision. Interview with a Commission official at DG Trade, Brussels, 15 June 2012.

Member States often raise issues of competences, which may undermine the EU's identity in the EDRC.

In light of the foregoing, it can be concluded that the EU holds a relatively strong position in the EDRC. It acquires this position first of all from its quasi-membership status in the Committee, especially since the introduction of the 'EU-wide' review in 2007 and the corresponding upgrade of the Union's position in the EDRC. When focusing on the EU representation, one can conclude that the Union holds a 'multilateral' identity in the EDRC. This means that the Commission represents both the Eurozone and the entire Union – in both cases a large group of EU Member States. This also explains why there is a lot of EU coordination in the EDRC. This emphasis on coordination, however, does not prevent that the EU's position in the EDRC is sometimes contested by the Member States, since a number of EDRC issues fall behind the Union's competences.

3.2.2 *The Development Assistance Committee*

The Development Assistance Committee (DAC) is one of the main OECD committees. It represents the world's largest (Western) donors, and is tasked to define and monitor global development standards. In so doing, the DAC hopes to improve both the quality and the quantity of development aid.[73] This is clearly reflected from the DAC's track-record, as it has fostered the development of a large number of important aid principles, such as the Paris Declaration on Aid Effectiveness or the International (and Millennium) Development Goals.[74] Also central to the DAC's work are traditional OECD practices such as Peer Reviewing and collecting statistical data, in casu on aid flows (e.g. Official Development Assistance).[75]

Before focusing on the EU's identity, it should be noted though that the DAC is also a very atypical part of the OECD, as it possesses a large number of distinctive features. For example, the DAC maintains more strict accession criteria then the rest of the OECD,[76] and is the only commit-

---

[73] DCD/DAC(2010)34/Final, *DAC Mandate 2011–2015*, 18 October 2010. OECD(60)13/§14, *Mandate of the Development Assistance Committee*, 23 July 1960.

[74] Richard Manning, 'The DAC as a Central Actor in Development Policy Issues: Experiences over het Past Four Year' (2008) 7 *DIE (Bonn) Discussion Paper*.

[75] DCD/DAC, 'Development Co-operation Report 2005', (2005) 7 *OECD Journal on Development*, pp. 132–147.

[76] While the OECD represents thirty-four countries, the DAC only has twenty-four members. Moreover a country can be a member of the DAC without possessing full membership of the OECD.

tee that is able to voice its own opinions without gaining approval from the OECD Council. The committee is also the only one that is headed by a permanent (and residential) chair; and while most other OECD committees only gather once or twice a year, the DAC meets at least once a month.[77] Therefore, one can conclude that the DAC is de facto an IO in its own right[78] operating within the OECD-structure – or as one of the DAC delegates puts it: "an OECD within the OECD".[79]

The DAC also proves to be unique when we take a closer look at the EU's identity in the OECD, as the Union upholds a much stronger identity in this committee than in the rest of the organization. This becomes clear when focusing on the different dimensions of the EU's identity. Starting with the legal status, the EU has always been a full member of the DAC while being a 'quasi-member' in the rest of the OECD.[80] This discrepancy goes back to the establishment of the DAG in 1960. At that time, the US faced growing balance of payments deficits, and was therefore keen to see other Western donors carry a greater share of the aid burden. This led to the establishment of the DAG. Remarkably the EEC was one of its original members, albeit represented by the Commission. This was felt appropriate given the latter's role in the European Development Fund (EDF).[81] Moreover, a large number of countries felt that EEC membership served their own interests.[82] Afterwards, when the DAG was adopted by the OECD in 1961, this membership status remained unaltered, and ever

[77] Ken Masujima, 'Good governance and the Development Assistance Committee: ideas and organizational constraint', in: Morten Bøås and Desmond McNeill (eds.), *Global Institutions and Development: Framing the World?*, London: Routledge 2004.

[78] This can be explained by the DAC's establishment history as the committee succeeded the Development Assistance Group (DAG), a Western IO established in 1960 in order to consult on development cooperation. In 1961 the OECD adopted the DAG (and renamed it), but the latter largely upheld its autonomous practices.

[79] Mr. Martinus Desmet, Paris, 17/01/2012.

Ken Masujima, 'Good governance and the Development Assistance Committee: Ideas and Organizational Constraint', in Morten Bøås and Desmond McNeill (eds.), *Global Institutions and Development: Framing the World?*, London: Routledge 2004.

[80] Carroll and Kellow, *supra* n. 3, pp. 207–209.

[81] Milton Esman and Daniel Cheever, *The Common Aid Effort: the Development Assistance activities of the Organization for Economic Co-operation and Development*. Ohio: Ohio State University Press 1967.

[82] Joren Verschaeve, 'The European Union in the OECD-DAC: An Exceptionally Strong Relation before and after the Lisbon Treaty', paper presented at the LISBOAN Network workshop 'EU External Representation and the Reform of International Contexts: Practices after Lisbon', The Hague, 21–22 February 2012.

since, the DAC is the only major OECD body in which the EU is represented as a full member.[83]

A second dimension of the EU's identity in the DAC relates to the clear understanding between the Union and its Member States on coordination. More specifically, the EU Delegation and all Member States represented in the DAC – including the observers – hold coordination meetings before every meeting of the committee. Moreover, the EU Delegation also organizes regular meetings with EU members that are not represented in the DAC, in order to involve them as much as possible. Finally, there also exists a clear understanding on the content of the EU coordination. As the DAC primarily serves as a forum for information sharing, the Union's default position is not to pursue a 'single voiced Europe'. However, if the DAC prepares more specific measures, the EU strives for a common European position.[84] In doing so the EU has been very successful, as is e.g. reflected by the run-up to the High Level Forums in Paris, Accra or Busan.[85]

A third dimension of the EU's identity relates to the Union's representation in the DAC. As discussed above, the Lisbon Treaty spelled a major change for the Union's representation in the OECD, as all Commission Delegations were replaced by EU Delegations in order to ensure a more coordinated and coherent external action.[86] Consequently, EEAS officials now represent the EU's development policy in the DAC. In reality however, this poses a number of problems, as there still is no clear division of labor between the EEAS and the Commission when it comes to development cooperation.[87] Moreover, the EEAS itself still lacks sector specific expertise in a number of important DAC policy areas, resulting in a continuation of Commission representation in a large number of subgroups and working parties of the committee.[88] To what extent this 'double representation' undermines the EU's identity in the DAC is still unclear. However, as the EU continues to be represented by two different institutional actors, this may eventually lead to multiple identities. This may occur in particular because – as some authors have argued – DG

[83] Helmut Führer, *The Story of Official Development Assistance: A History of the Development Assistance Committee and the Development Co-operation Directorate in Dates, Names and Figures*, Paris: OECD Press 1996, pp. 1–16.

[84] Interviews with DAC delegates and EU officials, Paris, 12–13 June 2012.

[85] Manning, *supra* n. 74, p. 14.

[86] Comelli and Matarazzo, *supra* n. 41.

[87] Jeske Van Seters and Henrike Klavers, 'EU Development Cooperation after the Lisbon Treaty: People, Institutions and Global Trends', (2011) 123 *ECDPM Discussion Paper*.

[88] Interview with DAC delegate, Ghent, 21 December 2011.

Development and Cooperation departs from a different development perspective than the EEAS.[89]

A fourth and final dimension of the EU's identity in the DAC is related to the intra-EU competences on development cooperation. When the EEC became a member of the DAC, the Commission lacked real development competences, as the Rome Treaty only foresaw in a small intergovernmental role within the EDF.[90] Consequently, the EEC possessed a weak identity in the DAC throughout the sixties, since the Commission was only able – and allowed – to take part in those discussions dealing with the EDF.[91] This gradually changed from 1970 onwards, since the Commission started to expand its development competences through its trade relations with the global south (e.g. *Lomé I*).[92] Because of this internal shift, the EEC abandoned its previous role in the DAC and became a more active and visible member of the committee. Nonetheless, the EU's identity was still hampered by the Commission's lack of capacities on development cooperation compared to other members of the DAC.[93] This fundamentally changed with the entry into force of the Maastricht Treaty as the EU was finally granted strong – albeit shared – development competences.[94] As a result, the Commission became one of the world's largest aid providers, initiating many activities in traditional DAC areas such as Policy Coherence for Development (PCD), Aid for Trade, or Aid Effectiveness.[95] This expansion of intra-EU competences clearly boosted the Union's identity in the DAC. Not only is the EU currently one of the DAC's largest donor, the Union also gained a lot of expertise, analytical capacities and credibility in a number of traditional DAC policy areas, in more recent years rendering it one of the central and dominant members of the committee.[96]

---

89 Van Seters and Klavers, *supra* n. 88.

90 Enzo Grilli, *The European Community and the Developing Countries*, Cambridge: Cambridge University Press 1993, pp. 5–74.

91 OECD/DA/M(1961–1965), *Summary Minutes of the 1st–60th session of the Development Assistance Committee*, consulted in Paris at the OECD, 17 January 2012.

92 Karen Arts and Anna Dickson, *EU Development Cooperation: from Model to Symbol*, Manchester: Manchester University Press, 2004.

93 DAC/M(1970–1977), *Development Assistance Committee: summary records of the meetings*, consulted in Paris at the OECD, 11 June 2012.

94 Then Art. 177–181 EC.

95 Jan Orbie, 'The EU's role in Development: a Full-Fledged Development Actor or Eclipsed by Superpower Temptations?', in: Stefan Gänzle, Sven Grimm and Davina Makham (eds.), *The European Union and Global Development: An 'Enlightened Superpower' in the Making?*, Hampshire: Palgrave MacMillan 2012, pp. 17–37.

96 Manning, *supra* n. 74, p. 14.

Therefore, taking all the aforementioned elements together, one may conclude that the EU upholds a very strong identity in the DAC. The Union derives this position from its full-membership the Committee, its strong competences on development cooperation, and the clear arrangements with its Member States on coordination. Only when focusing on the EU's representation in the DAC, one is confronted with a much weaker identity, since both the EEAS and the Commission represent the Union's development policy in the Committee. So far, however, this has not caused major issues, and thus not undermined the other dimensions of its identity in the DAC.

4. Conclusion

This chapter's central aim was to explore what 'international identity' the EU can be said to possess within the OECD. In so doing, we sought to contribute to the general EU–IOs literature, as the Union's relationship with the OECD has barely gained academic attention, despite the latter's important role in global governance and the strong historical ties between both organizations. The main finding of this inquiry indicates that the EU does not hold a single, distinctive identity in the OECD, but rather a multiplicity of identities. This is very remarkable, as in most international organizations the opposite is true. In order to explain this discrepancy, one has to look at the OECD's unique nature, realizing that it is an amalgam of over 250 committees, working parties and subgroups. Moreover, the OECD is one of the few IOs with a mandate covering the entire scope of EU competences. Consequently, there is no such thing as a single EU–OECD relationship; it all much depends on the particular committee or issue one is looking at.

Based upon these findings, we have developed a general framework in order to unravel the multiplicity of EU identities in the OECD in a more systematic way. More specifically, we argued that the Union's identity in each body of the OECD is determined by four important dimensions: (1) the EU's legal status; (2) coordination by the EU; (3) representation by the EU and (4) the nature of EU competences attached to the discussed issues. Moreover, we found that these dimensions vary – often considerably – between the different bodies of the OECD, which results in very heterogeneous set of EU identities. This finding clearly reflects from the case studies on both the Economic Development and Review

Committee and the Development and Assistance Committee. For example, while the EU is a full member of the DAC, it takes part in the EDRC's work as a 'quasi-member'. And while EU actors (both institutions and Member States) strive for common positions in the EDRC as much as possible, coordination in the DAC is less extensive, since the Committee's primary objective is to share information. With regard to EU representation there also exists a strong variation between both cases, as the Commission represents the EU in the EDRC in close cooperation with the ECB and (Euro Area) Presidency, while in the DAC the EEAS serves as primary representative, but in reality still shares this task with the Commission. Finally, while the DAC's mandate only covers shared, albeit important EU competences, the EDRC deals with the entire scope of Union – and even national – competences. In sum therefore, it can be concluded that the EU holds two very different identities in both cases: in the EDRC, the Union primarily has a multilateral role, representing the entire Eurozone or EU economy, while in the DAC, it holds a very strong identity but uses this first of all to represent its own aid efforts.

Lastly, it should also be noted that even though the Union does not dispose of a single or consistent identity in the OECD, compared to most other international organizations, it holds a rather strong position in the Organization in general. This can be explained by the fact that the EU holds at least a 'quasi-membership status' in all OECD bodies, and that most of these deal with socio-economic policies – areas where the Union often possesses considerable competences and expertise, and is consequently less contested by its Member States.

CHAPTER NINE

THE EU AND THE IMF: THE FINANCIAL CRISIS AS A CATALYST FOR A STRONGER UNION REPRESENTATION?

Laura Puccio

1. Introduction

The International Monetary Fund (IMF) was created at Bretton Woods in July 1944, with the aim of promoting monetary cooperation, facilitate growth and trade, and maintain exchange rate stability.[1] Such exchange rate stability was considered fundamental for the smooth development of trade relations.[2] It was to be achieved within the IMF through an arrangement known as 'Bretton Woods', whereby each Member was committed to maintain the parities of their currency with the US dollar, while the dollar would maintain a fixed dollar/gold parity.[3] The importance of exchange rate stability for harmonious trade relations was also recognized in the Treaty of Rome founding the European Economic Community, where Article 107 TEEC considered exchange rate policy of common interest. At that time there was no exchange rate arrangement within the Community, as all EEC members were also IMF members, and therefore exchange rate stability and monetary stability remained mainly outside the Community's competence.[4]

After the collapse of the Bretton Woods system in 1971, the EEC decided to strengthen economic and monetary cooperation. Indeed, exchange rate stability and monetary stability were considered fundamental for

---

1 See article I of the IMF Agreement.

2 As shown by the reference to exchange rate values in the General Agreement on Tariffs and Trade, even though the interpretation and application of the relevant articles is subject to debate.

3 For furthering reading on the Bretton Woods system and its evolution, see Andreas Lowenfeld, *International Economic Law*, Oxford: Oxford University Press 2008; id., 'The International Monetary System: A Look Back Over Seven Decades', (2010) 13 *Journal of International Economic Law*, p. 575.

4 Francis Snyder, 'EMU Revisited: Are we Making a Constitution? What Constitution are we Making?', in: Paul Craig and Gráinne de Burca (eds.), *The Evolution of EU Law* Oxford: Oxford University Press 1999, p. 417.

both the internal market and the common agricultural policy.[5] After several attempts to maintain an exchange rates arrangement, in 1993, the Maastricht Treaty codified the three stages of Economic and Monetary Union. That led to the adoption of the common currency, the Euro, by some Member States. Even EU countries not adopting the Euro are bound to the broader institutional framework for economic cooperation within the EMU. Moreover, aside from the two formal opt-outs countries (United Kingdom and Denmark), there is a presumption that the other EU Member States will adopt the Euro at a later stage.[6] The creation of the EMU, as well as the further development of financial regulation and the completion of the internal market, also modified the division of competences substantially with regard to financial, monetary and economic matters. As declared in the Vienna European Council Conclusions of December 1998, "the introduction of the euro will be a major event for the international monetary system".[7] The internal change in competence at the European level was mirrored by a change with regard to the external powers. Since then, the Union's institutions join the Member States in international economic and financial organizations, albeit that this happens in a rather scattered and diversified way,[8] depending on the precise subject matter (monetary policy, fiscal policy, financial services and macro-economic developments). Basically, the way they intervene depends on a complex horizontal and vertical division of competences in the external relations of the EMU. Therefore, even though monetary policy is an exclusive EU competence within the Euro area, and even though the IMF constitutes a monetary organization, the Member States have kept their individual seats there and the ECB has only been given an observer status, to be able to intervene on matters governed by EU law. The Council and the Commission also participate in some specific circumstances, as we will see and explain later. Voting power within the IMF remains exclusively in the hands of the Member States. Yet, if coherence is fundamental to create a

---

[5] René Smits, *The European Central Bank – Institutional Aspects*, Deventer: Kluwer Law International 1997, pp. 10–14.

[6] On the EMU as a double speed policy, see Francis Snyder, 'EMU – Integration and Differentiation: Metaphor for European Union', in: Paul Craig and Gráinne de Búrca (eds.), *The Evolution of EU Law*, Oxford: Oxford University Press 2011, pp. 687–716.

[7] European Council Conclusions, Vienna, 11 and 12 December 1998, III(A)(ii), point 14.

[8] See, inter alia, Jean-Christophe Poutineau and Marc-Alexandre Sénégas, 'L'Union Européenne et la stabilité mondiale', in: Muriel Le Barbier-Le Bris (ed.), *L'Union Européenne et la gouvernance mondiale – Quel apport avec quels acteurs?*, Brussels: Bruylant 2012, p. 256.

unified Union identity in external relations, and if coherence is understood as consistency, being the absence of conflict between external action and internal EU objectives and competences, a clear and effective distribution of powers across actors is necessary, in order to create synergies and avoid duplication.[9] The question is thus: can the Union ensure the coherence of its external relations, while relying on the diverse approaches of the Member States to the IMF and on the limited interventions of EU institutions inside the international organization?

With regard to EU–IMF relations, the absence of a single Union representation, or at least a single representation of the Eurozone, has always been a principal issue. Regular doubts have been voiced whether the current structure of the relationship is adequate for meeting the Union's external needs.[10] Indeed, under Article 220 TFEU:

> The Union shall establish *all appropriate forms of cooperation* with the organs of the United Nations and its specialised agencies, the Council of Europe, the Organisation for Security and Cooperation in Europe and the Organisation for Economic Cooperation and Development. The Union shall also maintain such relations as are appropriate with other international organisations.[11]

From a political and legal point of view, one may wonder whether the current framework and the maintenance of individual membership of the EU Member States within the IMF make any sense. Are the ways for the Union's institutions to intervene in the IMF sufficiently efficient, and do they permit the EU to speak with a single voice? On the contrary, the current, complicated institutional setting makes it difficult for the EU to do just that, which is one of the main reasons why the Union, and the Euro area in particular, are still considered a political dwarf in international financial matters. At the same time, the rise of Asian countries and other emerging economies within the IMF challenges more and more the current over-representation (if not collective power) of European countries and institutions.

---

9 See Marise Cremona, 'Coherence through Law: What Difference Will the Treaty of Lisbon Make?', (2008) 3 *Hamburg Review of Social Sciences*, p. 11.

10 The Commission took particular interest in the issue, and organized a conference in April 2009 (see <http://ec.europa.eu/economy_finance/articles/international/article 14724_en.htm>). In the current EMU external representation however, still no changes have been agreed and implemented.

11 Emphasis added.

To understand the current relations between EU, its Member States and the IMF, one has to look both at the competences of the Union's institutions with regard to the Economic and Monetary Union, as well as at the IMF's field of action. Both have to be considered jointly, and the legal picture needs to be completed by a political analysis that pays due regard to the context of the current financial and sovereign debt crisis. Paragraph 2 first briefly describes the current institutional framework for EU–IMF relations. Next, paragraph 3 focuses on the legal limitations within the IMF to a single EU representation, and the requirements (in particular in terms of power and capacity to act within the organization) for continued membership of the Member States. Hereafter, paragraph 4 analyses how the horizontal and vertical division of competences in the EMU has been organized to require both the involvement of ECB and the Council (through the Euro Presidency), and to allow for continued membership of the Member States. Finally, paragraph 5 sketches some of the persistent legal and political problems flowing from the current setup.

2. The Institutional Framework of the EU–IMF Relationship

As remarked already, the relations between the EU and the IMF involve both the Member States and the Union's institutions (the Presidency of the Council, the Commission and the ECB) in various and diverse capacities.[12]

With the collapse of Bretton Woods, the IMF mainly took on a supervisory function to ensure economic and financial stability and, in case of a crisis, offer technical and financial assistance.[13] The EU institutions have fully made their way, alongside the delegates of the IMF, in more informal international economic governance institutions such as the G7, G8,[14] and G20,[15] but also in the Financial Stability Board, where discussions are

---

[12] For a recent description of the institutional framework, see *ECB Monthly Bulletin*, May 2011 (available at <ttp://www.ecb.int/pub/mb/html/index.en.html>); Alan Hervé, 'The Participation of the European Union in Global Economic Governance Fora', (2012) 18 *European Law Journal*, p. 143.

[13] See Andreas Lowenfeld, *International Economic Law*, Oxford: Oxford University Press 2002, pp. 511–519 and pp. 545–614. See also Manuela Moschella, *Governing Risk – The IMF and Global Financial Crises*, Hampshire: Palgrave Macmillan 2010.

[14] The Commission, the ECB and the Eurogroup Presidency are not Members in the G7 or G8, but still participate regularly in the meetings.

[15] The EU is a full member of the G20 and is represented at ministerial level by the Commission and the ECB, while at the Head of State level, it is represented by the President of the European Council and the President of the Commission.

held on the regulation of financial markets and systemic risk. However, the EU's institutional presence in the IMF is more scattered, restricted to precise discussion items, and the Member States are still strongly attached to their traditional position of (sole) full members of the IMF.

The IMF is composed of a Board of Governors, an Executive Board, and sub-committees to the Board of Governors such as the Interim Monetary and Financial Committee (IMFC). All aforementioned organs are intergovernmental, and only IMF members enjoy the power to vote.

The Board of Governors consists of all the IMF members. The EU countries are normally represented by the head of their Central Banks or their Minister of Finance. The Board of Governors meets at least once a year, and decides inter alia on quota increases and the so-called Special Drawing Rights (SDRs). Subcommittees to the Board of Governors were created in order to discuss other specific topics. One of these is the Interim Monetary and Financial Committee, which advises the Board on questions related to global liquidity or institutional reforms of the IMF. The European Commission has an observer status on the IMFC.

The main organ concerned with the day-to-day decision-making is the Executive Board, to which the Board of Governors has delegated the main powers. The twenty-four members of the Executive Board are elected from constituencies on the basis of their relevance and economic importance, which determines their voting power. France, United Kingdom and Germany each form a single-state constituency, and are therefore constantly represented at the Executive Board. In multi-state constituencies, the chair is either given to the most powerful state, or it rotates among the group of countries that have similar and still dominant power. Italy's constituency is an example of the former type (a multi-state with the most powerful country holding the chair; also referred to as "dominated" constituency).[16] As Italy has a voting power higher than three percent, it dominates a group of countries which have a voting power lower than one (including Greece and Portugal). The Nordic-Baltic constituency forms a group of the latter type (a multi-state constituency with a rotating chair). There, the presidency rotates among the four most powerful Nordic countries, Sweden, Denmark, Finland and Norway. As the chair depends on the relative importance of the member, relative to other members of the same constituency, there is a tendency for countries to

[16] Peter Brandner and Harald Grech, 'Unifying EU Representation at the IMF – A Voting Power Analysis', *BMF – Federal Ministry of Finance Working Paper 2009/2*, p. 10.

choose the constituency in which they can hold more power. This was for example the case of Spain, which left the constituency of Italy to join a constituency with Latin American countries, and share the rotating chair with Mexico and Venezuela.[17] To some extent, the choice of Ireland to be in the constituency chaired by Canada can also be viewed as a way of giving more importance to the Irish representative in the IMF. Indeed, the Canadian constituency is mainly formed by small Caribbean states, which leaves Ireland – notwithstanding its weak voting power compared to other EU countries – to be the second biggest vote in the Canadian constituency. Ireland therefore enjoys a powerful position in the Canadian constituency, which it would not have had in a European-led one. Because of its position as the second most powerful country in the Canadian constituency, and since it is now possible for the chair (in this case Canada) to elect an alternate executive director, Ireland has also been handed that function.[18]

As mentioned above, the members of the Euro zone participate individually in the IMF. However, the Vienna European Council Conclusions of December 1998 stipulated that:

> The ECB, as the Community body competent for monetary policy, should be granted observer status at the IMF board. The views of the European Community/EMU on other issues of particular relevance to the EMU would be presented at the IMF board by the relevant member of the Executive Director's office of the Member State holding the Euro Presidency, assisted by a representative of the Commission.[19]

While the Commission and the ECB intervene within the IMFC, the ECB, as the main institution competent for monetary policy, received an observer status within the Executive Board,[20] while the Euro Presidency, assisted by the Commission, represents the Euro zone on other EMU positions within the Board (in particular with regard to exchange rate policy).

---

[17] Lorenzo Bini Smaghi, 'A Single EU seat in the IMF?', (2004) 42 *Journal of Common Market Studies*, p. 232.

[18] An overview of the current constituency formation is available on:<http://www.imf.org/external/np/sec/memdir/eds.aspx>.

[19] European Council Conclusions, Vienna, 11 and 12 December 1998, III(A)(ii), point 14.

[20] Decision No. 12925 (03/1), 27 December 2002, as amended by Decision No. 13414 (05/01), 23 December 2004, Decision No. 13612 (05/108), 22 December 2005, and Decision No. 14517 (10/1), 5 January 2010.

The Euro Presidency is held by a delegate of a Member State sitting in the Executive Board and representing the Eurogroup position.[21]

Alongside the observer status of the Union institutions, the EU Member States coordinate their position within the IMF either in Brussels, in a committee focusing on IMF issues and during ECOFIN Councils; or in Washington, where Union delegates meet regularly within the EURIMF, in a manner that mirrors similar gatherings of representatives at the UN in New York.[22]

Lastly, the Member State holding the Council Presidency delivers a speech at the annual IMF meeting, representing the EU. Here again, as in the above case of the Eurogroup, the Union is represented through a Member State as part of the Council, and not by the President of the European Council. The Commission and the ECB may assist at the annual meetings, inter alia the Commissioner entrusted with DG Economic and Financial Affairs, and the President of the ECB. It is striking to note that in October 2012, even though the formal EU speech was delivered by the Member States holding the rotating Council Presidency (Cyprus), said Commissioner organized a joint press conference with the ECB President.[23]

3. A Legitimate Framework? The Limits to Single EU Membership in the IMF Statutes

One may wonder why such a complex institutional framework was preferred over a single EU membership, or alternatively, a joint participation with the Member States, such as in the WTO. As Erik Denters argues however, it is important to not only consider the EU's vantage point, but also the IMF's legal perspective.[24] First of all, the IMF's membership rules

---

[21] In this respect the representation of the Eurogroup is different from the one in the G7 or the G20, where the President of the Eurogroup (Jean-Claude Juncker) attends with the President of the ECB. The Eurogroup is represented here through one of its Member States. See also Jean-Victor Louis, 'L'Union Européenne et la régulation de la finance internationale', in: Muriel Le Barbier-Le Bris (ed.), *L'Union européenne et la gouvernance mondiale – Quel apport avec quels acteurs?*, Brussels: Bruylant 2012, p. 278.

[22] On which, see further Hervé, *supra* n. 10.

[23] 'European Commission and the European Central Bank to hold press conference on the IMF/World Bank annual meetings', <http://www.euinjapan.jp/en/media/news/news2012/20121012/144502>.

[24] Erik Denters, 'Representation of the EC in the IMF', in: Mario Giovanoli (ed.), *International Monetary Law – Issues for the New Millennium*, New York: Oxford University Press 2000, pp. 211–224

have been the decisive reason for a continued membership of the Euro zone countries to the IMF, instead of a single Euro area seat.[25] Secondly, if Member States are to retain their individual membership, they also need to be able to fulfill their obligations under the EU Treaties. As we will observe below, these requirements were taken into account when drafting the EMU rules and dividing competences between the ECB and national central banks.

3.1 *The IMF Statute: Is the IMF Only For Countries?*

The IMF's membership rules, contained in Article II of the Agreement of the International Monetary Fund, provide that membership shall be open to other countries beyond the original members:

> Membership shall be open to other countries at such times and in accordance with such terms as may be prescribed by the Board of Governors. These terms, including the terms for subscriptions, shall be based on principles consistent with those applied to other countries that are already members.[26]

Joseph Gold, who extensively analyzed the question of IMF membership, sees the term "countries" as more flexible and different from the traditional understanding of sovereign states in public international law.[27] However, he contends that:

> Membership in the Fund is available to countries individually. No provision is made for joint membership of two or more countries that remain distinct political entities as countries. Even countries that have a common currency have separate membership in the Fund.[28]

Regional groups of states were not considered eligible; neither was an application from a currency union as a whole ever considered.[29] Contrary to the GATT, with its regulatory tool for regional agreements, the IMF did not make any references to monetary integration arrangements.[30] Yet, the question addressed by Denters and Gold concerns the issue of whether a

---

[25] Indeed the issue of IMF membership after adoption of the Euro was discussed in the EU Council in 1998.

[26] Article II(2) of the IMF Agreement.

[27] See Joseph Gold, 'Membership and Non-Membership in the International Monetary Fund', New York: International Monetary Fund 1974, pp. 43–52.

[28] Ibid., p. 68.

[29] Ibid.

[30] Moustapha Lo Diatta, *Les unions monétaires en droit international*, Genève: Publications de l'Institut Universitaires de Hautes Études Internationales 2007, pp. 161–2.

country that has outsourced its monetary policy is still able to perform its obligations under IMF law. Instead of discrediting the role of the Member States within the Fund, it points out which elements ought to be kept within their power in order to fulfill their international obligations.

3.2 *IMF Membership Based on the Capacity to Fulfill Obligations*

The preceding argument regards the authority and capacity to fulfill the obligations under IMF law as fundamental criteria for membership of that organization. Indeed, by looking at the applications of Italy, Austria, Germany and Japan, Gold demonstrates that full sovereignty and independence is not required for becoming a member. Instead, their applications were assessed on the basis of their capacity to act in foreign relations, verifying whether the country concerned would be able to perform its obligations under the IMF Agreement[31]

How does monetary integration affect this capacity? There are different agreements that can be pursued outside the IMF framework to cooperate in monetary matters. There are simple exchange rate agreements,[32] currency boards,[33] *dollarization*,[34] or agreements on a common currency. Whereas in a currency board, the right of coining money is relinquished, in a common currency this task is delegated to a common central bank. Exchange rate arrangements, on the other hand, oblige central banks to respect certain rules of the game, such as the obligation to maintain the exchange rate peg, constraining their freedom to determine their money supply.[35] In all three scenarios, the country gives up a part of its autonomous monetary policy. Indeed, the common currency can be defined as a very strict exchange rate arrangement peg, and the consequences are therefore similar; however, under exchange rate arrangements, the country has not *de iure* relinquished its monetary policy instruments. This is a very important difference with respect to the currency union agreements; for in currency unions, the countries relinquish their monetary policy

[31] Gold, *supra* n. 27, pp. 71–89.

[32] Whereby countries commit to maintain a fixed exchange rate vis-à-vis another currency or a basket of currencies.

[33] The introduction of a single currency for several countries.

[34] 'Dollarization' means the adoption of the currency of another country. For example, San Marino did not create a currency on its own, but adopted the Italian Lira, and subsequently the Euro when Italy became part of the EMU.

[35] On the so-called 'n-1 problem' in exchange rate arrangements, see Paul De Grauwe, *International Money – Postwar Trends and Theories*, Oxford: Oxford University Press 1996, pp. 17–60.

instruments and can no longer affect the peg that was irrevocably fixed at the creation of the single currency. Under Bretton Woods and the original Article IV of the IMF Agreement, whereby countries committed themselves to maintaining a certain par value with the dollar, other exchange rate arrangements were not a major problem for the Bretton Woods system. Indeed, if the rule of the game under Bretton Woods required central bank intervention to maintain the dollar peg, this would automatically trigger readjustments toward all other currencies of Bretton Woods countries (so-called triangular adjustments).[36] This would not have been the case for agreements created between countries outside Bretton Woods, in which case the country would have to realign its pegs under other agreements to respect its commitments under the system. Realignment is possible under an exchange rate regime, because the country can still manage its exchange rate policy. What would instead be the situation in a currency union? This was for example the core issue in the Malayan case, presented by Gold and also referred to by Denters.[37] A commission, and not directly a central bank, was in charge of managing the Malayan dollar, the currency of Malaya (the former name of Malaysia) and of five other dominions (including Singapore). The conclusion of the Malayan discussion in the IMF was that membership could be granted to the country (Malaysia) if, and only if, any monetary operations affecting the peg would be approved by Malaya. This rationale was subsequently followed in other cases, allowing individual membership to members of monetary integration frameworks.[38] However, this approach reached its limits when Singapore requested admission to the IMF on its own right.[39]

After the collapse of Bretton Woods, Article IV of the IMF Agreement revised the exchange rate arrangement. The amended provision requires simply that Member States ensure "to assure orderly exchange arrangements and to promote a stable system of exchange rates".[40] Regional or bilateral exchange rate arrangements, currency unions or exchange rate

---

[36] De Grauwe, ibid., p. 25.

[37] Gold, *supra* n. 27, pp. 106–113; Denters, *supra* n. 24, p. 217.

[38] Gold, *supra* n. 27, pp. 105–124.

[39] Ibid.

[40] Section 1 ('General obligations of members') of the revised Article IV of the IMF Agreement now reads as follows:

"Recognising that the essential purpose of the international monetary system is to provide a framework that facilitates the exchange of goods, services, and capital among countries, and that sustains sound economic growth, and that a principal objective is the continuing development of the orderly underlying conditions that are necessary for financial and economic stability, each member undertakes to collaborate with the Fund and

pegging could have been ways to attain this objective, even though the crisis of the 1990s moved floating exchange rates and inflation targeting to the core of current monetary policy frameworks.[41] But still, some other requirements rely on a country's capacity of being responsible for the choice of its exchange rate, for example in the case of competitive devaluation: "avoid manipulating exchange rates or the international monetary system in order to prevent effective balance of payment adjustments or to gain an unfair competitive advantage over the members and follow exchange policies compatible with the undertakings under this section". This is also true in any case for the requirement of fostering monetary and financial conditions in order not to provoke disruptions.

Another point that clarifies the question of whether a Member State without a central bank can or cannot fulfill its IMF membership requirements concerns the management of the Funds' resources. Each IMF member must provide to the Fund quotas, in currencies or Special Drawing Rights.[42] The IMF also allocates SDRsto its members that are to be used as reserve assets. Article VIII (4) of the IMF Agreement also requires that members have the capacity to buy its own currency in order to ensure the latter's convertibility. Can the management of these resources be outsourced without simultaneously losing the capacity of being an IMF member? As we will see, Europe's choice was not to create a single EU quota, but maintain the different Member States quotas. Consequently, notwithstanding the pooling of reserves within the European Central Bank, the EU had to leave some powers at the national level in order to allow national central banks to conduct such transactions with the IMF (detailed further below).

---

other members to assure orderly exchange arrangements and to promote a stable system of exchange rates.

In particular, each member shall:

(i) endeavour to direct its economic and financial policies toward the objective of fostering orderly economic growth with reasonable price stability, with due regard to its circumstances;

(ii) seek to promote stability by fostering orderly underlying economic and financial conditions and a monetary system that does not tend to produce erratic disruptions;

(iii) avoid manipulating exchange rates or the international monetary system in order to prevent effective balance of payments adjustments or to gain an unfair competitive advantage over the members and follow exchange policies compatible with the undertakings under this section."

[41] See further Rupa Duttagupta, Gilda Fernandez and Cem Karacadag, 'Moving to a Flexible Exchange Rate: How, When and How Fast?', (2005) 38 *Economic Issues*, pp. 1–30.

[42] Lowenfeld, *supra* n. 11, pp. 511–512.

Finally, the prohibition to impose limitations to current payments deserves a brief mentioning. In the EU, the Member States already transferred the corresponding competence to the supranational level, through the dedicated Chapter on the free movement of capital in the internal market.[43] Only under particular circumstances are they permitted to introduce such limitations themselves.[44]

3.3 *IMF Membership According to Object: Can the Currency Union Speak for the Country on All Relevant IMF Aspects?*

From the above discussion, it has become clear that monetary policy operations are important for fulfilling IMF obligations. This is obvious because – as emphasized by Denters – money exchange rates and the balance of payment form part of the Fund's general aims. As suggested by Article I of the IMF Agreement, the organization's overarching objective is cooperation in international monetary matters. With the breakdown of Bretton Woods though, this objective is mainly achieved through crisis management. The Fund's main activities in the post-Bretton Woods era have been surveillance of macro-economic activities and global liquidity, as well as technical and financial assistance in case of a crisis through stand-by arrangements. As crises have been triggered by balance of payment disequilibria and financial sector inefficiencies, the IMF's actions in crisis management have broadened beyond monetary policy choices to include financial sector regulation and any macroeconomic policy that can affect the balance of payments. In this context, we fundamentally agree with Denters when he argues that the IMF

> should concentrate primarily on solving monetary problems and thereby pave the way for growth and employment. Growth and employment should not be mistaken advocated as goals of the Fund in their own right.[45]

Growth and employment are definitely not goals of the Fund in their own right. As long as they restore competitiveness, they can however restore balance of payment disequilibria, and they are therefore still instruments to achieve the overarching objective. The same goes for fiscal policy. Conditionality attached to stand-by arrangements has covered several and

---

[43] See Art. 63, Art. 64 and Art. 66 TFEU.

[44] Only non-Euro area countries possess such a right under the specific circumstances of balance of payment disequilibria: see Article 144 TFEU.

[45] Quote from *Summary Proceedings of the 1994 Annual Meeting of the IMF Board of Governors* (Washington DC, IMF 1994), derived from Denters, *supra* n. 24, p. 219.

different real economic policies. It is possible to disagree with the concrete content of policy direction taken by conditionality, the way in which it is introduced, and its impact on democratic decision-processes, but it is very difficult to refute that conditionality must tackle real economy issues to restore financial and monetary stability.

Contrary to Denters' argumentation, the foregoing consideration leads us instead to believe that monetary policy competence alone is not sufficient. In reality, the objective of the IMF will be to counter balance of payment disequilibria, and this requires more and more focus on other policies, beyond the monetary one, that affect the balance of payment and economic fundamentals. Furthermore, if a financial or sovereign debt crisis occurs in a country that is part of a currency union while other countries are not affected,[46] then monetary policy cannot be used to restore the crisis,[47] and therefore crisis management must intervene on other decentralized policies. Moreover, even if it is true that a currency union creates a single balance of payment as a reference for the implementation of its monetary policy, it is also true that this single balance of payment remains fictional, in the absence of business cycle coordination within the currency union.[48] Indeed, this is presently the case in the sovereign

[46] This is called an asymmetric crisis, and it is characterized by intra-currency area disequilibria (in such a situation, the currency union economies' macroeconomic fundamentals diverge; they do not converge anymore at the level of the average aggregate used for monetary policy analysis to conduct the single currency).

[47] As monetary policy relies and affects only the aggregated values of the currency area, which are no longer representative as economies in an asymmetric crisis diverge, since the economic fundamentals of countries diverge more and more from the aggregated values of the currency area. In such a situation, the monetary policy does not find a single level of interest rate that is good for the whole currency area, and liquidity will have to be redistributed through open-market operations from countries in excess liquidity to countries in liquidity crisis. Moreover, when the credit market is impaired, this will affect the monetary transmission mechanism, and it will be difficult to make the monetary policy stimulus reach and affect real economy variables. In such a situation, monetary policy will therefore have a limited and constrained effect in solving the crisis. As a reference on the analysis of asymmetric crisis, see Paul De Grauwe, *The Economics of Monetary Union*, Oxford: Oxford University Press 2012, pp. 1–23; on the difficulties connected to the impairment of the monetary transmission mechanism, see the questions and answers to Mario Draghi's press conference of 6 September 2012, available on <http://www.ecb.int/press/pressconf/2012/html/is120906.en.html>.

[48] We refer here to situations where asymmetric crises are possible and the currency union is in fact not an optimal currency union as defined by Robert Mundell. According to Mundell, the perfect area for a single currency is an optimal currency area, which relies on business cycle coordination. In absence of business cycle coordination, i.e. an asymmetric crisis, the optimum currency area exhibits automatic stabilizers through price flexibility, intra-country labor mobility, financial market integration, or fiscal redistribution mecha-

debt crisis, where such disequilibria haunt the Euro area. Therefore, while originally the consultations of IMF members were only undertaken with EU Member States,[49] the Fund's choice to continue with both individual Members and Euro area-wide consultations under Article IV was probably most appropriate.[50] This required the intervention of both EU institutions and the Member States. The IMF's choice was extended to other currency areas.[51]

4. The EMU: An Incomplete Transfer of External Competences

The preceding reflections made clear that the IMF requires countries to be able to fulfill obligations in monetary policy, but also, in case of conditionality, in other economic policy areas such as fiscal policy, the labor market, financial regulation and structural reforms. With the creation of the EMU, the Union itself has received competences in the economic and monetary field. As mentioned above, competences in the pillars of the EMU are asymmetric. Article 3 TFEU mentions monetary policy for the Euro zone as an exclusive Union competence, whereas monetary policy of other Members States will be subject to a simple duty of coordination under Article 5 TFEU. The latter provision remains the legal basis for more general economic policy coordination for all Member States. Competences in financial markets regulations flow from both the EMU and the internal market competence. Below, these will be discussed separately.

4.1 *Monetary Policy for the Euro Area: Who is in Charge?*

On the one hand, it is true – as analyzed by Martha[52] – that the EMU has affected the Member States' capacity to act within the IMF, and

nism. See Robert Mundell, 'The Theory of Optimum Currency Areas', (1961) 51, *American Economic Review*, pp. 657–665. See also De Grauwe, *supra* n. 47, pp. 23–56 and 106–114.

[49] Cf. the early IMF applications of currency union members, reported in Gold, *supra* n. 27, pp. 105–124.

[50] While at the beginning, consultations for individual Member States should have been temporary, they were maintained. Euro-wide consultations were introduced subsequently. See Decision No. 11846 (98/125), 9 December 1998, and IMF Decision No. 12899 (02/119), 4 December 2002, as amended by Decision No. 14062 (08/15), 12 February 2008.

[51] See e.g. Decision No. 13655 (06/1), 6 January 2006, as amended by Decision No. 14060 (08/15), 12 February 2008, dealing with the modalities for surveillance over Eastern Caribbean Currency Union policies in the context of Article IV consultations with member countries.

[52] Rutsel Martha, 'The Fund Agreement and the Surrender of Monetary Sovereignty to the European Community', (1997), 30 *Common Market Law Review*, p. 749.

this is where the Union institutions intervene. On the other hand, the maintenance of the individual membership of the Member States has triggered a very peculiar vertical division of competence between national central banks and the ECB within the Fund. In that sense, as opposed to what normally would have happened under EU law,[53] it is not the international agreement – the IMF agreement – that was modified. Rather, the EMU organization was adapted to satisfy some requirements of the IMF membership of the Member States. Smits has inferred the necessity to create a joint action from Opinion 2/91,[54] where the ECJ proclaimed that:

> Cooperation between the Community and the Member States is all the more necessary in view of the fact that the former cannot, as international law stands at present, itself conclude an ILO Convention and must do so through the medium of the Member States.[55]

As the Community could not accede to the ILO Convention, Member States were to act in its place. However, we should not stop at this paragraph in the Opinion; for in the next, the Court emphasized that, even if Member States should continue to be the main EU international actors, there is a duty for "Community institutions and the Member States to take all the measures necessary so as best to ensure cooperation (...)".[56]

4.1.1 *The Transfer of Sovereignty on Monetary Policy and Exchange Rate Policy*

Monetary policy for the members of Euro zone falls within the exclusive competence of the EU (Article 3 TFEU), and is in the hands of the European System of Central Banks (ESCB). This entails a complete transfer of sovereign powers in the area of monetary policy decisions and exchange rate policies.[57] Article 127 TFEU hands the ESCB the following exclusive competences: (1) to define and implement the monetary policy of the Union; (2) to conduct foreign-exchange operations; (3) to hold and manage official reserves of Member States; (4) to promote the smooth operation of payment systems. The ECB and national central banks shall constitute the ESCB. Since the Euro area is not yet composed of all

[53] For example, if Art. 351 TFEU was applicable, or in any case through the application of Art. 4(3) TEU.

[54] Smits, *supra* n. 5, p. 441.

[55] ECJ, Opinion 2/91, *Participation of the Community in ILO Convention No. 170 on Chemicals at Work*, [1993] ECR I-1061, par. 36–38, par. 37.

[56] Ibid., par. 38.

[57] Martha, *supra* note 53, p. 749; Smits, *supra* n. 5, p. 431.

EU Member States, the ECB and the national central banks of the Euro area constitute the Eurosystem, and are in charge of conducting the monetary policy of the Union.[58] The decision-making bodies of the ECB govern the ESCB.[59] The ECB is thus the main decision-making institution of the common monetary policy, and only the implementation of the monetary policy is decentralized between the ECB and national central bank of the Euro zone. For these purposes, the ECB enjoys both legal personality and international legal personality.[60]

The exclusive competence of the ECB in the defining of monetary policy is however not mirrored in all aspects of the external relations with regard to that policy. The ESCB must *conduct* foreign-exchange operations consistent with Article 219 TFEU, which gives the main power of decision on foreign exchange rate agreements to the Council. The Council used this power with reference to arrangements concerning the Vatican, San Marino, Monaco, the CFA Franc, and the Cape Verde-Portugal agreement.[61] This horizontal outsourcing of external decision-making to the Council is particularly problematic and, as mentioned by Jean-Victor Louis, can cause "horizontal conflicts".[62] This is especially so because, as explained earlier, exchange rate arrangements influence and constrain monetary policy, and can therefore seriously limit the independence of the ESCB in defining its monetary policy. Aware of that link between monetary and exchange rate policy link, Germany desired to bestow more powers upon the ECB, whereas France preferred the decision-making to remain in the hands of political organs. Article 219 TFEU represents a compromise between these two positions, requiring the Council to either act on the basis of an ECB recommendation or, in the case of a Commission recommendation, only after consultation with the ECB (in an endeavor to reach a consensus consistent with the objective of price stability). The following procedure implies some deference of the Council for the exclusive competence of

---

[58] Article 282 TFEU.

[59] Article 129 TFEU and Article 282(2) TFEU.

[60] Article 9 of the Statute of the ECSB and ECB awards the ECB legal personality, and more precisely "the most extensive legal capacity accorded to a person under its law". International legal personality can be inferred from Article 6 of the Statute, where the ECB and NCBs are given express power to act in international institutions: "The ECB and, subject to its approval, the national central banks may participate in international monetary institutions."

[61] Zilioli and Selmayr, *supra* n. 65, pp. 218–221 and 225–228.

[62] Jean-Victor Louis, 'Les relations extérieures de l'Union économique et monétaire', in: Enzo Cannizzaro (ed.), *The European Union as an Actor in International Relations*, The Hague: Kluwer Law International 2002, p. 77.

the ECB with regard to monetary policy, and avoids substantial conflict. Indeed, an ECB assessment of a possible exchange rate arrangement would be based on its effect for the monetary policy objective of price stability, which is the cardinal objective of the common monetary policy under Article 119 TFEU. Even if the Council is able to say the last word on foreign exchange arrangements,[63] the obligation to respect the price stability objective for both monetary and exchange rate policy[64] renders any exchange rate policy that is considered to impinge on the price stability objective of the ECB's monetary policy a violation of EMU law. Therefore, if the ECB were to object on these grounds to a foreign exchange agreement decided by the Council, such an objection would have to be considered as *de facto* binding for the Council.[65] Still, this treaty-based limitation on the ECB's external competence is mirrored in the relations between the EU and the IMF as well. Indeed, whereas other topics of the common monetary policy are presented to the IMF by the ECB, exchange rate policy of the Euro is presented by both the ECB and the Presidency of the Council. The IMF rules are indifferent to the intervention of the political power of the Council in relation to exchange rate arrangements, which is purely dictated by an internal EU compromise. Even in the currently unlikely event of a single IMF membership of the Euro zone, power would be divided between the ECB and the Council.

According to Article 138 TFEU, the Council is also to decide about representation of the Union in external relations. In principle, external ECB action could also be constrained by the decisions of the Union's political organs. As scholars have noted however, such decisions cannot modify

---

63 As suggested by Louis, ibid., p. 84.

64 Article 119(2) TFEU.

65 Our position here occupies a middle ground between the line taken by Louis, who mainly sees a predominance of the Council's power, and the view held by Chiara Zilioli and Martin Selmayr, *The Law of the European Central Bank*, Oxford: Hart Publishing 2001, pp. 190–200 and pp. 203–206. In keeping with the ideas of the latter, our position recognizes the importance of respecting the objective of price stability and the independence of the ECB in carrying out monetary policy, while at the same time acknowledging that in this field, the competence to decide on exchange rate arrangements remains outside ECB competences. Other authors which argue for or against ECB external competence on exchange rate arrangement are Christoph Herrmann, 'Monetary Sovereignty over the Euro and External Relations of the Euro Area: Competences, Procedures and Practice', (2002) 7 *European Foreign Affairs Review*, p. 3 (defending a position opposite to Zilioli and Selmayr), and Norbert Weinrichter, 'The World and External Relations of the EMU – Fasten Your Seatbelts', (2000) 4 *European Integration Online Papers*, p. 12 (supporting Zilioli and Selmayr's claims).

and endanger the competences of the ECB awarded by the Treaties.[66] Again, the ECB should be consulted, and even though it is not explicitly mentioned as in Article 219 TFEU, any Union decision under the EMU Title may not endanger the price stability objective cemented in Article 119 TFEU. At the same time, when Article 6 of the ECB Statute grants the Central Bank the power to decide on the representation of the ESCB in international cooperation, and permits it to participate in international organizations, it also underlines that the power conferred in that provision does not prejudice Article 138 TFEU.[67] Finally, Article 138 TFEU also allows for the creation of a unified representation. It is possible that this provision was introduced with the hope that one day the Union could have a single membership within the IMF. As this provision is among those TFEU articles that apply only to Members States whose currency is the Euro, the TFEU explicitly foresees the possibility of a unified representation of the Euro zone (and not of the EU). This chimes with Article 3 TFEU, which clearly limits the transfer of sovereign powers in monetary policy from the Euro zone countries to the Union. For non-Euro area countries, the EMU only requires cooperation, but no transfer of sovereignty has occurred, and therefore they also get to keep all external competences in the area.[68] However, for these countries, the duty to cooperate and coordinate in economic and monetary field is still a hard obligation, also in their external relations.

4.1.2 *The External Competence of National Central Banks and Their Role in the IMF*

Powers with regard to external relations and external representation were expressly divided between the Council and the ECB (as the representative of the European System of Central Banks), and between the EU level and national central banks (NCBs). In the IMF, NCBs act as representatives of their own state and therefore as national agents, since only countries under Article II of the IMF Agreement can apply for membership. This is an interesting example of the *dédoublement fonctionnel* of NCBs within the EMU.

[66] Louis, *supra* n. 62, p. 82.

[67] See Article 6(3) of the Statute of the ECSB and ECB.

[68] See Article 141 and Article 142 TFEU. Those articles apply also to the opt-out countries, the UK (with some modification for Article 141(1) TFEU) and Denmark. See respectively Protocol 15 and Protocol 16, annexed to the EU Treaties (OJ [2010] C 83/201).

National central banks are an integral part of the ESCB, and as such, they act as agents of the ECB. Nevertheless, they retain some residual tasks as national agents, e.g. certain supervisory and regulatory functions in financial markets,[69] and at the national level, some of them are entrusted with extra competences in these fields. The latter applies also with regard to external matters. Indeed, the ECB Statute itself recognizes the possibility of the presence of NCBs alongside the ECB, or their solo performance in international organizations and negotiations.[70] For example, the role of the French Central Bank within the CFA Franc arrangement[71] and the NCBs external representation to the IMF are still considered national actions, as they function as representatives of the respective countries, and not as representatives of the Euro zone. Thus, NCBs carry out their functions wearing two different hats: as member of the ESCB and as national agents. The interrelation between these two identities is clearly subject to specific rules that bind their actions to the EMU system. Zilioli and Selmayr rightly point out that national actions of NCBs are exceptional,[72] and cannot interfere with ESCB objectives or tasks. They refer to this specific loyalty obligation of NCBs in the exercise of their non-ESCB tasks as 'system integrity'. This is emphasized further by the compliance obligation of Article 131 TFEU.[73] This requirement of consistency between actions of NCBs as national agents and the competences granted at the EU level (through the EMU) is mirrored in external action as well. After all, Article 219(4) TFEU states that Member States may negotiate in international bodies and conclude international agreements, without prejudice to the Union's competence and EU agreements pertaining to the EMU.

There are moreover no persuasive reasons why the more general duty of loyal cooperation under Article 4(3) TEU would fail to apply. Not only does it bind NCBs in the same way as the aforementioned EMU provisions, but equally treasury officials that may also represent the Member State at the IMF.[74]

---

[69] See Article 14 of the Statute of the ECSB and ECB.

[70] See Article 23 of the Statute of the ECSB and ECB.

[71] This continued function of the French Central Bank had to be accepted first by the Council (as we have seen, the Council is in charge of exchange rate arrangements in the Euro area).

[72] Zilioli and Selmayr, *supra* n. 65, p. 79.

[73] Article 131 TFEU reads: "Each Member State shall ensure that its national legislation including the statutes of its national central bank is compatible with the Treaties and the Statute of the ESCB and of the ECB."

[74] The potential role of article 4(3) TEU is discussed further in par. 5.2 below.

To ensure the capacity of Member States to maintain their own IMF quotas, contributions to the IMF are exonerated from the obligations of Euro zone members to hand over their foreign reserves to the ECB. Indeed, Article 30(1) of the Statute of the ESCB and ECB states that the NCBs shall provide the European Central Bank "with foreign reserve assets, other than Member States' currencies, Euro, IMF reserve positions and SDRs, up to an amount equivalent to EUR 50.000 million". Furthermore, Article 31(1) clarifies that NCBs shall be allowed to perform transactions in fulfillment of their obligations towards international organizations in accordance with Article 23. The second indent of the clause provides once again for a guarantee that such actions by NCB respect ESCB objective and tasks. Namely:

> All other operations in foreign reserve assets remaining with the national central banks after the transfers referred to in Article 30, and Member States' transactions with their foreign exchange working balances shall, above a certain limit to be established within the framework of Article 31.3, be subject to approval by the ECB in order to ensure consistency with the exchange rate and monetary policies of the Union.

Thus, NCBs must consult with the ECB in any area within the latter's competence.[75] On this basis, the ECB has been consulted on the IMF quota reforms, and how these conform to EMU law.[76]

4.2 *Fiscal and Economic Policy and Financial Regulation in the EU: The Asymmetric Competences of the EMU and Joint EU-Member State Actions in the IMF*

Fiscal and structural policies have always been at the centre of the IMF's conditionality. Financial regulation became more and more relevant to the IMF framework with the advent of the global financial crisis, in the wake of the Asian crisis, in particular through its assessments of reforms in financial market supervisions, and the drafting of the World Financial Outlook.

In the first area, the EU institutions only provide a coordination framework.[77] Consequently, sovereignty remains firmly in the hands of

---

[75] See Article 127(4) TFEU.

[76] For two examples (pertaining to a Euro and non-Euro country), see Opinion of the European Central Bank of 1 June 2012 on the increase of Hungary's quota with the International Monetary Fund (CON/2012/45); Opinion of the European Central Bank of 9 November 2011 on the payment by the Banco de Portugal of an increase in Portugal's quota with the International Monetary Fund (CON/2011/89).

[77] See Article 5 TFEU.

the countries concerned. This would restrict the political capacity of a single Union seat. The same goes for the second area in which joint EU and Member States participation is required. Indeed, the 2008 financial crisis has triggered an increased amount of actions at the EU level in the field of financial regulation.[78] Nevertheless, in fields where the EU has not acted, the relevant regulation has remained national. The same goes for supervisory and prudential competences. Those traditionally rested with the NCBs and the Commission, and only specific tasks were partially performed by the ECB.[79] The new European System of Financial Supervision includes the European Systemic Risk Board, and the three European Supervisory Authorities (the European Banking Authority (EBA), the European Securities Market Authority (ESMA) and the European Insurance and Occupational Pensions Authority (EIOPA), but also national authorities whose role has not been supplemented at the European level. In these areas too, application of Article 4(3) TEU cannot be discarded a priori. Over time, financial regulation, which used to be mainly national, has more and more become a shared competence. Therefore, in accordance with established case law, the duty of cooperation is applicable.[80]

Notwithstanding the particular characteristic of economic policy coordination under Article 5 TFEU,[81] it also binds Member States to respect certain obligations. This flows for example from the provision in Article 121 TFEU, which states that Member States "shall regard their economic policies as a matter of common concern and shall coordinate them within the Council". The economic policies of the Member States are to contribute to the objectives of the Union and follow the guiding principles of stable prices, sound public finances and sustainable balance of payment.[82]

---

[78] Inter alia, communication and guidelines to ensure compatibility of liquidity provisions to banks with state aid rules, the creation of the European Banking Authority, European Securities Market Authority and the European Insurance and Occupational Pensions Authority.

[79] See Article 25 of the Statute of the ESCB and ECB. The role of the ECB in prudential supervision will be increased by the proposed legislation on a 'Banking Union'.

[80] On the duty of loyal cooperation in the context of shared competences and coordination of Member States' positions, see ECJ, Case 266/03, *Commission* v *Luxembourg*, [2005] ECR I-4805; Case C-433/03, *Commission* v *Germany*, [2005] ECR I-6967; ECJ, Case C-246/07, *Commission* v *Sweden*, [2010] ECR I-3317.

[81] Article 5 TFEU does not foresee any transfer of competences to the EU level, as is instead the case for exclusive competences under Article 3 TFEU and shared competences under Article 4 TFEU. Article 5 TFEU sets up a framework for coordination of Member State policies.

[82] See Article 120 and 119 TFEU, respectively.

All these principles must be complied with in the determination of internal policy, but apply equally on the external front.

5. Problems Caused by the Fragmentation of EU Representation within the IMF and the Sovereign Debt Crisis

5.1 *Legal and Political Problems Flowing from the Fragmented EU Representation at the IMF*

The fragmentation of EU representation at the IMF raises a number of legal questions. For starters, while with regard to the Euro zone, the EU has exclusive competence in monetary policy, one may wonder whether the Union should not have replaced those Member States within the IMF, following the parallelism between internal and external competences within the EU. In reality, the Union's institutions were only granted observer status, while Member States have retained their traditional position within the IMF. As we observed, remarkable about the IMF–EU relation is that not the IMF agreement was modified as a result of EU integration,[83] but rather, the Member States were given competences within the EMU monetary pillar, in order to maintain their position within the IMF. Would maintaining this status quo be compatible with EU law? In other words, does the current arrangement affect the exercise of the ECB's competence, and its independence, as enshrined in Article 130 TFEU? The main 'insurance policy' here is the loyalty clause enshrined in the EMU legal framework that binds each institution involved (be it national or European), to act in accordance with EMU tasks and objectives.

The second, and perhaps most discussed problem of all with regard to EU–IMF governance pertains to the voting balance within the IMF, and in particular the balance between European and developing countries within the Executive Board. The retained individual positions of the Member States, and their dispersion over various constituencies in order to increase the individual Member State power, excites complaints

[83] Many authors suggested that the EU should require amendment of Article II of the IMF Agreement and pursue Union membership. We already mentioned that, beyond Article II, the participation of Member States would need to be flexible, because of their powers in other economic policies that are of concern to the IMF, even if the Fund's objective is purely monetary. For further analysis of the possible amendment of Article II and its limitations, see Der-Chin Horng, 'The ECB's Membership in the IMF: Legal Approaches to Constitutional Challenges', (2005) 11 *European Law Journal*, pp. 814–821.

of 'Too much Europe' from the side of developing countries. Indeed, if one looks at the table of the constituencies, over nineteen multi-country constituencies, five are headed or have an alternate head from a European country, and one is currently not headed by a European country but will be after rotation (the constituency with Spain). To these one must add the three single country chairs of Germany, France and the UK. In total, of the twenty-four Executive Board directors' positions, Europeans could potentially hold up to nine chairs.[84] The successive reforms in 2006, 2008 and 2010 result in a substantial loss of voting power of larger European countries, in favor of smaller and developing countries.[85] The 2010 reform, which still needs to be formally implemented, requires advanced European economies to reduce their combined Board representation by two chairs.[86] This trend is not going to be altered; for the moment however, its slow-moving path forms a less urging incentive for the EU Member States to retract and form a single constituency, as suggested by Bini Smaghi.[87] Both the single constituency and the single EU seat would produce the problem of a polarization of power between the US and the EU, and therefore, these innovations might be resisted by developing countries as well as the US.[88] Additionally, a rationalization of the European chairs (through either a unified representation of the Union or the Euro zone, or through a single constituency unifying all Member States) is politically resisted by many EU Member States that fear to lose substantial voting power within the organization.[89]

Beyond legal and governance issues, it is important to consider how the EU can effectively play a role within the IMF with the current setup. Already during the Asian crisis, in order to discuss financial matters, the importance of the IMF for the EU was emphasized.[90] The current crisis

---

84 See 'IMF Executive Directors and Voting Power', available at: <http://www.imf.org/external/np/sec/memdir/eds.aspx>.

85 See Brandner and Grech, *supra* n. 16.

86 See 'IMF Executive Board Approves Major Overhaul of Quotas and Governance', available at: <http://www.imf.org/external/np/sec/pr/2010/pr10418.htm>. The European Commission issued a similar proposal: see Communication from the Commission, 'A blueprint for a deep and genuine Economic and Monetary Union – Launching a European debate', COM(2012) 777 final/2.

87 Bini Smaghi, *supra* n. 17, pp. 229–248.

88 On a single EU seat, see also Hervé, *supra* n. 10, pp. 158–161;

89 See *ECB Monthly Bulletin*, May 2011 (available at <http://www.ecb.int/pub/mb/html/index.en.html>, p. 96.

90 European Council Conclusions, Vienna, 11 and 12 December 1998, III(A)(ii), point 16: "The European Council welcomes the report on strengthening the international financial system, which shows that Member States share a common outlook on the appropriate

has certainly brought this importance back to theforeground. Indeed, the accent on reforming the IMF has been strong in Europe, at least up until the outbreakof the sovereign debt crisis, which has moved interest away from IMF reforms to EMU reforms. Currently, discussions on global financial reforms seem more centered on the informal meetings of the G20 and G8, which are however mostly insisting on European reforms. One may therefore wonder whether the IMF, and the Union's position within it, is truly of fundamental importance to Europe. The first remark that should be made in this respect relates to the collaboration that the EU institutions (in particular the Commission) have established in the past with the IMF. This collaboration predates the current loan facilities, and can be traced back to the IMF involvement in Turkey after the Turkish financial crisis of 1999. The IMF reforms there, in particular as regards financial market supervision and independence of the central bank, followed the lines of the Union's acquis, to be adopted as part of the process of EU accession. More recently, the 2007/2008 subprime crisis badly affected the Central and Eastern European Countries and the Baltic States, particularly Latvia. These countries requested help under the EU funds for balance of payment disequilibria (based on Article 143 TFEU) as well as from the IMF. The meeting of the conditions is supervised by the European Commission as well as IMF officials. These countries were not part of the Euro zone, but the cooperation between the Commission and the IMF did prove useful for the Euro zone members in the sovereign debt crisis. Due to the belief in a single balance of payment for the entire zone, no fund was set up in the EMU framework for individual Euro countries in case of a severe asymmetric crisis. Thus, an asymmetric crisis would have to be dealt with through the own fiscal resources of the Member States. Greece, lacking the maneuvering room to cope with the crisis, faced the consequences, which gave rise to the sovereign debt crisis, as well as a spill-over to countries on the periphery of the Euro zone. Lacking the funds necessary to face the predicament, Greece obtained bilateral loans from other Euro zone countries, and an IMF standby arrangement was concluded. The conditionality requirements were introduced through EU law on the basis of Article 136 TFEU.[91] The creation of the EU loan facilities (the EFSF and

responses to the global financial crisis. Europe shall play a decisive role in elaborating a new international monetary and financial system (...) The IMF is the cornerstone of the international monetary and financial system (...)."

[91] Council Decision of 10 May 2010 addressed to Greece with a view to reinforcing and deepening fiscal surveillance and giving notice to Greece to take measures for the

the ESM)[92] still involves the IMF in monitoring conditionality, and the ECB calls for the IMF to be involved in monitoring the conditionality of bond purchases under the new Outright Monetary Transactions scheme. Moreover, even if the Camdessus report[93] on IMF reform has not been adopted, the future debate on how to regulate monetary and financial markets in order to avoid new global liquidity crises and disequilibria will probably still remain centered around the IMF. The weakness of the EU representation in the IMF, and the consistent weakening of its position due to the current crisis, did not allow the EU to export efficiently beyond its borders its normative and regulatory progresses in financial market regulation. The initial ambitious program that would see Europe "play a decisive role in elaborating a new international monetary and financial system" is far from being realized. A more cohesive and compact action of the Union and the Member States within the IMF would be the first response.

5.2 *The Duty of Loyal Cooperation and Its Potential Role in EU–IMF Relations*

From the above discussion, it can be inferred that it would be politically difficult to change the current representation of the EU Member States within the executive organ of the IMF. Changes, if any, will probably result from the pressure of emerging developing countries (as demonstrated in the last IMF governance reforms). However, a continued Member State representation, and even their fragmented presence in various constituencies, should not be seen as an obstacle to the creation of a European shared identity within the IMF.

We agree with Cremona[94] and Casolari[95] that the role of the duty of cooperation under Article 4 TEU must not be underestimated in

---

deficit reduction judged necessary to remedy the situation of excessive deficit, OJ [2010] L 145/6.

[92] See also See *ECB Monthly Bulletin*, May 2011 (available at <http://www.ecb.int/pub/mb/html/index.en.html>, p. 96.

[93] Michel Camdessus, Alexandre Lamfalussy, Tomasso Padoa-Schioppa et al., *Reform of the International Monetary System: a Cooperative Approach for the Twenty-First Century*, 8 February 2011, Palais-Royal Initiative, available at: <http://www.global-currencies.org/smi/gb/telechar/news/Rapport_Camdessus-integral.pdf>.

[94] Marise Cremona, 'Member States as Trustees of the Community Interest: Participating in International Agreements on Behalf of the Union', *EUI Working Paper LAW* 2009/17.

[95] Federico Casolari, 'The Principle of Loyal Cooperation: A "Master Key" for EU External Relations?', in: Steven Blockmans and Ramses Wessel (eds.), 'Principles and Practices of EU External Representation', *CLEER Working Papers* 2012/5, p. 11.

cases where, notwithstanding an exclusive or shared EU competence, Member States continue to be the main representative of the Union in an international organization. It has already been mentioned that the ECJ allows Member States to be representatives of the Union in international organizations, when the latter do not allow the EU to become a member itself.[96] When in a matter of exclusive Union competence, the Member States should thus be seen as proxy of the European institution, while in shared competences, they would wear a double-hat as sovereign countries and as EU Member States. In both cases, the duty of loyal cooperation intervenes as the guarantor of coherent Member State action within the international organization, with due respect for their Union law obligations. The initial case law focused on procedural duty of cooperation, understood as a best effort obligation. As highlighted by various authors,[97] the duty has evolved into a substantial one. In particular, with regard to exclusive EU competences, the duty takes the form of an obligation to abstain from unilateral actions. This situation was mainly represented by the *IMO* case.[98] The latter pertained to a unilateral proposal submitted by Greece within the framework of the International Maritime Organization. Even though the EU is not part of the IMO, the relevant subject matter fell under EU competences. Therefore, the Court declared that Member States could not unilaterally submit proposals, since Member States must de facto act jointly in the Union's interest, as a proxy of the EU institutions within the international organization. As Delgado and Larik point out, the fact that the Union (then still the Community) disregarded the proposal submitted by Greece, and therefore might have ignored its own duty of cooperation, did not excuse Greece from acting unilaterally within IMO.[99] Drawing a parallel with the EMU and the IMF, an action that pertains to the Union's exclusive competences, e.g. on exchange rate arrangements and monetary policy decisions, are to be submitted through the ECB in its role as observer, and Member States cannot act independently.

---

[96] ECJ, Opinion 2/91, *supra* n. 50, par. 36.

[97] See, inter alia, Cremona, *supra* n. 94; Casolari, *supra* n. 95; Andrés Delgado Casteleiro and Joris Larik, 'The Duty to Remain Silent: Limitless Loyalty in EU External Relations?', (2011) 36 *European Law Review*, p. 524; Christophe Hillion, 'Cohérence et action extérieure de l'Union européenne', *EUI Working Papers LAW* 2012/14; Elefteria Neframi, 'The Duty of Loyalty: Rethinking its Scope through its Application in the Field of the EU External Relations', (2010) 47 *Common Market Law Review*, p. 323.

[98] ECJ, Case C-45/07, *Commission* v *Greece*, [2009] ECR I -701.

[99] Casteleiro and Larik, *supra* n. 97, p. 532.

In an area of shared competences, where decisions have been taken at the EU level to negotiate jointly, this brings with it a duty for Member States to cooperate before acting independently. From the *Inland Waterways* cases,[100] it followed that this duty was merely a duty of cooperation and consultation, but in the *PFOS* case,[101] it became a substantive duty. For, by acting individually, the Member State was considered to violate the concerted decision taken at EU level (regardless of how informal that decision was). Here too, we can draw a parallel with the common positions taken within the ECOFIN Council and the EURIMF. Delgado and Larik have already warned about the seemingly limitless development of the duty of loyal cooperation,[102] and perhaps it goes rather far to take it into consideration for every aspect of the concerted approach to IMF issues. However, a common position agreed upon in this informal setting (if not the EURIMF concerted positions, at least those that are confirmed by the Council) on matters of common concerns for the Union (or the Euro zone) should bind the Member States (the members of the Euro zone), as that flows from their very basic duty of good faith, and the necessity of an effective coordination mechanism to ensure unity in the Union representation.

6. Concluding Remarks

The Union's representation at the IMF is an example of the complexities involved in the delimitation of EU external relations competences. The Economic and Monetary Union is characteristic of a double-speed and asymmetric policy. Indeed, while some Member States have united in a currency union, others have (for now) chosen to preserve their own currency. While economic policy is only subject to coordination, for members of the Euro zone, monetary policy is an exclusive competence. Nonetheless, the latter competence knows a considerable degree of decentralization, and there are some areas of residual national competence, e.g. (up to a certain amount) the management of certain central bank reserves. This is reflected in the different ways in which EU institutions are involved with respect to international economic and monetary relations, and their

---

[100] ECJ, Case 266/03, *Commission* v *Luxembourg*, [2005] ECR I-4805; Case C-433/03, *Commission* v *Germany*, [2005] ECR I-6967.

[101] ECJ, Case C-246/07, *Commission* v *Sweden*, [2010] ECR I-3317.

[102] Casteleiro and Larik, *supra* n. 97, p. 532.

current representation within the IMF. From that point of view, the creation of the common currency, adopted by (currently) seventeen members, has not resultedinto a prominent role of the EU within the IMF, in the same way as the conclusion of the customs union changed the Union's position in the GATT and the WTO. Still, while the Member States appear to have maintained their traditional positions, both the ECB and the Commission participate at the IMF within their area of competence and enjoy an observer status. The current institutional setup flows from the EMU division of competences as well as from the current IMF membership rules, which restrict full participation to countries. The EMU framework was drafted with the intention to continue the participation of Member States within the IMF, even though the legal possibility for a decision leading to future unified representation was introduced. However, the continued action of the Member States within the IMF is still constricted through the various loyalty clauses in the EU Treaties. Already in 1998, the Vienna European Council of December 1998 declared that:

> [C]oherence and effectiveness require that it shall be able to speak with one voice on issues of particular relevance to economic and monetary union. The European Council encourages the Commission, the Council and the Member States to take the necessary action to ensure a timely and effective preparation of common positions and common understandings which can be presented to third parties in international fora.[103]

The preparation of common positions within the ECOFIN Council and the EURIMF is (de facto) the main way in which coherence can be realized within the framework of EU–IMF relations. One could wonder then whether the recent trends in the case law of the ECJ do not trigger the application of a duty of loyalty every time a common decision and position is taken, even in informal forums such as the EURIMF. Considering the contemporary lack of political will to implement reforms in terms of seat and IMF constituencies, more uniform actions in the IMF could be prompted by a greater adherence of the Member States to their duty of loyalty towards EMU tasks and objectives. In the future though, it is more likely that the greater political opposition of Member States towards rationalizing their IMF chairs will be countered by sustained pressure from developing countries.

[103] European Council Conclusions, Vienna, 11 and 12 December 1998, III(A)(ii), point 15.

CHAPTER TEN

'NAME ME YOUR FRIENDS, AND I WILL TELL YOU WHO YOU ARE' – THE UNION AND THE MEMBER STATES IN THE GLOBAL ARENA

Henri de Waele

1. Introduction: The Union's Incremental Global Presence

The past decades have been marked by a nearly irrepressible advance of the EU into the world of international organizations. As yet however, full Union membership of such organizations remains a relatively rare occurrence. It has obtained this status in the EBRD, the WTO, the FAO, the Hague Conference on Private International Law and the Codex Alimentarius Commission. It is not a member of the other specialized UN organizations, the UN itself, the IMF, the World Bank, NATO, or the Council of Europe. Also, it has not acceded either to the ILO or the IMO, which can be considered surprising in light of its broad powers as regards social and maritime policy.[1] Nevertheless, even when not integrally taking part, the EU has certainly achieved a greater visibility, and exerted a growing influence on the activities of its global partners.[2]

The relations between the Union and a select number of international organizations has been the subject of the research carried out in the foregoing chapters, with a view to exposing its position and participation, as well as the external perceptions of that position and participation. As duly realized in advance, the organizations concerned display a considerable substantive heterogeneity, and were not designed on the basis of a uniform institutional blueprint. This has overall resulted in a neat panorama, but impedes the drawing of too general conclusions. At the same time, several common trends and recurring patterns could all too easily be spotted, and at this stage deserve to be underscored.

---

[1] Piet Eeckhout, *EU External Relations Law*, Oxford: Oxford University Press 2011, p. 223.

[2] Frank Hoffmeister, 'Outsider or Frontrunner? Recent Developments under International and European Law on the Status of the European Union in International Organizations and Treaty Bodies', (2007) 44 *Common Market Law Review*, p. 67.

As explained earlier, the international identity of the EU encompasses all the means and forms, both tangible and intangible, through which it manifests itself at the international level. Furthermore, since identity is a question of standpoint, a capturing of the entirety calls for the inclusion of different standpoints.[3] In the preceding analyses, the construction and representation of the Union has been assessed from multiple angles. This has ultimately made it possible to juxtapose the different experiences, test our provisional assumptions, and draw some general conclusions with regard to the EU's emerging international identity.[4]

2. Adaptability and Context-Sensitivity of the Union's Profile

A first expectation pertained to the adaptability and context-sensitivity of the Union's profile. From the outset, we assumed the EU's identity to have a chameleonic quality, and the viability of its emergence to be determined by the specific setting. This is perhaps exemplified most vividly in (the modalities of) its partaking in the OECD. As observed, the latter's decentralized structure is extremely sophisticated, resembling a complex amalgam of committees that pursue their own agendas in varying ways. Consequently, the EU's stature within the OECD has been seen to vary in tenor and significance, depending on the particular issue (and corresponding committee) at stake. A similar malleable *habitus* appears evident within the IMF, where a single Union identity as such is prevented from arising due to the absence of a truly unified system of representation. For one thing, the distinction between Euro and non-Euro area countries does not go unnoticed, with the situation being exacerbated further by the attendance of the Council, the ECB and the Commission, alongside the Member States (and their central banks). With respect to the WTO, the Union's identity is largely defined by its internal market activities, but the context of this organization offers sufficient flexibility for it to pursue non-trade values, which it has done quite emphatically, even before WTO dispute settlement bodies. The EU thus bases

[3] Ian Manners and Richard Whitman, 'Towards Identifying the International Identity of the European Union: A Framework for Analysis of the EU's Network Relationships' (1998) 21 *Journal of European Integration*, pp. 237–8.

[4] Of course, the inferences drawn in this chapter cannot and do not bear any pretense of universal validity.

its international trade identity on multilateralism, but simultaneously makes clear that other (internally endorsed) objectives can often take precedence.

Apart from this continual changing and adjusting from the side of the Union, in accordance with the needs and the possibilities within an organization, we assumed that the less politicized the specific environment, the more receptive the latter would turn out to be.[5] This has held true for the UN, in view of the struggles to acquire the enhanced observer status, but there was more here that lent credence to the thought. For instance, within the Human Rights Council, the Union faces a predominant 'regional bloc mentality', and an especially strong presence of the Organization of the Islamic Conference and the African Group. All the same, cases such as the Human Rights Council's Special Session on Darfur and the EU's participation in the negotiations on the moratorium on the death penalty indicated that, in the end, the particular political constellation is decisive for the Union's potential to significantly impact on the decision-making process, rather than the legal and institutional architecture of the relevant forum. Similar thoughts prevail with respect to the NATO, where the EU at present is not and cannot become an official member either. As with the UN Charter, the Union itself, in contrast with its Member States, is not subject to the obligations of the NATO Treaty. So far, no attempts at a greater legal *rapprochement* have been made, with the 'Berlin Plus' arrangement constituting the only formal nexus.[6] Within this context, there also exists no (reciprocal) support for moving beyond the 'living apart together' arrangement.

3. Interlinking the Union's Official Position, Identity and Performance

One might believe the EU to cut a finer figure in forums where its position is more solidly anchored. Thus, its identity would be weaker to begin with in organizations where it merely holds an observer status, or

[5] Moving beyond the obvious point here that not all international organizations allow for Union membership.

[6] Apart from the commitments undertaken in the form of treaties on specific topics; see e.g. Agreement between the European Union and NATO on the security of information, [2003] OJ L 80/36.

(as such) does not take part at all.[7] Indeed, the Union's official legal position seems to determine its stature and influence, but a more complete presence does not guarantee an actual 'speaking with one voice', and therefore does not guarantee a truly effective performance either.[8] In the ILO for example, after the precursor of the EU had become an observer, instead of abating, the friction with the Member States increased. Especially in the 1983–2000 period, the views of the latter (often supported by their national social partners) diverged considerably from those of the Commission. Rather than functioning as a catalyst for greater harmony, the shared participation in this forum hampered the formation of a structural united front. The story of the WTO illustrates though that full membership offers no panacea. To this, the precedent of the FAO, discussed in the contribution on EU–UN relations, can be added. For despite the Union institutions and Member States taking pains to work out an internal arrangement to enable a smooth concerted practice there, this did not obviate the need for repeated statements with respect to the division of competences.[9] Moreover, a substantial inequality is retained due to the EU being ineligible for election, designation or participation in FAO bodies where only countries are accepted.[10]

Conversely, a complete formal absence does not lead to outright invisibility, as evidenced by the analysis of the situation in the Council of Europe. There the EU is neither a member nor does it enjoy the status of observer, as the legal arrangements underpinning both organizations do not allow for this. What they do allow for is mutual assistance and cooperation, and over the years various forms of indirect contact have been established. In addition, the EU may send representatives to the meetings of several Intergovernmental Committees of the CoE, and it takes part in four CoE bodies which were set up as (enlarged) partial agreements. On top of this, the EU has signed and ratified numerous CoE treaties. Yet, we noticed a same discomfort here as flagged above, essentially arising from a fear

[7] Even when the Member States are to act as its 'trustees' there, the likelihood of fragmentation is still invariably greater.

[8] Cf. Knud Erik Jørgensen and Ramses Wessel, 'The Position of the European Union in (other) International Organizations: Confronting Legal and Political Approaches', in: Panos Koutrakos (ed.), *EU Foreign Policy – Legal and Political Perspectives*, Cheltenham: Edward Elgar 2011, pp. 282–3.

[9] In the same vein e.g. Inge Govaere, Jeroen Capiau and An Vermeersch, 'In-Between Seats: The Participation of the European Union in International Organizations', (2004) 9 *European Foreign Affairs Review*, pp. 165–7.

[10] See Article II(9) of the FAO Constitution.

of duplication, which was most palpable in the period surrounding the launch of the Union's Fundamental Rights Agency. After the EU accedes to the ECHR, the Union shall be entitled to take part in sessions of the Committee of Ministers of the CoE and obtain the right to vote there, but this might once again increase rather than diminish the potential for division. On the other hand, the failed attempt at creating a 'European Security and Defence Identity' within NATO could be taken to mean that, whenever the Union is unable to join, a unitary presence does not immediately follow from synchronized efforts from the collective of Member States.[11]

In sum, the EU's profile in a certain organization may have a lot to gain from a more extensive involvement, but this cannot be called a hard and fast rule. Moreover, it hardly guarantees a truly unitary representation, mainly due to the fact that the environments in which the Union operates *to the exclusion of the Member States* are few and far between. In turn, whereas a 'European influence' might be quantifiably greater when the Union and the Member States operate alongside one another, this situation is anything but conducive to the rise of a uniform identity, and could just as well hamper the effectiveness of the performance. At the end of the day though, the importance of loyal cooperation and coordination between the Member States or (if applicable) the Union institutions and the Member States, could trump that of formal, partial or non-participation of the EU itself.[12]

4. Interlinking Formal Competences, Identity and Effectiveness

In the introductory chapter we already noted that, while the Union's external action mirrors its internal dynamics to a considerable degree, its internal decision-making and external representation are still different things. Naturally, at the heart of the matter lies the division of competences between the EU and the Member States, with a shared Union competence producing the mixed participation in international organizations

[11] Apart from the fact that, within NATO, such synchronized efforts have on the whole not been that regular an occurrence.

[12] But cf. Jørgensen and Wessel, *supra* n. 8, p. 285, who contend that *neither* formal membership *nor* improved coordination are sufficient preconditions for a higher EU impact within a given policy field.

described above. When the joint presence of the EU and the Member States does not do all that much to advance the emergence of structural common positions, the blame may logically be placed on the non-exclusive quality of the Union's powers – even when an exclusive power does not immediately yield *effective* performance either. The weak image within the IMF can be largely explained on this footing: despite the Council being tasked to ensure a unified representation within international financial institutions and conferences, matters are compounded by the EU's competence only being exclusive with regard to monetary policy for the Member States whose currency is the Euro.[13] Internally as well, the EMU only requires cooperation from non-Euro area countries, but these get to keep their relevant external powers.[14] To be sure, the legal duty to cooperate and coordinate in economic and monetary field did not cease to apply to these countries, but does not automatically iron out all possible conflicts of interest.

The study of the OECD partially corroborates this thesis, since the nature of the Union's competences on issues residing within the organization's scope of activities was found to have a marked impact on the Union's identity there. Especially when exercising its exclusive powers, the EU upholds a strong and often leading role in the OECD. Amazingly however, the Union occasionally even represents the Member States in areas where it lacks competences altogether, which suggests that even in the absence of formal authority, at least an impression of 'European homogeneity' can be conveyed. By the same token, in the WTO, in spite of the Court's determining that the EC did not have the competence to conclude agreements in the area of trade in services and trade related aspects of intellectual property rights, the Commission has made no bones about playing an active role in these fields.[15] In contrast, while inside the EU, competences pertaining to the Area of Freedom, Security and Justice are shared,[16] three Member States have secured a special position with respect to the adoption of internal acts. Ireland and the United Kingdom may decide ad hoc whether they participate in a specific measure; Denmark is not bound by such measures at all. Consequently, the EU is prevented from representing

[13] See Art. 138(2) TFEU and Art. 3(1)(c) TFEU.
[14] See Art. 141 and Art. 142 TFEU.
[15] Opinion 1/94, *Competence of the Community to conclude international agreements concerning services and the protection of intellectual property*, [1994] ECR I-5267.
[16] Art. 4(2)(j) TFEU.

the entire franchise in the Hague Conference on a certain dossier, even when it would otherwise be granted leave to do so, and is formally disconnected from these three countries from the very beginning. The discrepancy between the situation here and in the OECD is understandable when realizing that the latter functions in an advisory capacity, whereas 'hard law' is frequently brought about within the confines of the Hague Conference and the WTO.

It seems clear in any case that when competences are divided in an asymmetric fashion, the Union institutions and Member States should tread carefully, which holds *a fortiori* if the EU possesses exclusive competences in a certain field, but the relevant international organization does not permit it to join. The idea of letting the supranational interests be advanced and defended by proxy looks fine on paper, but reality has repeatedly demonstrated that the perceptions of the 'common interest' can vary radically in the eyes of the 'trustees'.[17] The weakness of the theory becomes even clearer when we realize that it attempts to reverse the order of play posited by political scientists, as the Union seeks to hold the reins as a principal, employing the Member States as its agents. Rather, given the ubiquity of mixed participation, the Member States more often have the opportunity to use the Union as their conduit whenever that would work to their advantage – or if that cannot be achieved, obstruct the implementation of unwelcome proposals tabled by the Union acting on its own accord.[18] Therefore, in line with what one would expect, an uneven internal distribution of powers raises the chance of garbled external perceptions, precluding the rise of an overarching identity, and reducing the chance that the EU successfully attains its goals.

5. Delineating the Union's Identity – Vacuous, Transcendent, Indissoluble?

We argued before that various takes are conceivable in the delineation of the Union's identity. To begin with, the identity can be qualified as

[17] When the nature of EU competences is intrinsically fuzzy, such as those pertaining to the CFSP and the CSDP, the Member States can arguably not even be obliged to pursue a common interest within a forum like the NATO.

[18] See e.g. Eugénia da Conceição-Heldt, 'Variation in EU Member States' Preferences and the Commission's Discretion in the Doha Round', (2011) 18 *Journal of European Public Policy*, p. 403.

wholly vacuous in itself and merely derivative, coinciding (at most) with the sum of the individual identities of the Member States. Alternatively, a transcendent identity may be observed which arises from their combined actions, with the EU and its Member States being perceived as still separated, but strongly interconnected parts. Lastly, one could consider the latter as no longer separate and having dissolved within the greater whole, becoming part of an indissoluble Union construct. Although the views from the global arena collected in the previous chapters do not all point in the same direction, the detailed scrutiny performed there has enabled us to discern the main contours of the EU's identity in the eyes of its international partners.

The first option would probably be quite appropriate for typifying the view from the NATO. Once the Union as a polity started to become more active in the area of security, it ostensibly reached a new level of self-consciousness. Under the current Treaties, its intention to become a more prominent stakeholder in the military field is eminently visible. Hereby, the principal acknowledgment of 'NATO primacy' and the stressing of the importance of the Transatlantic Alliance could, on the one hand, be seen as an integral part of the EU's identity as an international actor. On the other hand, this abstract posture carries little practical relevance. For, as illustrated by the intervention in Libya, in the many situations in which NATO is chosen over the EU, this occurs de facto, not as a matter of law. Furthermore, even when one should attach value to the text *sec*, it expressly underscores that, at least at present, a common defense is not yet part of that identity. To be sure, beyond the legal realm, there are cautious signs of a more transcendent appreciation, predicated on the fact that when the EU started to bear arms, it remained a community based on the rule of law with a deeply integrated economy, which was flexible enough to respect the parallel identities of its Member States. However, with the Union's institutions completely sidelined, including the High Representative for Foreign and Security Policy, the non-European NATO members cannot be faulted for detecting little more than a collective of countries from roughly the same region, with occasional shared interests.

In a similar vein, as was demonstrated in relation to the UN, the Union's international identity inherently includes the respect for the principles of the United Nations Charter. What is more, the extensive references to the United Nations in the European Union's founding Treaties reflect a constitutional attitude from the side of the EU vis-à-vis the UN system. That attitude forms in itself part of an emerging international identity which, as testified by the award of enhanced observer status by its peers, appears to have acquired a definitive transcendent quality.[19] This thesis is readily extendable to the IMF and the Hague Conference for Private International Law.

On a broad reading, not limited to a narrow understanding that clings to its formal observer status, one can say that there exists an even more uniform Union identity within the ILO. Over the course of the past decades, the interaction between the two organizations has intensified forcefully, and is not impaired by the fact that many ILO labor standards provisions do not touch upon exclusive Union competences, but mainly deal with shared ones. Furthermore, its identity would seem to coincide with the emergence, between 2000 and 2010, of a more coherent and integrated European social model, combining economic, employment, social and environmental objectives, and the exploitation of its external dimension by both the EU institutions and the Member States. Together, they have managed to impress their conception on international partners, and can often be seen to speak with one voice, despite being firmly separate and unequal from a 'law in the books' standpoint. This is – mutatis mutandis – also the situation in the Council of Europe, in light of the prevalent European approach to fundamental rights.[20] Importantly, these experiences show once more that identity is not per se conditional on membership.

Within the framework of the WTO, the Union's profile looks to have superseded that of the Member States. In this context, it has profited from something that might be called a distinctly European approach to international trade, placing a keen emphasis on reciprocity, comfortably nestling itself alongside the ways of thinking of (inter alia) the US and Japan. Largely owing to its exclusive competence, this has arguably transformed the franchise into a hermetic and indissoluble whole. Hereby, the residual powers of the Member States, notably in the field of transport services, exemplify that the distribution of competences does not necessarily coincide with the nature of the emerging identity.[21]

---

19 Though not always to the liking of all EU Member States: for instance, October 2011 saw a harrowing quarrel when the British delegation to the UN blocked more than 70 EU statements to UN committees, because it insisted those statements should be delivered on behalf of the "EU and its Member States" instead of on behalf of the EU. See Julian Borger, 'EU Anger over British Stance on UN Statements', <http://www.guardian.co.uk/world/2011/oct/20/uk-eu-un-statements-wording>.

20 Again, notwithstanding the handful of countries that prefer adopting the pose of 'persistent objector'.

21 Cf. Art. 207(5) and Art. 4(2)(g) TFEU.

An enigmatic picture arose in the discussion of the OECD framework, where the EU is represented as a full member in one of its major bodies, the Development Assistance Committee. In the multitude of other OECD committees, it enjoys a lesser position, which offers more leeway for the Member States to define and voice their own opinions. This results in the Union possessing a single distinctive identity in the DAC – but elsewhere, one that basically consists of the sum of the Member States' individual identities. For that reason, in this particular organization, the perceptions vis-à-vis the EU of non-European countries understandably waver between the first (vacuous) and the second (transcendent) reading.

6. Union Representation and the Impact of the Lisbon Treaty

In the introduction to this volume, it was predicted that issues of representation were certain to crop up, considering the post-Lisbon proliferation of offices with external tasks or ambitions. Since the total number of actors did not witness any meaningful decrease, and the gap between CFSP and non-CFSP decision-making was not entirely closed, the friction was assumed not to have abated all that much, despite the evaporation of the Community.

The implementation of the Lisbon Treaty has indeed not been a perfectly smooth process, and was marked by an absence of political guidance with regard to EU representation at multilateral organizations. In addition, the EEAS has had a rough start, after a launch that was slightly overdue. Nevertheless, the first dust has begun to settle. The European Council President has, for example, worked out an (informal) understanding with the President of the Commission.[22] The exact details of the agreement remain shrouded in secrecy, but a recurring pattern is emerging for some settings, with Mr. Van Rompuy and Mr. Barroso deciding on a case-by-case basis who will present the Union's views on other occasions.[23]

---

[22] As acknowledged by Mr. Van Rompuy himself in the general activity report 'The European Council in 2010' (available at <http://www.european-council.europa.eu/media/161695/qc3010507enc.pdf>), p. 12.

[23] For example, at G20 meetings, they form part of the EU delegation together, taking the floor depending on the subject of the discussions (CFSP or not). They also jointly participated in the 2010 and 2011 EU-US Summits. See also Peter Van Elsuwege, 'EU External Action after the Collapse of the Pillar Structure: In Search of a New Balance between Delimitation and Consistency', (2010) 48 *Common Market Law Review*, p. 992; Henri de Waele and

The former has exercised the novel speaking rights at the United Nations, where his broader activities are adequately synchronized with those of the High Representative.[24] The Commission Delegation and EU Council Liaison Office have merged into a Union Delegation under the authority of the HR, representing the EU in both the CFSP field as well as in other matters. The newly merged EU Delegation is also in charge of coordination. Moreover, the EEAS has progressively taken up the chairmanship of the relevant EU meetings in Brussels, so that the coordination there mirrors that in New York.[25] The net result of this intensified attuning of views is that a common position of the Union can nowadays be established on almost 95 percent of UN resolutions.[26]

In the OECD too, great advances have been made. With the Community erased from the picture and the EU finally receiving international legal personality, the nameplates at the OECD now display 'European Union' as well. The Commission Delegation in Paris was replaced by a Union Delegation, operating as a part of the EEAS. The latter's diplomats represent not only the EU institutions, but also issue statements or declarations every time a common position is reached on issues falling within areas of exclusive or shared competences. In reality, the Member States continue to take the floor quite often, but a convention has been established that, once there is a commonly agreed position, Member States will merely complement and not contravene it, besides permitting the Union Delegation to speak first.

In a diachronic perspective, the participation of the Union in the ILO underwent a remarkable intensification as early as 2003, despite the Commission partaking only as an observer on behalf of the Community. The alleged spur behind this development was the desire to promote the social dimension of globalization. From that point on, the Commission proved capable of presenting a plethora of common EU initiatives or

---

Hansko Broeksteeg, 'The Semi-Permanent European Council Presidency: Some Reflections on the Law and Early Practice', (2012) 50 *Common Market Law Review*, p. 1065.

[24] See e.g. Herman Van Rompuy, 'Address to the 66th United Nations General Assembly General Debate', 22 September 2011, EUCO 78/11; id., 'Address to the 67th General Assembly of the United Nations', 26 September 2012, EUCO 178/12.

[25] Emanuele Giaufret, 'The EU in the UNGA Third Committee', in: Jan Wouters, Hans Bruyninckx, Sudeshna Basu and Simon Schunz (eds.), *The European Union and Multilateral Governance. Assessing EU Participation in United Nations Human Rights and Environmental Fora*, Basingstoke: Palgrave Macmillan 2012, p. 73.

[26] The enhanced status has come at a diplomatic cost, in that it relegated the Union to speaking after the other nations; previously, the individual Member States holding the EU Presidency spoke higher in the 'pecking order'.

policies in the general debates at the International Labour Conference, in a Working Party of the ILO Governing Body, and succeeded in setting the agenda in various other committees. The provisions of the Lisbon Treaty did not lead to a real watershed, but gave rise to substantial confusion among the Union's partners. This confusion stemmed from the multiple interventions by different Member States in representing the Union position, pursuant to the 'burden-sharing principle'. Furthermore, around that time, Member States avidly began to pursue positions that were difficult to square with the Treaties, secondary legislation or vested practices. In these years, it also became ever more noticeable that beneath the surface, the vaunted European culture of social dialogue was not applied with equal rigor across the Union.

In comparison, matters have proceeded unperturbed at the Hague Conference. That no significant alterations were required here and no new representational conflicts arose might be testimony to the sterling character of the voting rules, which were established long before Lisbon's entry into force. As noted, whereas every delegation has one vote, the erstwhile Community was allowed to exercise a number of votes that corresponded to the number of Member States that had transferred their competence to it on the topic in question. Post-Lisbon, if the Union exercises that right, the Member States continue to refrain from exercising theirs, and vice versa. Of late, the attempts at actually aligning the positions on particular dossiers have turned out to be neither more cumbersome, nor less.

These samples make patently clear that, whereas the Lisbon Treaty appears duly operationalized in most respects, here and there the interplay between the EU and its constituent parts can still prove fractious. This is incontrovertibly caused, first and foremost, by the innate ambiguity of the Member States. On the one hand, they are willing to persuade international organizations to open up and grant the Union access when that strengthens their political leverage. On the other hand, they entertain few scruples about reducing the Union's visibility and undermining its actions when their interests would otherwise be jeopardized.[27] In certain forums they consciously strive to reduce the influence of the EU institutions, take distance from, or renounce their claims and statements.[28] Notwithstanding the ever-expanding duty of loyal cooperation, the Lisbon reforms have not eradicated this obstinacy, and quite possibly, no

---

[27] Govaere, Capiau and Vermeersch, *supra* n. 9, p. 167; Eeckhout, *supra* n. 1, pp. 233–4.
[28] Cf. *supra*, n. 19.

future Treaty amendment will ever manage to do so.[29] The sundry codes of conduct drafted by the Commission do alleviate the pain, and have facilitated coordination in some places, but have (alas) not been greeted with universal enthusiasm.

At the same time, the problem should probably not be overstated. It is rare for the Member States to oppose the Union institutions *en bloc*, and although their views regularly differ, one may notice a growing support for the emancipation of the EU as an actor in its own right.[30] Additionally, based on the accumulated evidence in the preceding chapters, it would be wrong to pit the two against one another, as if they were natural adversaries engaged in constant turf wars. If that were true, it would be impossible for any semblance of a European identity to take root; yet the WTO and ILO experiences, amongst others, point in a wholly contrary direction.[31]

All in all, perhaps the Lisbon Treaty has not produced sufficient new opportunities to ensure a structural harmony, or perhaps these opportunities have simply not been sufficiently explored yet. Evidently, the EU failed to rise to the challenge at the Libyan civil war in 2011 – but albeit too late, *did* eventually agree on the launch of a military operation.[32] The setting up of the EEAS has so far proceeded sluggishly, but does hold a most notable promise. When deployed in full, the Union's external representation looks destined to take a great leap forwards.[33] As unlikely as

---

[29] Cf. Mauro Gatti and Pietro Manzini, 'External Representation of the European Union in the Conclusion of International Agreements', (2012) 49 *Common Market Law Review*, p. 1734, pointing out how the Member States, in the conclusion of mixed agreements, continue to rely on pre-Lisbon practices that no longer have any legal ground.

[30] In the same vein Scarlett McArdle and Paul James Cardwell, 'EU External Representation and the International Law Commission: An Increasingly Significant International Role for the European Union?', in: Steven Blockmans and Ramses Wessel (eds.), 'Principles and Practices of EU External Representation', *CLEER Working Papers* 2012/5, p. 101.

[31] In the Union's external environmental action as well, specifically its policy on climate change and green biotechnology, the formation of its international identity has been seen to take place *across* the EU institutions and the Member States. See Kathrin Birkel, *We, Europe and the Rest – EU Discourse(s) at Work in Environmental Politics*, Enschede: Ipskamp 2009, pp. 179–80 and 184–5.

[32] See Council Decision 2011/210/CFSP of 1 April 2011 on a European Union military operation in support of humanitarian assistance operations in response to the crisis situation in Libya (EUFOR Libya) [2011] OJ L 89/17.

[33] See further e.g. Steven Blockmans and Marja-Liisa Laatsit, 'The European External Action Service: Enhancing Coherence in EU External Action?', in: Paul James Cardwell (ed.), *EU External Relations Law and Policy in the Post-Lisbon Era*, Berlin-Heidelberg: Springer 2011, p. 135; Bart Van Vooren and Ramses Wessel, 'External Representation and the European External Action Service: Selected Legal Challenges', in: Steven Blockmans and Ramses Wessel (eds.), 'Principles and Practices of EU External Representation', *CLEER Working Papers* 2012/5, p. 59.

it seemed at the turn of the last century, the Member States have permitted the Union to develop a diplomatic arm, which has impacted with astounding force on the role of venerable Commission DGs, even in a hybrid organization like the OECD.

7. Substantive EU Impact on its International Partners

Now reverting once again from an outside-in to an inside-out perspective, one may wonder whether the international partners have undergone any modifications as a result of their dealings with the EU. Here, of course, the amendment of their constitutions to allow for Union accession, undertaken e.g. by the Hague Conference for Private International Law, forms a most striking occurrence. Admitting it as an observer was significant enough, but would prove just the first step, owing to the tenacious support of the Member States for a further upgrade. The negotiations leading to the Conference's 2005 Statute led to such an agreeable synergy that this trajectory could serve a broader purpose, as a handy model for the future. Naturally, the recognition of R(E)IOs had already become a fairly widespread practice before, with an entity like the WTO opening its doors for the participation of any willing regional trading blocs from the very beginning. Nevertheless, despite the many potential barriers to entry flagged at an earlier stage, the EU is somehow capable of giving rise to the thought, or actually manages to persuade other IOs, third countries, as well as its own members, that its joining would be mutually beneficial. For sure, some of those 'on the receiving end' are well aware of the legal or political advantages. The Union's accession to the ECHR is for example highly anticipated by the Council of Europe, since thereby, for the first time in history, a supranational organization voluntarily submits its acts to external supervision by a court of another international organization.

Even if in the long run, there is no reason to rule out full membership of the CoE, in certain external environments, the barriers to entry are extremely difficult to overcome. This goes above all for Article 4 of the UN Charter, which only allows states to join. Yet, with the UK and France occupying two out of the five permanent seats in the UN Security Council, the EU theoretically bags thirty percent of the votes there. Were the Union one day to secure full UN membership, its accession would be bound to bring an end to this situation. Conversely, the present setup entails an overrepresentation, which might have been the final straw to set a reform in motion – but so far did not.[34] Paradoxically then, whereas the main gates to this grand keep are nigh impregnable (the UN Charter), an easier entry is provided via the backdoor (the operation of the Security Council). At any rate, this case demonstrates that the Union's impact on the institutional structure of partner organizations can sometimes be absolutely negligible.

Lastly, in the ILO, an invaluable political impact is apparent, as opposed to a legal one. For within the International Labour Conference and Governing Body, the EU has gradually become a positive force, capable of neutralizing or softening negative positions of third parties. Interestingly, here and in the Council of Europe, the contacts at the highest political level are premised on exchanges of letters. When the rules of the organization concerned preclude intenser forms of coordination, this may constitute an elegant middle road for the Union to assert its interests, and exert a waxing indirect influence.

8. Repercussions of the Sovereign Debt Crisis

Shortly before the sovereign debt crisis hit home, the EU had shaped up from a humble instrument of regional economic organization to a prominent global political presence. In the introductory chapter to this volume, the crisis was assumed to have appreciable consequences for the ways in which the Union relates to the world. After all, outsiders cannot fail to have noticed the tensions eating away at the foundations of the supranational edifice. In an ironic analogy, the widening internal ruptures were unavoidably to have an external counterpart.

The repercussions of the crisis are visible indeed, but on the whole, the fragmentation is less severe than we presumed, by leaving the core of the European identity unaffected. Also, the impact is not perceptibly greater in organizations where the Member States continue to partake individually (e.g. the OECD), in comparison to those where the EU wields virtually exclusive competence (e.g. the WTO). The emerging international solidarity, coinciding with the desire to prevent a cataclysmic domino effect, has assuaged imminent clashes within the International

[34] Cf. Eric Suy, 'Certain Other Perspectives for a Reform of the United Nations Security Council', in: Eva Rieter and Henri de Waele (eds.), *Evolving Principles of International Law* (Queen Mary Studies in International Law: 5), Leiden: Martinus Nijhoff Publishers 2012, p. 91.

Monetary Fund. Unpropitiously though, this had the oblique effect of shifting the prime interest to EMU reforms, away from the – equally pressing – IMF reforms.[35]

As described, the European Commission worked together with the ILO Office in exploring adequate responses to the impending financial catastrophe. The crisis strained the Union's identity most heavily during its 'second phase', when the promotion of austerity was prioritized by (inter alia) the Eurogroup, Commission and ECOFIN Council. Elsewhere, this changed the perception of the EU's agenda, and confused third parties with regard to the centrality of the Union's social model. International partners believed that employment and social policy had been sidetracked as dimensions that were subordinate to the economic and financial priorities. It was only at the subsequent stage that the message came through that key provisions in the Treaties, such as the horizontal social clause and the article spelling out the role of social dialogue, had not in fact been suspended.

While the EU aspired to play a greater role in international financial institutions, its attempts had little success before the crisis, for the Member States did not believe Union participation to have much added value for this policy field.[36] The tables are turning now, for better or for worse. As already indicated in an earlier chapter, it remains to be seen whether, after the imminent refurbishment of the EMU, the continued individual presence of the Member States on that echelon still makes legal and political sense.

9. Conclusion: 'Name Me Your Friends …'

Ten years ago, two eminent political scientists posited that the EU's international identity can be broken down into several elements. For starters, despite its newly gained competence for military action and the acquisition of the necessary resources, they argued that it is pacific. Second, with its liberal-democratic agenda centered on peace, liberty, democracy, the rule of law and human rights, it was alleged to be principled. Third, with its preference for deliberation and dislike of polarization, one may label it consensual. Fourth, with its variety of governance modes sprawled across

[35] Chiefly necessitated by the current overrepresentation of European countries and institutions within the IMF.

[36] Jørgensen and Wessel, *supra* n. 8, p. 283.

different levels and locations, it predominantly carries a network-character. Fifth, its decision-making, consultation and legislation processes render it a politically open rather than a closed system. In combination, these elements ought to signify that the Union's identity not merely defies classification in Westphalian terms, but is consciously counter-Westphalian.[37] Though the approach in the foregoing chapters was decidedly more legal than political science oriented, a number of these features did indeed come to the surface. At the very least, this gives a boost to the credibility of the inferences that were drawn in the previous paragraphs.

Regardless of whether the Union construct is non- or counter-Westphalian, and notwithstanding the rise of ASEAN, Mercosur, the Andean Community or the African Union, it knows no true equivalent at the present day and time. In that light, some might be disappointed at the finding that still today, in various forums, its identity retains a derivative quality. Probably most grievously, in that most general of international organizations, the United Nations, the EU is often viewed as a cohesive group of UN members rather than an actor in and of itself. Exactly in an organ like the 'Third Committee', where the Union is expected to be most visible as a 'soft power' and maximally make its influence felt, it is quintessentially perceived as the expression of the political will of its Member States.[38] To an extent, this is also reflected in Resolution 65/276.[39] In all other milieus where the EU's profile is articulated weakly, or even appears entirely vacuous, the political reality represents a hard break with the legal theory, making a mockery of the autonomy postulate cherished by the European Court of Justice. Occasionally, the founding Treaties corrode this axiom themselves, for instance in the repeated stressing of NATO primacy in the TEU. Such principled subservience is not reflected anywhere in the case law, shedding doubt on whether juxtaposed analyses of the legal and the political sphere can truly complement one another, or convey the impression of excessively arcane disciplines irrevocably placed at loggerheads.

---

37 Ian Manners and Richard Whitman, 'The "Difference Engine': Constructing and Representing the International Identity of the European Union (2003) 10 *Journal of European Public Policy*, pp. 398–9.

38 To the 'Third Committee', the General Assembly allocates those agenda items that relate to social, humanitarian affairs and human rights issues which are thought to affect people all over the planet.

39 A/RES/65/276, particularly in point 1(d) of the Annex, where EU representatives are expressly permitted to "present proposals and amendments orally as agreed by the States members of the European Union; such proposals and amendments shall be put to a vote only at the request of a Member State".

All the same, the two walk together in their acknowledging of the Union's systemic specificity and its unique contribution to the international institutional landscape. Moreover, the emancipation of the EU as an actor in its own right is an incremental process, as the experiences recorded in the foregoing chapters corroborate.[40] If the Union were eventually to gain a universal formal recognition among its external partners, the observations of political scientists could finally be (re-)aligned with the position of the supranational judiciary. In this scenario, at long last, its identity hinges less on internal perceptions and pronouncements, but becomes chiefly discernible on the basis of the nature and quality of the relations it maintains with other global players. That outcome would confirm the classic wisdom that who you are is determined just as well by where you decide to manifest yourself.

[40] Cf. McArdle and Cardwell, *supra* n. 30, p. 101.

INDEX